DATE DUE

DE 1 0 98			

DEMCO 38-296

RANDOM HARVEST

RANDOM HARVEST

by

JAMES THOMAS FLEXNER

Fordham University Press
New York
1998

Copyright ¤ 1998 by JAMES THOMAS FLEXNER
All rights reserved.
LC 98-10780
ISBN 0-8232-1730-2

Library of Congress Cataloging-in-Publication Data

Flexner, James Thomas, 1908-
    [Selections]
    Random harvest / by James Thomas Flexner.
        p. cm.
    ISBN 0-8232-1730-2
    1. United States--History. 2. Painting, American--History. I. Title.
E178.6.F652 1998
973--dc21   98-10780
                                                                 CIP

Printed in the United States of America

CONTENTS

Publisher's Note

For almost three-quarters of a century James Thomas Flexner has been a published author. Though he admits in his autobiography, *Maverick's Progress,* that some of his childhood poetry was published in 1925, here he dates the beginning of his career with the dissemination, by Harvard University, of his commencement address in 1929.

After a brief stint as a newspaper reporter and some lean years writing fiction, Mr. Flexner found his true writer's pen in nonfiction, with the publication in 1937 of *Doctors on Horseback,* the first of his twenty-eight books.

Since then, virtually no arena of nonfiction publishing has escaped him: radio interviews and television scripts, newspapers articles and op-ed pieces, magazines, speeches, book reviews, journals, and books. He is the winner of a National Book Award and a special Pulitzer Prize, and a member of the American Academy of Arts and Letters.

His particular interest is the story of America's past—her history and her art—and he investigates it with grace, style, and wit. What follows is a harvest of his occasional writings, both published and unpublished, arranged initially chronologically and then at random.

Taking a note from Mr. Flexner in one of these pieces, we invite you to "get yourself quiet, for [his] is not a narrative that moves rapidly to any objective like a superhighway which burrows under all umbrageous country lanes. Put on your slippers, place a drink by your elbow, and resolve to ramble imaginatively with the author through vanished times. His avowed object is to make you acquainted with a great many people. He himself finds them all interesting because he is eternally amused and excited by the human race."

HARVARD ADDRESS

My formal entrance into the great world at my graduation from Harvard was, as here revealed, dramatic and remarkable. Not only did I address at the university commencement (1929) the largest live audience that I was ever to encounter, but the speech I delivered, copiously distributed by the university, was like a red flag to bulls to the conventional art faculties across the nation that were still preaching "art for art's sake."

Poetry in a Machine Age

The dominant note of the present age is industrialism. To convince yourself of this, it is only necessary to read any history of modern civilization, or to study the output of the Ford factory, or, best of all, to try to do for ten minutes without anything produced by machines. Industrialism is not confined to the cities. The wheat that makes our bread is cut and bound by mechanical harvesters. No modern farmer can get on without a tractor and a Ford car. In fact, there is no phase of life in American today which has not known the inroad of the machine.

What is the place of poetry in this world of steam and steel? Can you write a sonnet to a city? May the hero of the epic travel in the subway? Or, on the other hand, may poetry disregard the present day, fleeing to nature or the past? Can a city dweller write convincingly of flowers, or a man of the twentieth century praise Greek gods? How may poetry deal with a machine age?

Great poetry must have reference to the great movements of its time. When kings ruled the world in power as well as name, tragedy could deal with the fall of kings. A complete study of either Shakespeare or Chaucer would give a better idea of his time than many a history book, as no important elements would be found missing. The flowers of the fields are still beautiful, but since they are not a part of the dominant movement of modern times, no poet can make from pure descriptions of them truly great verse. His work, however finely wrought, would represent only a minor phase of life; it would not be universal.

Man—Background for Nature

Still, most of our contemporary poets make man a background for nature, rather than nature a background for man. Their verse, though never great, is often pretty. The secret of such success as they have lives in the fact that they are using words which have already been impregnated with poetic feeling. It has been asserted that candles lend themselves more to poetry than electric lights because they are more material to us as sensitive beings. Compare the number of times you have read by candle light to the number of times you have read by electricity, for thus you will find which is more material to you. But it is nonetheless easier to write of candles. They have been used in verse so often that the very mention of them brings beautiful associations. Anyone can write competently about the moon, for the very word "moon" has, through much use, become in itself a poem. Yet for that reason it is harder to compose great verse about the moon.

Since old words grow dead through overuse, and since new words grow up to describe new phenomena, we may not allow our poetic diction to be dominated by the usage of the past. Wordsworth rebelled against such a principle in order to use the language of industrialism, for the diction of poetry must keep up with the diction of its age. Otherwise verse will be as pretty and sterile as that of our nature poets.

The greatest verse had never been a picture of inanimate objects: art is a human thing that must deal with men's problems and men's actions. When Schiller said that nature was the only flame that kindles the poetic soul, he was going against the precedent of all the great writers of history. Homer resorted to nature for similes with which to describe man. Shakespeare used the woods and fields as a background for human action. Even Wordsworth projected an allegory of life into nature before he felt justified in writing about it.

In truly great poetry, then, the actions of life, the tragedies and triumphs, the vacancies and passions, the hopes and fears of men are expressed in such a manner that through them shine the eternal human verities that form the basis of all meaning. The poets who are most universal in virtue of their imaginative reason are likewise as a rule those who realize most intensely the life of their period. In the France of 1840 there was so huge a gap between the romantic poetry and real life that the poetry was empty, dead. Sainte-Beuve recognized this fact. Eventually the sterility became so obvious that the conservative French Academy gave in 1844 as a subject for their annual poetic contest The Discovery of Steam. Maxime DuCamps, in his preface to *Les Chants Modernes*, which he intended for a manifesto of a new movement opposing the Parnasse, declared that the marked artistic decline in France was because literature, instead of marching forwards, was going backwards. He said: "when steam is discovered, we sing of Venus; when electricity is discovered, we sing of Bacchus. It is absurd!" Perhaps Montaigne summed it all up when he said that we seek for other conditions because we do not know the use of ours.

THE PRODUCT OF TRIVIAL EVENTS

If poets nowadays try to write as if the industrial revolution had never happened, they are doomed to failure. A man's life is more made up of the myriad insignificant minutes he has lived than of the few hours he remembers. A thousand trivial events have combined to make him what he is: the beat of his feet on the pavement during random walks; the shine of an electric light over his shoulder; the rumble of a street car which he did not notice as he studied. These innumerable trivialities, rising inevitably round him, each one making a tiny impress on his consciousness, force him to be a man of his period. Though he wishes to be a man of the Middle Ages, though he steeps himself in the literature and culture of past centuries, no matter; even as he reads of Tristram and Iseult the horn of a passing truck colors his mind. He is shackled down to his own age: he never fully understands knight errantry.

A man of the twentieth century, then, must find the essence of life through the accident of his own age. He must write for a world of airplanes, and steam shovels, and street cars. But his work will be vital only if he has caught within the meshes of his temporal scheme the universal verities of life.

Even our pastoral poetry must deal with peasants as they are now. The most rural farmer has undergone a certain amount of industrial influence. The smallest towns boast movie theaters and telephones. If we are then to penetrate into the backwaters of life and write pastorals, we must still take machinery into account.

Fleeing contemporary conditions often makes a work of art too expansive and therefore superficial. When you are trying to escape from the real, you must throw overboard restraint, which has an irritating way of bringing you face to face with facts. Assuming this necessity as a virtue, most modern writers believe that they can understand men by letting their own emotions expand. Thus they are led into a fallacy, for only through making yourself as universal as possible can you understand the universal. By restraining all the accidental and individual parts of your nature, you must find within yourself the fundamental realities of life. If, on the other hand, you let yourself go, you will multiply the distinctions between yourself and other men. Your work will become self-expression in its lowest form. Like some contemporary ladies, you will be able to write of nothing but your own love affairs.

Many justify their escape from the real by asserting that they are seeking the ideal. Too often, the only quality of this ideal is lack of actuality. The more other-worldly art gets the less reference it has to men living on earth; it can only offer the reader an escape from actual problems which, as a rational being, he ought to consider. Of what use is a Utopia which has no reference to Man? The only ideal worth striving for is one that grows out of actual conditions and is therefore tangible.

Yet we must consider the manner in which the results of the industrial revolution may be used in poetry. Obviously, the verse may no more argue for industrialism than against it; may not point out that the development of cheap automobiles gives the working man an opportunity to spend his Sundays in the country. It is not the function of poetry to debate controversial ideas. Poetry is the expression of emotion, and good argument is not emotional. Verse takes the results of controversy once the question is settled, and by heightening these with emotion, makes them more acceptable to the mind.

A poet may not content himself with describing machines, for the machines of one generation are different from those of the next. An ode to a 1920 airplane would be out of date in 1929. Authors may no more forget that such machines exist for men than that the men they write about are living in a machine age, traveling in automobiles, talking over the telephone, lighting their houses with electric lights. Poets must see the essence of life through the accident of their own time, but their emphasis must nonetheless be on the essence. Then their work will be immortal. No one fights nowadays with a sword for a weapon, and a shield and a breastplate for defense, but Homer is still read and admired.

NEW YORK HERALD TRIBUNE

After being graduated from Harvard (magna cum laude) in 1929, I had the stupendous good fortune to secure a job that would have been envied by newspapermen all over the United States: a reporter, under the famous city editor, Stanley Walker, on the *New York Herald Tribune*, then the major competitor of *The New York Times*. Six days a week I wrote at least one story that went to hundreds of thousands of readers. This was a marvelously educating adventure, but the stories, being by intention topical, do not, except for the few quoted here, fit into such as volume as this.

LEOPOLD AUER

Leopold Auer was kingmaker among violinists and himself a king.* For two generations he was hailed as the supreme teacher of virtuosos. His death marked the closing of an epoch. He taught for forty-seven years at the Imperial Conservatory of Music in Petrograd, and he was "soloist to his majesty" of three Czars. When the Russian revolution smashed everything he had known and loved, he came to New York in his seventy-third year, a penniless exile, who had, in his own words, "cast into discard his entire past, except its memories."

But, although New York is separated from Petrograd by half a world, he found to his delight that it already harbored many of his greatest and most beloved pupils, who had also fled from Russia and who were already idols in the New World. Efrem Zimbalist, Mischa Elman, Jascha Heifetz, Toscha Seidel, and a myriad lesser lights flocked to the lonely old man from whom they had learned their magic in the days of the Czars.

Employing the boundless energy that had always been characteristic of him, he quickly accustomed himself to New York. Though puzzled for a while by the skyscrapers and the rush of traffic, he eventually found the New World to his liking. No sooner had he become an American citizen, in his eightieth year, than he delivered a speech against prohibition.

He had planned to give up teaching, but when future American virtuosos flocked to his door he lacked the heart to turn them away. Soon he became a familiar figure in New York. All musicians grew to love this jolly little man, whose white beard bristled, while his eyes flashed with uncontrollable temperament and his tremendous vitality surrounded him like an aura.

Most of New York's major violinists had studied under Auer at Petrograd. So it is that musicians cannot gather now without sadly discussing

---

*An earlier version of this essay, entitled "The Teacher of Masters," appeared in the *New York Herald Tribune* on July 27, 1930.

the little man who scolded them terribly to their eternal profit. For the myriad stories that circled round the kindly gentleman who threw Paul Strassevitch down stairs for musical impiety and who berated Heifetz and Elman like a fishwife have suddenly turned from gossip into legend.

The master class for violinists, Auer's disciples recall with amusing clearness, was held at 2:35 P.M. They will never forget the exact minute, because Auer had insisted upon such punctuality that the pupil who was ten seconds late was either excluded from the lesson or scolded for ten minutes. Auer appeared so punctually himself that Zimbalist often set his watch by the master's entrance.

A few days ago Strassevitch described a typical scene in the classroom. The pupil who had arrived earliest played first, while the others apprehensively waited their turns and the inevitable group of visiting masters strained forward in their chairs. Being carried away by the music, Auer was transformed from a courtly gentleman of the old school to a musical fanatic. In his desire for perfection he lost all control of his emotions.

His hands clasped behind his back, his head cocked to the right side and his eyes bright with excitement, he strode up and down the room with a cigarette fuming eternally at his lips. He would pause for a moment to stare absently out of the window, but then, as the tension grew, he would circle the class like a bloodhound on a hot trail, suddenly appearing before his startled pupil, ducking under his arm and staring into his face while he played.

When his pupil performed skillfully, Auer's excitement and love of music would manifest itself in public praise, Strassevitch said. But woe to the unfortunate that struck a false note. The master would be suddenly angry. He would push the offender's elbow, often breaking the bow and sometimes the violin. He would scold and scold. But the pupil, though abashed, would be grateful for the show of anger, for it proved that Auer thought he could do better. When a stupid pupil played badly, but as well as could be expected, Auer bore it in silent misery.

Like all born teachers, Auer was not forced to rely on pedagogy and formal methods. The genius that burned in his mind struck a responsive chord in the minds of his gifted pupils. The art of music defies definition in clumsy words; it must speak in its own way to those who understand its idiom. Auer had little to offer to the lesser musicians, who required exposition and explanation. Mere polite performers could go elsewhere and Auer was glad to see them go.

By inspiring rather than teaching Auer forced his pupils to develop from within; theirs was no superimposed training. "Sincerity, sincerity," he used to shout to his disciples. "Never mind what I know, play what you want. I don't like that—but it's all right, go ahead!" It has often been remarked that, considering their common origin, Auer's pupils have a remarkable diversity of style.

Auer could teach well because he could play well. In his youth he, too, had been a famous virtuoso, although it was said that his hand was too small. His arduous concert experience which started in his thirteenth year enabled him to prepare his pupils for the emergencies of the concert stage) where a hot day may make your violin almost impossible to tune, or a dining car dinner may temporarily enervate your genius.

Auer had been a musical pioneer in his youth. When he came to Petrograd, Russia was going through the birth pains of a national music. While the conserative critics stormed, Tchaikovsky, Balakireff, Rimsky-Korsakoff, Cesar Cui, Borodin and Moussorgsky were composing music based on national traditions. In the days when the struggle was hard, Auer supported the new school and gladly performed their works when he conducted the concerts of the Imperial Russian Musical Society.

But when Auer traveled across the Atlantic in his old age, he was unable to make the adjustment to what has sometimes been called the national music of his home. Jazz, he said, was only a passing phase. When jazz was no more, the United States would be the musical leader of the world, as it was already the musical center.

Broun "Crashes" City Flophouse to Study Jobless

One of the largest bums in history, stylishly dressed in torn tuxedo trousers, a crumpled brown coat and socks into which holes had been cut with scissors, shuffled last night into the Municipal Lodging House, 432 East Twenty-fifth Street, so disheveled and forlorn that the hard-boiled attendants rushed to give him a plate of applesauce, the delicacy which is kept for the most downtrodden.* Within an hour, however, a wondering group of attendants and hoboes had gathered around the large stranger in possibly the first political meeting ever held within "flophouse" walls.

Heywood Broun, Socialist candidate for Representative in the 17th Congressional District, had journeyed to the lodging house to study unemployment at first hand. He had planned to remain all night, but when he was recognized so often that he could no longer keep the knowing ones quiet he set out for home slightly disappointed, although much impressed with the cleanliness of the lodging house.

Hope Nearly Dashed on Dollar

Afraid that admission would be refused if he were found solvent, Mr. Broun carefully audited the cash in his pockets so that, after paying the taxi driver, who took him to within a block of the house, he would have only a dime left. The first near misfortune of the evening came when Mr. Broun put his hand in his pocket as he entered the "flophouse" and found a dollar he had overlooked. With a quick gesture of a veteran hobo he dropped the bill in a corner, hoping it would be found by some needy bum and not by the husky policeman who was eyeing him suspiciously.

---

*An earlier version of this essay originally appeared in the *New York Herald Tribune* on October 31, 1930.

The Socialist candidate then shuffled over to the free-lunch counter, where the attendant handed him a cup of coffee and some beef stew without any beef. Taking another look at the large man standing before him, the attendant reached beneath the counter and brought out a heaping plate of applesauce.

"Here, take this, my man," he said. "Cheer up. Things will be better pretty soon."

Sitting at the same table with the Socialist candidate were a few professional hoboes, who ate their food with a greedy absorption, but the majority were young men, dressed in the remains of well-cut clothing. They stared with hostility at the watery stew.

Youth "Too Tired" to Eat

"Here take this. I've got to get used to this food, but I'm too tired tonight," said a tall youth dressed in a spotless trench coat. Mr. Broun refused the plate, but it was eagerly grabbed by an old hobo across the table, who later made off with the candidate's applesauce.

The meal over, Mr. Broun hurried to the registration window after having pledged to secrecy an attendant who recognized him. He stood in a long line of hoboes, who waited with obvious humiliation for the required questioning. When he finally reached the window, Mr. Broun was asked his name, age, religion, last employment, place of birth, and the address of a near relative to be notified if he did not survive.

He fibbed glibly about coming from a small town in Pennsylvania, and said, with a break in his voice, that he had no near relatives. He was told that as he was not a citizen of New York he could only come to the house once a month. Then he stood in another line for ten minutes until all the hoboes were herded down to the cellar, where they had to sleep on the floor because the ordinary bunking accommodations already were overcrowded.

The genial Socialist had hardly received his blanket when he ran into a fellow-spirit.

"I was a big politician in Cincinnati, where I come from," a Negro announced. "Yes sir. I worked for equal rights between the races. Yes sir. But I says to them colored boys who want to do it all at once, 'You boys is going too fast. After all we're black and they're white. Take it slow,' I says. As soon as I make $200, I'm going back to Cincinnati. If I have $200 I'll be elected."

Mr. Broun agreed that racial friendship could not be promoted to rapidly, since the greatest battles were won a little at a time. Then he asked the Negro if he was a Socialist, but on the subject of political parties the "Cincinnati politician" was a little vague.

A small, unshaven man gleefully slammed the Socialist's back.

"Why, Mr. Broun," he cried, "don't you know me? Only a week ago when your picture was in a tabloid I was standing right behind you. And it came out in the paper. Don't you remember?"

"Sh-h," replied the Socialist, "don't let on that you know who I am."

With a sage nod, the old man walked off whistling.

DEPARTS WITH GOOD WISHES

The cellar where Broun was holding court was a large room with white-washed walls. The entire floor space was covered with blankets, each containing a man. Some slept, a few stared sullenly at the roof, but most of them swapped stories of their experiences. Not one but had immediate hopes for the future. Mr. Broun listened with sympathy, and then drew the talkers out with questions.

Finally, however, all the attendants and many of the inmates had discovered who he was. Some sleepers rose from their blankets to wish the Socialist a successful campaign. A bizarre crowd of stern, blue-uniformed figures and unshaven men in underclothes collected to wish Mr. Broun good luck.

But there was no secret now, and Mr. Broun decided it would be useless to stay for the night. He was a marked man, and everything would be staged for his benefit. So he shook hands and departed.

SPURNED BY A TAXI DRIVER

Faced with the problem of getting home, Mr. Broun blithely hailed a taxi. The driver took one look at the Socialist's weird costume and waved him back.

"Hello, buddy," he cried, and drove on.

Finally an aged cab crept up the street. The doors, it later developed, were hinged with wire. One window handle was jammed, while the other twirled easily but without effect. This ancient equippage stopped at Mr. Broun's call and the candidate, who had passed the day speaking at street meetings, sank to the hard seat with a sigh of relief.

"I was very favorably impressed with the lodging house," he said when he got settled. "It was by no means as sordid as I expected. I thought the attendants were most polite and sympathetic to the unemployed. Perhaps the most fascinating point about the whole thing, however, was the way each of the men had some dream ahead of him. Each knew that better things were right around the corner."

HARVARD'S MUSE FOR WRITING

The youngest tradition of the oldest college in the United States is seventy today. "Copey," as he is known to Harvard, and Professor Charles Townsend Copeland, as the title pages of books read, is now three score years and ten.* He was feted last night at the New York Harvard Club by the Charles Townsend Copeland Association, a group of his students, including some of America's foremost writers, who have banded together for the one purpose of expressing their appreciation of a teacher and a friend. "Copey" has a private alumni association.

For twenty-five years Harvard's most loved professor has journeyed to New York to read aloud to his disciples who gather from all over the country. He is one of the few remaining masters of the lost art of reading to audiences. His rich, melodious voice, his unerring ear for the subtleties of rhythm and his stage presence have already become part of the Harvard tradition.

More than a brilliant reader, "Copey" is the exponent of the old-fashioned idea of personal education. Year after year, in his courses, English 12 and English 5, he selected only a few of the most promising undergraduate writers, labored with them and loved them, criticized them harshly, sometimes, but always inspired them. Understanding their personalities, he helped them to develop themselves.

He has had a great influence on American culture, through such pupils as Walter Lippmann, Heywood Broun, Conrad Aiken, Kenneth MacGowan, John Dos Passos, J. Brooks Atkinson, Robert Littell, Herman Hagedorn, John Reed, Robert E. Sherwood, Edward Sheldon, Earl Derr Biggers, Frederick L. Allen, Richard Connell, David Carb, John Marquand, Robert Burlingame, Waldo Pierce, Willard Huntington Wright, Marshall Best, and Maxwell Perkins.

Shunning publicity for himself, "Copey" has been content to let his pupils represent him before the world. Each of his readings is prefaced

---

*An earlier version of this essay, entitled "Silent Partner of Authorship," appeared in the *New York Herald Tribune* on April 27, 1930.

with a request that if there be any reporters present, they will not write up anything he says. Even in the sanctity of his own room, when he is receiving friends, he has his eye out for scribblers.

On one occasion Tom Prideaux, the editor of "The Yale Literary Magazine," journeyed to Cambridge to see if Harvard is as barbarous as reported at New Haven. The first thing he did, of course, was to call on "Copey." The Yale man was introduced in his official capacity and everyone waited for the professor to be impressed.

"Copey" fixed Mr. Prideaux with his eye. "Young man," he said, "I trust that you are not planning to write any sketches."

Scribner's for years had been trying to persuade "Copey" to write his autobiography. Finally, one of their representatives, despairing of less violent methods, telegraphed "Copey" that he was coming to Cambridge on the next train to get the first installment.

"Come up eight years from now," "Copey" wired back. The autobiography has not been written.

But "Copey" cannot hide his light under a bushel, for the light is too strong. Little by little the whole world is beginning to learn about the personal triumph of this retiring little man, who has written few books himself, but many through his disciples.

The most famous of the books that "Copey" has written—for he did write some—is *The Copeland Reader*, an anthology of his favorite selections for reading aloud. This had become standard all over the country for oral recitations.

He is also the author of *The Life of Edwin Booth* and the editor with various collaborators of *The Letters of Thomas Carlyle to His Youngest Sister*, Tennyson's *The Princess*; *Representative Biographies*, and *Selections from Wordsworth, Byron, Shelley and Keats*. He was made a doctor of literature by Bowdoin in 1920.

"Copey's" books all dealt with the preservation of the past. He was intensely interested in the lives of modern men which, he felt, could best be shaped by contact with the classics of the old days. But he had no interest in modern inventions. He has never liked telephones that break into the silence of meditation with their jangling. So, when he agreed on Christmas to read over the radio, all Boston was startled, and you may be sure there were few radios that were not functioning that night. More recently he has been hounded for the talking pictures, but it is doubtful if he will agree to pose. For how could he come down from the screen to keep the audience from coughing?

Students with colds long ago learned to keep away from "Copey's" readings, which take place several times a year at the Harvard Union, in Cambridge. He requires silence.

When he reads he has to have a special lamp on his desk, and however perfectly it is fixed, he must rearrange it. Then he takes a second pair of glasses from his pocket, wipes them deliberately and starts to put them on his nose.

Suddenly he lays them down again and glares at his audience fiercely. If anyone coughs or as much as shuffles his feet, he says, something terrible will happen. The audience holds itself still. He raises his glasses again, but just at that moment a truck rumbles by the open window. Will no one close the window? The window is shut and the audience stiffles in frightened silence.

Then "Copey" startes to read with all the magic of his personality and all the beauty of his voice. It is usually something from the Bible or Dickens. His voice rises and drops to the rhythm of great prose. The audience forgets all about shuffling feet and coughing. The spirit of a great actor transforms the eccentric little man behind his eccentric lamp; he is "Copey" no longer.

His voice, though rich and firm, is built on the clipped sentences of New England speech, just as his character, for all its tolerance, rests on the austerity of righteous men who have struggled for generations with rocky, barren soil.

About two years ago, when ill health forced him to resign his professorship and give up his formal teaching, old graduates moaned that Harvard would never be the same again. But they reckoned without the magnetism of this little man with a huge intellectual head who stares from beneath oversize glasses like a kindly lion.

For "Copey" continues to live on the top floor of Hollis Hall, a beautiful old building erected at Harvard in the fabulous days when Massachusetts was still a British possession. During the revolution, Colonial soldiers were quartered in his room. And now modern undergraduates walk up the steps worn by the Yankee boys of '76, to knock on the door behind which "Copey" lives.

From the outside, his room resembles that of any undergraduate, except for the presence of a hairy doormat that went out of style fifty years ago. But once past the threshold, the student has stepped into all the glamour of the past.

"Copey's" room, full of the crooks and crannies of old buildings, is still lighted by oil lamps. Its owner has never capitulated to electric lamps, which would, he feels, give too harsh a glare. One lamp especially is the guardian of "Copey's" disciples, for it is placed in the window as a signal to the initiated that he is home to receive visitors and carry on the high talk that is his joy.

Every Wednesday night the room is filled with his undergraduate friends and his old pupils come back from all over the world. Each is seated according to his importance, the most distinguished receiving the best chair and the undergraduates often being forced to sit on the floor. Then "Copey" sinks into the huge armchair by the fireplace, half-lighted by a student lamp and surrounded by innumerable photography of friends and admirers, outstanding among them being pictures of Mrs. Fiske.

There is a story that whenever Mrs. Fiske comes to Boston he writes her: "Minnie come over to 'Copey's.'" She never fails to come.

There is probably no subject under the sun—or over it, for that matter—which has not been discussed in these audiences of "Copey's." The little old professor may hold forth, to the delight of his circle, on the proper way to cook spinach, or he may discuss books, to their edification.

One day, with his friends gathered around him, "Copey" was bewailing the advances of modern science, which were threatening to get the better of him at last. The glass chimneys on his student lamps broke every once in a while and had to be replaced. But lamps of the luxurious type designed for large houses were being used so little that it was more and more difficult to get new chimneys. He was in despair.

His life had been lived under the genial influence of oil lamps. They shone on his childhood in the little town of Calais on the Maine coast. They were in his blood. They had given his grandmother light when she read Pope's *Odyssey* to him, her daughters, and servants as they made Thanksgiving pie.

Nothing could be more natural for a boy from Maine than to go to Harvard. Having been graduated in 1882, "Copey" went to law school for a year, but did not like it. Then he made a series of attempts to adjust himself to the world, among other things spending seven years as a dramatic and book critic on a Boston newspaper. In writing about plays he learned, perhaps, the histrionic art so valuable to him in his readings. Finally, at the age of thirty-two, he became an instructor in the Harvard English department.

In 1905, years before Harvard College really was conscious that such a man was teaching in Cambridge, "Copey's" private alumni association was formed with the object of bringing him to New York every year for a reading.

The Charles Townsend Copeland Association began modestly with fifteen members, but now more than 250 disciples belong to it. In addition to being spread out over the whole United States, its membership has penetrated into Europe and the Orient. Disciples often travel half way across the continent to attend its meetings.

"Copey" is so highly revered that an elaborate ritual has grown up around his New York appearances. For weeks before he arrives there is a rapid-fire exchange of letters between him and the officials of the Harvard Club, so that none of his wishes may remain unanticipated.

"Provide me with a glass of buttermilk whenever I want, but especially regularly and methodically at meals, Friday, Saturday and Sunday," "Copey" writes. It is done.

He is always met at the train by a special committee from the association, usually numbering one or two famous writers and a bank president or so. A porter from the club is brought so "Copey's" bags will be properly handled and a special valet is waiting at the club door to unpack them the moment he arrives. His room is heated to an exact figure by trembling attendants who remembered what happened the year it was two degrees too cold.

On the night of his reading "Copey" is received at the door of his room by a special delegation which escorts him downstairs to the hall, where a special reading lamp is waiting, where the windows on the noisy streets are specially closed and the listeners with colds especially well stocked with cough drops.

Usually the meetings of the association are full of amused reminiscence of old college days, but one became tragic because the memory of John Reed, who had died a Communist, entered the Harvard Club from which he had been expelled when being tried as a radical spy. Reed, who died in Russia a Soviet hero, had been "Copey's" favorite disciple. "Copey" was not a Communist and could not quite understand.

Heywood Broun, writing in *The New Yorker* describes the meeting thus: "two springs had gone by since John Reed died when 'Copey' got up to face some fifty of his former pupils. There had been other speeches, all humorous in tone. To-hell-with-Yale talks and so on. The men were the sort that could be found in any cross-section ten years out of college. Bankers and bond men and a few writers, and all of them good fellows. Nobody spoke of John Reed. He had been dropped from the Harvard Club when he was tried for espionage along with the other editors of *The Masses*.

"But 'Copey' didn't make any jokes at all this time. He talked about Reed and his brilliance. He said that this man who died in Moscow had gone through utterly for a cause which he ['Copey'] could not possibly believe. And then he added that it didn't make much difference about his own belief. Jack had believed. That was important. 'Copey' said that sometimes he worried because a lot of the men who came away from Harvard and from him didn't seem to give much of a damn about anything. To go through completely with anything in which you had faith was all that mattered.

"Nobody could possibly tell whether you were right or wrong anyway until a hundred years had passed. For that one evening Reed was honored in the Harvard Club and the Kremlin. 'Copey' knew now that there had been no break in the tradition which he had worshiped. The boy from 1910 had not sinned against the creed of gallantry. It was a brave thing to be a pacifist."

John Reed was not the only one of "Copey's" disciples to become well known. Others earned leadership in many lines; they became business men and bankers and, above all, writers. Many of his scribblers grew, partly through his teachings, to exert great influence.

"Copey's" pupils have been most outstanding in the theater. Kenneth MacGowan had much to do with the founding of the Provincetown Players, where such men as Eugene O'Neill got their start. It was the first successful subscription theater in New York. J. Brooks Atkinson and Robert Littell are among the "Copey" disciples who, as dramatic critics, arbitrate between the public and the stage.

"Copey" helps collect the news of the whole country, for the offices of papers are overrun with his disciples. He supplies every pupil who receives a B-plus or an A in his courses with one of his famous "to whom it may concern" letters. As the lettter explains that the bearer is one of "Copey's" accredited disciples, it is reputed to be good for a job in any Eastern newspaper office.

Conventional professors of English wondered how "Copey" managed to turn out so many writers. He was a most unconventional teacher. "Copey" had no use for the painstaking German scholarship and burrowing into sources. He committed the capital sin among professors of never conning roots and the derivation of words in order to become a Doctor of Philosophy. Therefore he was an instructor for seventeen years and had already become the idol of the undergraduates before he was promoted to assistant professor. Seven more years elapsed before this man who dared to boast he was not a scholar of philosophy was made associate professor. Eight years later his recognition came at last, when he was appointed Boylston Professor of Rhetoric and Oratory, one of the highest honors in the English Department.

Immediately, four enterprising disciples discovered a ruling made in Colonial days when Harvard was an informal country college, permitting the Boylston Professor to keep a cow in Harvard yard. The discovery was greeted by "Copey's" followers with whoops of joy. They determined to buy him a cow. Only by expressing stern disapproval did Professor Copeland manage to avert the catastrophe and remain cowless.

"Copey's" classes were more a dramatic performance than a lecture. Having glared his pupils into silence and a horror of coughing, he talked about whatever came into his head. The lightning of his wit was quick to strike any student who committed a sin that ranked with coughing—that of coming late.

On one occasion three men drifted into the lecture roon when "Copey" was already talking. He allowed an ominous silence to fall for a moment. Then he said simply: "All Gaul is divided into three parts."

As he talked good-naturedly about this and that and without any seeming plan, he revealed an appreciation of literature that was more likely to inspire his pupils than any listing of dates or discussing of influences. Because he loved literature so well himself and because he felt its beauties so deeply, he showed his students how to love and feel. That was all he cared about.

Above all, "Copey" inspired his pupils to write. They might scrible about whatever they pleased, as long as the result was not boring. "The only damning fault against a piece of writing is dullness," he once said.

Twice a month the pupils in English 12 and English 5 had to climb to his lamplighted room and read their compositions aloud. "Copey," the great reader, felt that rhythm was all important and that it could best be evaluated in the spoken voice. And how hollow many phrases sounded as "Copey" listened, writhing politely, sometimes, at an especially bad phrase.

Since "Copey" loved his pupils, they took even his harshest criticisms in good part. The students who came to know this little man, staring fiercely from behind oversize glasses, found they had a real friend. "Copey" had a place in his heart for all and many a queer, ungainly boy found refuge there and came out at last a man.

For "Copey's" disciples are not the conventional followers of the ordinary professor. Some sport Phi Beta Kappa keys, but more are on the verge of being dropped from college. Many of the intimates of the lamplighted room are the kind that just cannot keep out of trouble. A motley crew, and not one very suitable for a professor, the doctors of philosophy think.

But "Copey," descended from Puritan ancestry, has his own rigid code, to which his students must adhere. If they are gentlemen in the sense of the word which means much more than well-bred, they are respected by this unconventional man who objects heartily to being called "Professor Copeland."

DREISER BRINGS PESSIMISM BACK FROM U.S. TOUR

From the point of view of the Herald Tribune, *this was the most controversial of my many stories: no reporter was supposed to name a personal bet, and what Dreiser had said here would be waving a red flag in the face of the* Herald Tribune's *readers. On the following day, the story did not appear. Or on the second day. But it was run on the third day with a contrary editorial. In the long run, though originally outraged, the editors were pleased since it gave them the opportunity to demonstrate a basic editorial policy. The bet revealed very much for many. The story was widely reprinted in America and somewhat abroad. It appears in Dreiser bibliographies.*

Theodore Dreiser has returned from his voyage of exploration through the United States more than ever a pessimist.* Yesterday he fumbled silently with the papers on his desk for ten minutes before he suddenly rose, drew himself to his full height and exclaimed, "All newspaper interviews are stupid. For years I have not seen one that is worth anything. I will bet you $10 that you cannot get into your paper the things that I am going to say."

The wager was taken up, and the novelist enthusiastically discussed the ills of the universe for an hour and a half. Since modern business and financial developments have made American citizens into nothing but "trudging asses," there is no great contemporary American literature, he said. If there is to be any in the future, it will have to take the form of satire or expressions of despair.

HARDLY AN INDIVIDUAL REMAINS

"The constitutional government of America is abdicated. In every state in the Union there is no such thing as representative government," Mr.

---

*An earlier version of this essay appeared in the *New York Herald Tribune* on July 8, 1930.

Dreiser complained. "America is controlled by trusts that function as government. They have the power to tax, which is the power to destroy.

"The mental capacity of our school teachers is practically nullified by business authorities dictating what they may teach. They must denounce bolshevism and keep their mouths shut on Darwinism. The great educational thing, they are told, is the flag, and it is the duty of every citizen to be 100 per cent American—in other words, a damn fool."

He said that big business movements are making it impossible for men to express themselves as individuals. Because they cannot hope to succeed in small, private enterprises. American citizens have lost their initiative and their power to think. There is hardly any such thing as an individual left in America, he said.

LITERATURE PRACTICALLY KILLED

When asked if these things would kill American literature he rose from his chair in excitement. "They have already practically done so," he exclaimed. "Just name me a single great writer. And supposing there were one, what chance would he have of being popular?

"What do the books concern themselves with nowadays? Why, with a little love affair, perhaps, or people's marital experiences for twenty years, or the adventures of some dub in the detective world, or how terrible the world looks to some dub who has never looked at it at all."

Mr. Dreiser attacked introspective novelists who "cannot step out into the world and survey it as it is." They were not writers at all, but merely autobiographers. He had hopes, however, that despite all modern handicaps, American literature would become great.

LIFE HERE INVITES SATIRE

"Life is life. It may be a lolling, fat, disgusting thing, but in the hand of a master it would become a very sardonic thing. The life of America today, fast verging as it is on social tragedy, should lend itself to satire and irony. Or, perhaps, we might have a literature of despair like that of Dostoievsky. That might be a good thing. Conditions here are in many ways similar to those in Russia before the revolution."

As Mr. Dreiser talked, a silky wolfhound, three feet tall, lay curled at his feet. The big sitting room in his duplex apartment at 200 West Fifty-seventh Street was decorated with several modernistic pictures, large as barn doors, and on one side was a painting of Mr. Dreiser when he was younger. Lolling in a straight, uncomfortable chair, the novelist kept rolling and unrolling his handkerchief. He spoke with great intensity, never taking his eyes off his interviewer.

"I have returned from a tour which I took to revive my understanding of America," he said. "I am more convinced than ever that the country is headed for great social changes that will frustrate the life of the ordinary individual unless they can be checked by a really important stand on the part of the intellectuals."

Traces Rise of Rackets

He said that everywhere he went he found that corporations were functioning as government. Indiana had established the doctrine that it was illegal to enter "unfair competition" with anybody. This, he said, was used by chain hotels to close their small competitors.

Having attacked the telephone and railroad companies, he said that in Minnesota a radical newspaper had been suppressed by big business interests on the ground that it was a public nuisance. Graft and crookedness in government was the principal topic of every newspaper he had seen during his travels.

Small dealers cannot make a living unless they band themselves together into racketeering groups that serve to shut out competition by illegal methods, Mr. Dreiser said. Because the "trusts" kept them from getting a profit on their crops, farmers could not make a living.

Only Misery Stirs People

"Nothing will be done until 50 or 60 per cent of the people of the United States feel the pinch that follows the right of the corporations to tax them to death," he said. "The only thing that will stir the people is misery. They are not miserable enough yet, but they soon will be. Men could organize this land so it could support three or four times its population without any misery.

"I have never seen a land more beautiful. It is self-sufficient, it could close its borders and live without any contact with the outside world. It could live beautifully."

Mr. Dreiser rose from his chair. "Be sure to mail me that $10," he said.

MR. DREISER IS INTERVIEWED

Americans, says Theodore Dreiser, have become mere "trudging asses." He has just made a tour of America and he knows. Business dictates what the schools may teach. The trusts have ruined the farmers and have ruined literature. "Because they cannot hope to succeed in small private enterprises, American citizens have lost their initiative and their power to think." So they read and write nonsense, and will continue to do so until they suffer more. "The only thing that will stir people is misery. . . . They are not miserable enough yet." . . .

Thus the author of *Sister Carrie* and *An American Tragedy*, sitting in his duplex apartment close to Carnegie Hall, with his blooded wolfhound lying at his feet. We are not sure just what it all goes to show, unless it be that novelists should never be interviewed, or that Mr. Dreiser's digestion is better on his country estate in Mount Kisco than in the City of New York, or that a man may be a great novelist and still be something of a fool.

Mr. Dreiser is indisputably, whether judged by the verdict of those critics who, hirelings of the capitalistic press, write for the American public, or by that of the beautiful, free Europeans, or even by the verdict of coarse, materialist sales, one of the outstanding American novelists. He has an uncanny power to probe the mysteries and describe the weary inevitabilities of the human soul. He has a profound and sympathetic understanding of the somber banalities that lie beneath the surface of human lives; he paints them ruthlessly and realistically, yet with a curious affection quite alien to the sterile mood of some of his more rebel-minded imitators. Yet this same man, with a chance to make deductions and to utter something akin to philosophy, falls into absurdities.

"They are not miserable enough yet!" What pathetic nonsense! Would Dreiser prescribe misery for himself and his friends? If he believes that the success of his own novels corrupts his artist's soul, why does he keep his wolfhound and his duplex apartment? It is true enough that the machine age—not in America alone, but in the whole world—has stamped its imprint upon the minds of men and has made them feel like midgets in the immediate and overwhelming presence of a world which to their ancestors was remote and unimportant: but the answer is not more poverty.

Mr. Dreiser may write another great novel as a fruit of his tour of America: but he will do better as a novelist than as a sociologist. His own life belies his dour outlook: his own hard-earned success is indicative of a growing change in America.

THEODORE DREISER

July 7 – 1930

Dear James Flexner:

Fair enough.

You win

Incidentally this makes me
slightly less pessimistic

But lay aside one of this Enough
to buy me a drink on sight.

The loser always needs a
drink

Theodore Dreiser

LAST MANHATTAN FARM SOON WILL GIVE UP STRUGGLE

For the first time in all its history Manhattan Island is threatened with becoming entirely an urban place and harboring no farms within its limits.* Census figures announced yesterday revealed that the farms in New York County had dwindled from five in 1920 to one in 1930. And Mrs. Joe Benedeto, lessee of the final farm, said last night that her little block of vegetables at 213th Street and Broadway is about to be obliterated by the encroachments of the city, thus divorcing Manhattan from agriculture forever.

A part of the cabbage patch has been shaded for a long time by a sign reading "Entire Block for Sale or Lease." A few days ago, according to Mrs. Benedeto, it was almost sold; so it was that standing knee-deep in corn, Benedeto shook a defiant pitchfork at the skyscrapers that loom to the south of his little garden. But he knew it was no use.

As he stood there a subway train rushed over the Tenth Avenue trellis that casts its early morning shadow across his vegetables. Frightened by the roar, his few chickens clucked and huddled. Silently, he returned to the red brick farmhouse under the subway.

Yesterday afternoon several neighbors sat sullenly in the farm yard, shelling corn. They said very little. When they spoke it was to tell of the farms they too had once owned, but which had now become apartment houses or new yards for the Interborough subway.

"I had two farms within a block of here once, but the subway took them," said Peter Rhere, now a caretaker for the city. "I am getting disgusted with the town: there is nothing to live for, nowhere to go. When I need a little amusement, I come here to weed and get my hands in honest soil again. I shall leave the city when this farm is sold." The others nodded gravely.

"Farm life is happier, more comfortable," Rehre continued. "These

---

*An earlier version of this essay appeared in the *New York Herald Tribune* in August 1930.

apartment houses have come too close. Where I shall go when this is sold there will be no one sitting on your neck, bothering you all the time. I will be up very early in the morning and work until the heat comes. Then I will rest until the cool of the evening and work again: I will be sensible, not mad like these city people who work in the heat of day."

Rehre was interrupted by the shouts of a vegetable vender who was driving down the street in the cart that had brought him in from the country. When he saw Manhattan's last farm he began to laugh. "Oh, wotta joke!" he cried as he galloped away."

FARM OCCUPIES BLOCK

New York's last farm occupies a full city block bounded by Broadway, Tenth Avenue and 212th and 213th Streets. From a distance it looks like a vacant lot, but when you come close you see surprising variety of vegetables laid out in orderly squares. There are corn, beets, spinach, tomatoes, string beans, carrots and cabbages. Stretched across one corner a lonely clothes line bears the family washing.

Behind the square the two-story farm house is the little patch of gravel that serves as a yard. A police dog lives in a crate. In one corner grow a few sunflowers, too weak to turn their faces to the sun. There is a jumble of old ginger ale crates and a few empty bottles. To one side rests, probably forever, a Ford with 1929 license plates.

TRAINS BOTHER CHICKENS

Manhattan's last farm boasts an outhouse made of unpainted boards and having no floor. In it are a few shovels and rakes. Right under the shadow of the subway is a chicken coop inhabited by two dozen chickens who cannot get used to the trains.

Mrs. Benedeto stood in a shed washing tomatoes. She would not be sorry to see the place sold, she insisted. She did not like to have people saying "Mr. and Mrs. Benedeto are farmers." People lost caste in the city if they are farmers, she said. When the place was sold her husband would get a job in an office and then things would be better.

"And, anyway, things have not been very good for farmers this year," she continued. "See, all my corn has been dried by the sun, and prices have gone down so low that I cannot make money. People come by and want to buy a bag of tomatoes for five cents. How can one make a living?"

Mrs. Benedeto had nine children as well as two cats and a dog to support, she said. And the people who drive by in cars always wanted things she did not grow. City dwellers do not realize that oranges refuse to grow on a truck farm. They do not realize that it is hard to grow things in the city. But she could say at least this for city farming: There are no crows to steal your crops. However, there are little street urchins. She threw up her hands in despair.

Over her head hung a sign reading: "Christmas trees will be sold here." When her eye fell on it she frowned.

"There is nothing in the Christmas tree business unless you can get a whole load," she said. "It was an idea of my son. But it did not work. What chance have we small farmers nowadays? Yes, it is better that my husband go into an office."

Rehre, who had been listening silently, rose and excused himself. "Well, I guess it's time for me to get to my dinner," he said.

"All you ever think of is eating," said Mrs. Benedeto.

"No," he replied. "You know. I wouldn't walk six feet for the best steak on earth. What I like is good fresh vegetables, just out of the ground. Your own vegetables that you have worked over and watched grow. I shall get all of that in a little while when this farm has gone and I have left the city. And I shall never come back, for what would be the use?"

WHERE SHEEP AND CATTLE MEET

Two miles and a half above sea level, Cloud Peak rules the Bighorn Mountains of Wyoming.★ Though only a trifle lower than Pike's Peak, it has never received publicity, so only an occasional sheepherder knows of the three lakes that form its diadem: Misty Moon, round as its namesake; Helen, surrounded by eternal snow, and Solitude, where trout swim back and forth through the reflection of the peak, which looms only slightly above.

The country is honeycombed with parallel brooks whose canyons leave between them pyramids of crumbling rock hundreds of feet high. Over these the endless trail climbs, dropping sometimes so steeply that your horse slides helpless in a cloud of red dust.

When I first rode this trail, clouds hung so low they seemed to brush my forehead. Back in the valley it was raining, but I could see through the gray streaks miles beyond to sunny hills. My horse was tired and jumpy and the lone pack animal took every opportunity to make for the brush.

The silence was suddenly broken by a strange, melancholy clamor coming from many throats. Like some inarticulate folk music, it was dull and almost toneless, yet filled with infinite nostalgia. I knew I was catching up with a herd of sheep. Soon they were on all sides of me, crawling through the rocks like overstuffed caterpillars. One in every hundred had a bell. I rode through them for a long time.

Having forded a stream and circled a cliff, I saw Lake Helen stretched out before me. An old man sitting on a rock watching the sheep pass seemed so much a part of the landscape that I did not notice him till two dogs rushed at me, barking. As I cantered curiously toward him he stared at me silently, but with interest. When I had tied my horse next to his the dogs ran up, anxious to be petted.

Only then did he take his pipe from his mouth, "Don't pat them

★An earlier version of this essay appeared in the *New York Herald Tribune* on February 2, 1930.

dogs. I never pat them. Kindness ruins good sheepdogs. Kick them, and they'll do what you want."

He must have been seventy. His face was pasty and a few long white bristles decorated his receding chin. But he looked kind and obviously was delighted to have someone to talk to.

"It's a terrible day," I remarked, and in a moment he was telling me all about himself in a high, bodiless voice.

"You see, I come from Baltimore. When I was a young fellow—sort of like you—I ran away from home and enlisted to fight Indians, but by the time I got here they were all gone, so I became a sheep man, and, by God, I'm proud of being a sheep man." He eyed me hostilely.

"You should be," I said.

He smiled. "Yea. We're teaching those cowboys that this is a sheep country. They'll all be broke soon." He laughed. "In the old days there were more millionaires living in Cheyenne than anywhere else in the world, for there wasn't any fences then, so their cattle ranged at will over three states. But when the freeholders came in and built fences it ruined the range.

"One night the boss rangers brought an army of cutthroats up from Texas in a special train and sent them marching down through Wyoming to murder the freeholders. So the inhabitants of Boulder organized an army which surrounded the cattlemen and would have killed every one of them if the government hadn't butted in."

By this time we were enveloped by a cloud that blotted out the mountains and the lake. Walking up and down in his excitement, he seemed a slightly more material form shaped by the mist. His voice, grown thin with anger, was part of the wind.

"Then we brought the sheep in," he continued, "long lines of them that came for days and days. The cowboys said we were ruining the ranges and the waterholes, so they reached for their guns again, but we were ready for them.

"One night they burst into camp and set fire to our sheep wagons and tried to blow up the sheep. I had an old .45 army revolver. I was proud of it. I don't know how many of them I got, for it was dark, but we saved three of the wagons and most of the sheep.

"And the next time they tried it we gave it to them just about the same, though we were only half as many as they. The congressmen wouldn't do nothing because they, too, were cattlemen, but at last the dirty sons of guns shot a Frenchman, and the French government started crabbing, so Congress had to butt it.

"After that it didn't take long. You can see for yourself that the country's ours. In a few more years the last cowboy will cash in and go East like a sissy, or else take up the sheep business."

The mist drew back suddenly, revealing a pack train almost at our feet. A cowboy I had known in the village, his Stetson sagging under the weight of rain, led the long line of pack animals. When the cowboy noticed my companion his face grew hard.

"Hello, sheepherder!" he sneered.

"Hello, cattleman!" was the sullen reply.

The cowboy turned to me and said sharply, "What are you doing here?"

"I'm going to camp tonight at Solitude." Being in too good a mood for hard feelings, I smiled conciliatingly, but he would not smile back.

"You'd better move along with me, then, and not hang around here." He rode over and untied my horses.

The shepherd's little eyes narrowed with anger. Fearing trouble, I swallowed my pride and mounted.

"You ride behind and keep them going," he ordered so gruffly that I could not help being amused.

We rode in silence for a long time. When I could see Lake Solitude glimmering dimly through the mist he turned to me.

"What's the big idea of talking to that sheep man? He'd as soon shoot a man as talk to him. They're a rotten lot, those sheepherders!"

SKIPPER DEFIES RESCUE FROM
SINKING HOME

If an honest, fearless sailorman and his wife cared to sink on their barge in full view of the patients at Bellevue Hospital, it was not the business of any woman doctor to interfere, Julio Almstandt, seventy-one years old, and a former city lifeguard, exclaimed yesterday.★ The same thing held for the police. In fact, it would take more policemen than there were in New York State to get him off his barge even if it was almost under water.

Almstandt's floating home, which for two years has been moored in the East River behind Bellevue Hospital, began to list seriously Sunday night, so alarming Dr. Beulah Rhoden, acting medical superintendent of the hospital, that in an attempt to save its owner she brought on an exciting struggle in which the seventy-one-year-old sailor worsted the police, his long years at sea having taught him that a barge could not sink very far in eight feet of water.

The trouble started, Almstandt explained, when his hand pump got out of order last week. By Saturday night the water had risen over the floor of the little cabin he had built on the barge, and which he had divided into a bedroom, a "parlor" and a "dining salon." Undismayed, he took his wife, who is sixty-five, upstairs into the "sun parlor," which protrudes from the top of the cabin. Nothing makes a sailor feel more at home than a little water on the parlor floor, he meditated.

RIVER RISES TO OCCASION

Then the river began to pour in through the open seams that are usually above the water-line. During her daily inspection, Dr. Rhoden was horrified to notice that the craft was settling fast. She rushed down to the

---

★An earlier version of this essay appeared in the *New York Herald Tribune* on September 3, 1930.

wharf with an escort of hospital police and called Almstandt out of the sun parlor.

"My dear man, you must get off immediately; your ship is sinking," Dr. Rhoden said, or words to that effect.

Ever an old-world gentleman of the sea, Almstandt pulled at his forelock. "Madame," he said, "you are undoubtedly right. But I have sailed the sea, man and boy, for seventy-one years and I have saved 200—or was it 300—persons from drowning. All my people were sailors. I hate to tell you, Madame, that this ship is not sinking. Even if it was, I am the captain, and I could not leave it. Good day." Smiling at the ignorance of land lubbers, he returned to the sun parlor.

Anxious to save the old sailor from himself, Dr. Rhoden sent the chief of the hospital police to persuade him of his danger. But the policeman did not get a chance to get a word in edgeways. Almstandt having suddenly remembered that he had once been an employee of the Department of Justice and had arrested 200—or was it 300—radicals and that he was not an amateur policeman like the hospital officer.

Then Dr. Rhoden called the 15th Precinct Police Station. Just as Almstandt got comfortably settled in the sun-parlor, two policemen came to call. Did he realize his ship was sinking? they asked.

Then Almstandt discovered to his joy that he had gone to school in Staten Island with one of the officers, he said yesterday. He invited both of them into the sun parlor and they all smiled at seeing the water get nearer and nearer to the bedroom ceiling. In any case, the patrolmen meditated, they had no power to drive a man off his own property.

When the policeman departed, Almstandt decided he had been bothered enough, so he conferred with his wife as to the best way to reestablish public confidence. She suggested that if two women passed the night on the barge no one could doubt that it was seaworthy. Flossie, his wife's best friend, was invited in and the three slept peacefully, lulled by the water and parlor.

Yesterday morning, Almstandt awoke to see his ice box floating merrily out to sea. This annoyed him. Things had gone far enough, he decided. So he shipped his wife off to the country to wait till their home was dried out. They he called some of his friends and set about pulling the barge up close to the hospital wall, where the water is only two feet deep at low tide.

Hotel Sleepers Aid Science by Counting Sheep

The vital question of whether people manage to sleep in hotels and, if so, how it happens will be scientifically settled at last by Colgate University.* The experiment will start this morning when each guest at the Hotel New Yorker will receive a printed questionnaire asking him how he slept and what he did last night to make him sleep that way.

To the "Good morning, Mr. Jones, it is 8 o'clock" which usually wakens the guests, the questionnaire will add such searching questions as "What time did you get to bed last night?" and "Were you more active yesterday than you usually are?"

It is hoped that the experiment, which was inaugurated by Dr. Donald R. Laird, director of psychology department at Colgate, will yield data which will facilitate the slumber of visitors to big cities and will aid the tired business man to rest. The relation of city noises and city life to sleep will be ascertained.

No Mention of Liquor

The guests will be asked whether they enjoyed getting out of bed, whether they awoke easily and felt cheerful. If they dreamed, they will be asked whether they enjoyed it.

The effect of New York's night life on those unaccustomed to it will be investigated by asking the following questions: "Did you drink coffee with your evening meal last night? How many lumps of sugar did you use yesterday? How many pieces of candy did you eat yesterday and did you eat within two hours of going to bed?" There will be no mention of intoxicating liquors.

The guests, who will be expected to sign their names to the question-

---

*An earlier version of this essay appeared in the *New York Herald Tribune* on May 20, 1930.

naire, will be asked their ages and how much they weigh. Their home towns, their occupations and whether they are in New York for business or pleasure, also will be asked.

MUCH ADO ABOUT NOISE

Excitement and worry will be listed among possible disturbing influences. Others will be: Noise from police or fire sirens, from trolleys or trains, from taxis or automobiles: the effects of lights shining into the room and of not being tired on retiring.

Telephone operators at the New Yorker, on whom will fall the task of waking the guests for questioning, yesterday expressed hope that Dr. Laird's studies would bring successful but not too successful results. They hoped he would do something about the man from Oklahoma who, unable to forget his ranch, insisted on being called at five o'clock each morning. The elderly gentleman who wants to be wakened every hour to take pills might also be improved, they felt.

But, they said, it would be rough on them if Dr. Laird's experiments produce too successful results. Even now, they explained, most guests have to be called twice.

DEAN OF AMERICAN MEDICINE

A WORLD-WIDE CELEBRATION, WITH PRESIDENT HOOVER HEADING THIS
NATION'S OBSERVATIONS, WILL BE HELD ON APRIL 8 TO MARK THE
EIGHTIETH BIRTHDAY OF DR. WILLIAM H. WELCH, OF JOHNS HOPKINS, FOR
FIFTY YEARS THE CHIEF INSPIRATION OF AMERICAN MEDICAL EDUCATION.

The idea that contagious diseases are caused by invisible animals and
plants which attack men from the food they eat and the air they breathe
was regarded, only fifty-five years ago, as the stupid theorizings of philosophers and laughed at by all respectable scientists.* When medicine
was at this low ebb, Dr. William H. Welch, known to doctors as "the
dean of American medicine," was graduated from the College of Physicians and Surgeons at Columbia University. He was forced to study
abroad because an adequate medical training could not be secured in the
United States. But since then, largely through the influence of the Johns
Hopkins Medical School, with Dr. Welch as dean, and the power of
innumerable foundations on which Dr. Welch has served, American education has risen to equality with that of all other countries except,
perhaps, Germany. And so American doctors were enabled to play their
part in the international battle with germs that was soon to come.

And now, when Dr. Welch is celebrating his eightieth birthday, with
the President of the United States heading the committee to do him
honor, the war on germs has been so completely won that the young
minds of American medicine are turning to other battlefields where the
armies of man still flee before unfathomed diseases that appear like spec-
ters out of the night of man's ignorance and against whom there is no
appeal. Aiming no longer to destroy exterior plagues, the medical generals of today are mobilizing against ills caused by the treachery of the
body itself.

His birthday, a week from this Tuesday, will be the occasion of an
international celebration. Most of America's distinguished scientists will
go to Washington, where the main celebration will be held, with Presi-

*An earlier version of this essay appeared in the *New York Herald Tribune* on March
30, 1930.

dent Hoover delivering the principal address. Many important university centers in the United States and abroad will hold simultaneous ceremonies, and it is hoped that all will be tied together by an international radio hook-up.

Dr. Welch does not feel that the span of three score years and ten a man may expect through biblical precept has been increased by the remarkable advances of science. The length of a man's life, he believes, is regulated by heredity. But in the past few men have lived long enough to let old age kill them—now many do. This is the triumph of modern medicine.

Laughing at prohibitionists who claim they have aided doctors in lengthening men's actual lives, Dr. Welch says that during his years of research he has found no evidence that moderate drinking shortens life.

The fifty-five years during which Dr. Welch has been shaping medical destiny cover practically the whole bacteriological era. He was graduated from medical school a short time before medicine was transformed by the scientific demonstrations of the germ origin of disease. Although Pasteur had been working for a quarter of a century, he had not, in 1872, attacked the problem of human infectious diseases. Koch was still unknown.

But all the way down the long stretch of history philosophers had sat back and observed epidemics theoretically, without the advantage of microscope or scientific method. Wondering why plagues which started with a few concentrated cases should widen their malignant influence until whole cities were stricken, they established the doctrine of "living contagion," which corresponds roughly with the theory of scientific bacteriology.

But, as always, the doctors scorned philosophical medicine. They believed that diseases were caused by filth or by such contamination of the air as produces bad smells. In those days public health and the fighting of epidemics were thought of in terms of street cleaning and sewage, which goes to prove that although theories are bad, their conclusions may be better.

Dr. Welch had already been out of medical school for one whole year when Robert Koch, an obscure German scientist, isolated the bacillus which causes anthrax, a malady of cattle. The germ origin of contagious diseases had been scientifically established!

But American doctors went on playing with bad smells as if nothing had happened. Dr. Welch traveled and studied all through Germany and Austria, went back to New York, accepted and rejected academic positions, built a laboratory or so and, finally, went to Johns Hopkins in Baltimore. But even then, nine years after Koch's discovery, the germ theory was not universally believed.

"Koch's experiment was received with a great deal of skepticism in the United States," Dr. Welch explained. "When I left New York I doubt if any doctors except Austin Flint, who was regarded as an old foggy, accepted it. Then came discovery after discovery based on it, but American doctors were not willing to see the truth for a long time. Germany and France both accepted it rapidly, but England was as slow as we."

The inability of even the leading American doctors to recognize verity when they saw it was one of many inducements why Dr. Welch went to The Johns Hopkins University; the American medical world needed education above everything. The stage had to be set before there could be productive research.

Dr. Welch, although he had done valuable experimental work, stands out in the forefront of American medicine as an educator. He has been the teacher and inspiration of our great investigators. Who knows in the the background of how many great discoveries looms the portly figure of the "dean of American medicine"?

Dr. Welch is rotund. He possesses the amiability for which portly men are famous, but none of the softness; though immense in body and mind, he is flabby in neither. Well read on all subjects, he knows where his knowledge ends. But what has endeared him to generations of doctors is the warm personal interest and the childlike joy he takes in all the world offers. The passing of eighty years has made him walk a little slower, but even now he thrills to everything that is new.

There is hardly an honor which the American world has to offer that it has not laid at Dr. Welch's feet. He has been president of the Congress of American Physicians and Surgeons, the Association of American Physicians, the American Association for the Advancement of Science, the American Medical Association, the National Academy of Sciences, the American Social Hygiene Association.

He is a fellow of the American Academy of Arts and Sciences, the College of Physicians and of three English associations—the Royal Society of Medicine, the Royal Sanitary Institute in London, and the Royal College of Physicians in Edinburgh. In addition he belongs to honorary societies in Germany, France, Belgium, and Italy.

Describing the American medical schools of his youth, Dr. Welch said: "Everything was lectures and nothing was taught practically except anatomy. Although we had some examples of men with great native ability who, despite the bad American training, succeeded, the majority who became leaders studied abroad.

"This was because American schools were attuned to the pioneer condition of the country. With the rapid growth of population and communities, due to immigration and the pressing of civilization westward, there came a great need for doctors, and more doctors, who had to be supplied quickly. Independent medical schools grew up in profusion, unconnected with universities and for the most part giving miserable instruction.

"The remedy consisted in forcing doctors to have practicing licenses. In my day anybody who received a so-called medical degree from any school, reputable or otherwise, could attempt to cure the sick. But when prospective doctors faced the necessity of passing examinations for a practicing license, they had to study in a school with standards high enough to get them by. As a result, the total number of medical schools has been cut in two during a period when the law schools doubled."

But the legal necessity for good medical schools did not create them. It was the privilege of Johns Hopkins, under the leadership of Dr. Welch, to show the way.

When in 1878, Dr. Welch returned from his two years' study abroad he was offered a position at the College of Physicians and Surgeons, then probably the leading medical school and therefore a great opportunity for so young a man. But he refused in order to go to the Bellevue Hospital Medical School which, although a more obscure institution, allowed him freedom to set up a pathological laboratory, the first of its kind connected with an American school. His method of letting the student find out for himself by experiment was so immediately successful that very soon the College of Physicians and Surgeons capitulated and set up a laboratory too.

Six years later Dr. Welch was called to Baltimore. The Johns Hopkins Hospital was approaching completion and the thoughts of President Gilman and the trustees of the university were turning toward the establishment of the medical school provided for in Mr. Hopkins's original gift. Seeking a leader to guide the new enterprise they invited Dr. Welch to become professor of pathology in the university and pathologist to the hospital. Having studied for another year in Germany Dr. Welch arrived at Johns Hopkins in 1885. As soon as the new medical school was established he became dean.

"The state of medical education when the Johns Hopkins Medical

School was started," Dr. Welch modestly explained, "was most favorable to the development of such a school as we had in mind. As early as 1880 there had been efforts to improve the medical schools of this country. By then the Harvard Medical School, the school at Ann Arbor, and a few other medical schools had already taken steps to improve the standard. There was consequently an eagerness on the part of the medical profession to see the establishment of a school of a higher order than any which existed at that time. We felt that to add one more similar medical school to the list of those already existing would be of little service to the community or to the country or to the cause of medicine."

When Dr. Welch went to Johns Hopkins, pathology, the study of the diseased conditions of the body in all their aspects, was not being taught as a unified science. Every university had one department of bacteriology, the study of germs; another of histology, the study of tissues or "microscopic anatomy," and a third of pathological anatomy, but the professors did not correlate their teachings or in many cases even agree.

Under Dr. Welch's leadership the study of all diseased conditions began to develop systematically, utilizing for its advancement the materials and methods not of one branch of science merely, but of all branches, main and collateral. On this foundation the great American structure of experimental pathology was reared.

In explaining the next step, Dr. Welch said, "American colleges had been developed to train men for few professions except the clergy, so the adjustment of medicine to the college was a very serious problem. We threw back into the colleges two years of training that were in Germany part of the regular medical course. We had to do this because students here enter medical school two years later than they do there."

Thus the Johns Hopkins Medical School, with Dr. Welch as dean, was responsible for the "pre-medical courses" which make the college lives of future doctors not all one football game. The other medical schools soon followed the lead of Johns Hopkins. By requiring for entrance preliminary training in physics, chemistry, and biology, they received their pupils with a sound basis of elementary fact.

Other innovations made by the Johns Hopkins Medical School under Dr. Welch's leadership include putting such faculties of clinical medicine as anatomy and physiology on the full-time basis. It was felt that professors who carried on flourishing practices simultaneously with their teaching could not give enough of their time and energy to their academic duties. Few other medical schools have accepted this point of view. But Johns Hopkins made a still greater innovation. "Our fundamental idea," Dr. Welch explained, "was that research and instruction should go hand in hand; that the best teachers are interested in the scientific advancements of their subject. We believed that productive research was more important than undergraduate training."

To understand the vast significance of this attitude we must realize that medicine as a profession is not necessarily the same as medicine as a science. The average practitioner is no more a scientist that the average lawyer is a creative jurist. Both take laws, be they civil or medical, and apply them to definite cases, but they do not create.

Like every great movement, the advancement of healing requires the co-operation of two types of men: the rare thinkers who build new rungs in the never-ending ladder of man's advancement and the many stalwart followers who make the ignorant world climb.

Largely under the influence of Johns Hopkins the standard of American medical education grew steadily like the sturdy trunk of a tree, and when the time came the fruit also was not lacking. Within the fifty-five years of Dr. Welch's career scientific medicine rose to a position of importance in American culture.

A large part of our constructive medical investigation has been done in the Rockefeller Institute of Medical Research of New York City. Dr. Welch played a major role in the founding of this, the first independent research institution in the country, and he has from the beginning served as the chairman of its board of scientific directors.

The Rockefeller Institute carries one step further the theory that productive research is more important than undergraduate training. Within its walls men who have proved that they belong to the small fraternity of scientific pioneers are sheltered from academic duties and allowed to spend all their time on research. They do not have to interrupt their experiments to teach a class of first-year students that bugs are bugs.

Resigning at seventy from the active leadership of the Johns Hopkins Medical School, Dr. Welch felt too young to retire. So, with the aid of $7,000,000 presented by the Rockefeller Foundation, he founded the Johns Hopkins School of Hygiene and Public Health, conceiving it so broadly that it has been copied all over the world. When, a few years later, the British government rebuilt its school of hygiene in London, they modeled it on Dr. Welch's creation.

In many countries the most brilliant students of public health were selected and sent to study under Dr. Welch, the necessary funds being supplied by the Rockefeller Foundation. Thus, in every corner of the world, questions of life or death, involving millions of people, of all races, are determined by the "dean of American medicine" through his pupils.

Having fashioned the groundwork for medicine in the United States, Dr. Welch turned to world problems. He has been from its inception a trustee of the international health board which has conducted public health work in more than fifty countries, fighting effectively from the tropics to the poles such diseases as hookworm and malaria.

In 1916 he was a member of that commission sent to China by the Rockefeller Foundation, which organized the Peking Union Medical College and Hospital, as a model from which the Chinese might learn what other nations already knew of the alleviation of suffering and the blessings of science.

In his seventy-fifth year, Dr. Welch resigned as director of the school of hygiene to take over the chair of the history of medicine. Thus the dean of American medicine will spend the last part of his fruitful life in retrospect, looking back over the long years of science; smiling at the days when disease was explained by original sin, or too much blood pressure, or filth; living again the graphic years of his life when medicine was rising to new glories not without his help and looking to the future, confident that the work to which he dedicated himself will go on from new glory to new glory in the cause of humanity.

In surveying the position to which American medicine has climbed, partly under his guidance, Dr. Welch recently said, "Although many Germans now think that the United States is the world leader in medical education, I feel that Germany still is in the forefront, though not so outstandingly as in my youth. We undoubtedly have come up tremendously.

"In scientific medicine, we now have men who rank favorably in all fields with the workers in the same lines in other countries. Since science is international, the question of who is the world leader is meaningless, but you may be sure that we nowadays have nothing to be ashamed of.

"In world medicine my active fifty-five years have been revolutionary. There has been an immense accumulation of new knowledge that has enabled us to control the spread of many diseases—cholera, yellow fever, diptheria, plague, typhus, malaria and so on.

"The only contagious diseases that we have not really learned how to control are of the respiratory type, such as pneumonia and influenza. They have baffled us, though we know that they are largely related to the accummulation of people in cities and that they are directly conveyed.

"As to the future—the directions are doubtful, but the progress in bacteriology has been so tremendous that the interest has shifted away from infectious dieseases. The young men now are working on diseases of nutrition, chronic diseases and diseases of the heart, because we have so little information about them. The discovery of insulin, which cures diabetes, is a result of this trend.

"The doctors of today, no longer satisfied with attacking the invisible enemies that invade men's bodies, are now making war on the treachery of the body iteslf. Like the religious men of old who aimed to increase your spiritual stature by curing the soul within you they soon may, by regulating your pituitary glands, increase your physical stature. But be that as it may, they are now working on 'hormones,' the gland secretions in the body which harmonize all its actions."

Looking back over his eigthy years, Dr. Welch said: "The expectation of life has gone up tremendously, but there has been no increase in the span. A fixed span of life is a part of the human machine. Longevity is hereditary, so the best thing you can do to live to a ripe old age is to pick your ancestors carefully.

"It has been contended that each man has a given stock of energy which he can use up by years of intense living and that thus his life is shortened. I doubt it. The deepest thought doesn't involve as much energy as the traction of the arm. Energy is measured by the loss of heat, and only recently have we developed a calorimeter delicate enough to register the energy used up in thought.

"In the last fifty-five years it has become much more likely that you will live out your span. Because a larger number do this than ever before, there has been a great shifting in the age distribution of the population."

"But," said Dr. Welch meditating with a contented smile, "I don't think the elder statesmen have made such a success of things that you can look with enthusiasm on the increased average duration of life. Young men under forty do all the productive thought in the world. If a man has done significant thinking when he is young, as he lives on he can deepen those thoughts and develop them. But there is little hope for a man who has done nothing before he is forty."

SHORT STORIES

I FELT THE BEACONS

He looked at her and looking felt the unbelievable relief of one who has suddenly recovered from a black disease.* Is it possible, he asked himself, that this is she and my heart has not stopped beating?

She had come down the stairs into the little bar as she had always come and sitting there at the usual table, his heart pounding with terror, he had looked up to see her draw near as she had often drawn near to him in dreams. For the first split-second of looking he saw only her legs, but he would have known those lovely, nervous, race-horse legs anywhere in the world ("They're like a chorus girl's," she had used to say with her terribly intimate smile that was both happy and shy because he knew her legs so well.) And since she seemed to come down the stairs with such slowness in that half a minute of time, her legs were one separate impression from her face. He saw her face and it was impossible to believe that something which had lived so long only in his heart was outside too and that this was she coming down into the little café where they had always met.

Amazedly, like Pygmalion when the statue he had dreamed began to move, he watched her descend the steps with the slowness of centuries and the speed of light. She paused, looking out over the café as she had always done, and he saw her tighten the lids round her huge, near-sighted eyes to focus them better that she might find him there among the other men in the room. And when he saw this gesture that was only hers and that he had loved with all the rest of her so blindly, his nerves tightened, waiting for the stab of pain that was sure to follow. And then he knew with the most terrible relief that he was well again, that in these two years the fever had left his blood, and, suddenly, so great was the joy of his discovery, he was close to tears sitting there at the little table where he had waited for her with dry-eyed anguish so many unforgettable hours.

She had seen him now and her eyes widened again and on her lips

---

*An earlier version of this essay appeared in *Esquire* (July 1936), pp. 51-52, 198-201.

appeared a frightened little smile. She is very pale, he thought. And then, in an unbelievable instant of time, she was standing before him with her hands outstretched. As he stood up to receive her, he looked into her face, and they stared at each other before either spoke or he took her hands. In that first deep look he did not know what he saw—there was meaning there to be pondered long and never really known—he only knew that she was grave and remembered that her gravity, although it clouded the prettiness of her face, had always been his favorite of her moods.

Finally, he reached out with terror toward her hands. What will happen, he wondered, when I touch this flesh again? Trembling, he took her slim fingers, and then once more he was overcome by such relief that he felt weak and dizzy. Joyously he lifted his eyes to see that the mournful expression of her eyes had not changed although her lips had softened into the mischievous smile with which she had so often teased him. He dropped her hands and stood there, still looking at her.

"May I sit down?" she demanded, affectionately mocking his clumsiness that he had not asked her.

"Please." He pulled out her chair and when as she sat her cheek passed close to his, he wanted to kiss her there in the crowded room, to hug her out of thankfulness that he loved her no longer. "That's a new dress," he said.

"Do you expect to know all my clothes after two years, you idiot?" Her laughter fitted in his mind over the laughter he remembered.

"Do you come here often now?" he asked.

She hesitated a moment. "No, I haven't been here since—since you ran away." In the melancholy depths of her eyes there dawned a timorous smile that as she talked grew gradually stronger. "For it was flight, wasn't it? Or do you still like to think that you left me in righteous anger. Putting the hussy in her place, was that it?"

Hypnotized by the changing expression in her eyes, he said nothing. She shook her head quickly, and her eyes became opaque. "Well," she said, "it's been a long time, hasn't it, and now you've come back and here we are again. It's a funny world. And as for me, I'm a staid married woman. Why," she cried, "I've been married a year!"

"Yes, I'd almost forgotten you were married."

She looked at him sharply, her lips tightening. "You mustn't forget!" Then she smiled. "But come: what sort of a host are you? You haven't even ordered me a drink."

After he had beckoned to a waiter, she asked for a Tom Collins. "You mean a John Collins," he corrected. "Will you Americans never learn to speak the English language?"

"Don't be so out of date," she replied gayly. "The English language went out of date twenty years ago. It's the American language now."

Miraculously, they were launched on one of their old subjects of laughing argument, one of the few subjects they had ever been able to discuss lightly, and as they made the ridiculous points that they had made so often, time ran backward until all the hatred and anguish had not been. They spoke lightly, as if he had never fled across three thousand miles of ocean and called her every evil name he could think of, as if she had never torn up his letters unread.

How long they argued thus he did not know, for this moment and the moments that were gone fused into an unbroken reality that was as long and yet as instantaneous as the meaning of their lives. Finally she said, "You English have a frightful nerve to assume that your dialect must be correct. The only people who still speak Elizabethan English are the hillbillies in the Ozark Mountains, so perhaps our modification is better than yours. As my husband says—" She paused but then went bravely on. "My husband says only the Americans now have the vitality to coin new speech."

But it was useless to go on. Her words had invoked the years between them and again they were strangers sitting in a familiar bar where they had been very much in love. And because he had forgotten that those years had ever been, their surging return restored the jealousy he had hoped he was imune from now.

"Your husband? Tell me, what sort of a fellow is he anyway?" He heard the tightness in his voice and cursed himself, as he had often done, that he could not keep it from her. But when he looked up he saw that she was too absorbed by her own sensations to notice his. She stared at the drink she stirred. Her face had become haggard as it sometimes did in an instant and its one blemish, her over-large mouth, was evident. Eagerly his mind seized on this blemish, tried to magnify it, saying to itself, "You see, she is not as pretty as she was." But it was no good; agony welled up in his diaphragm, and sitting there after two convalescent years he was as miserable as he ever had been.

"My husband?" she said, still stirring her drink. "He's very charming. You'd like him, I'm sure."

"What does he work at?"

"He's advertising manager for the northeastern agency of Universal Motors."

"Does he talk shop when he comes home at night? You must know the difference between a differential and a transmission now."

"Don't. You mustn't make fun of him. I thought you were bigger than that."

"I'm sorry." With a sense of degredation he felt swelling within his flesh again the jealousy that had for so long grown there like a cancer, and this recurrence after two years and the illusion of health seemed to be the epitome of all the jealousies he had ever known.

Once again he leaned from the window of a dark room; he had switched off the light for even in his despair he remembered that people must not know that he had a key to her apartment.

Beneath him the unbroken stretch of asphalt that usually swarmed with cars testified to the late hour; the street-lamps reflected murkily on the grey, litter-swept pavements.

It was unbelievable that New York could be so quiet. He was conscious of the ten thousand sleepers who lay, all horizontal, in the black houses around him; he alone waked, trembling, his nerves tightened for a sign of her return.

Three million women slept under the halo tossed upward by the city lights, three million women breathed softly as she breathed each dawn with her head on the pillow beside him; it is unfair, he thought as he leaned out of the window empty and broken, that I should love her so much and that she does not return.

Already it was almost two hours past the time she had promised she would be back from her date with William. At first he had been furious, rehearsing bitter words with which to greet her, but long since his fury had evaporated into a prayerful desire that his agony stop; he felt like a sick child who cannot believe that the universe would strike down the innocent so cruelly.

With seering concentration he listened for the footsteps that presaged still invisible walkers; each time the gaunt, recurrent sound fumbled at his window, he knew it must be she and his tension loosened, but the faces that showed in the lamplight were always the faces of strangers.

Over and over he reminded himself that always she was late but always she came home at last. "The little devil," he said out loud, "couldn't be on time even if she tried," and he forced himself to smile, but his ears as they strained for her steps did not hear his words, and it was someone else's lips that smiled. Determined to regain mastery of his own body, he walked to the mirror, and stared into his own eyes. "What are you afraid of?" he asked himself, speaking slowly as if to a half-witted child. "You know there's not one chance in a thousand she has run off with William."

But his logic was the vain flashing of a match in the darkness of an abyss without end; he was falling down, down, beyond hope, beyond reason, beyond everything but the desire for her return.

In an agony of fear that he had missed her, he hurried back to the window and the old comedy of the recurring footsteps went on.

And then suddenly the girl in the pool of lamplight beneath him was she. Seeing the springy step with which she walked, her arm under her escort's arm, he did not need to see her eyes to be certain they were soft with the afterglow of a delightful evening. And instantly, before he had time to feel relief, he was angry, furious that she could be happy while she put him through such misery. Clenching his fists in rage, he walked to the door and listened for her step on the stair. He let her open the door with her key and then accosted her in a flood of furious speech.

The little smile that had been on her lips vanished. She looked at him in amazement, stunned for a moment like one who had come from bright light into darkenss. Then she shut the door behind her, threw off her coat, and stood with her back to the wall, facing him while he raved on.

As she stood there in the dress he loved because it showed the beauty of her shoulders, a deeper emotion surged beneath his anger: the sheer, simple joy of having her back again, of watching the movement of her face, of knowing that he would put his arms around her. Above all he wanted to put his arms around her, to hide his face in her bare shoulder and weep as a child who has been hurt weeps, but he stood six feet from her and poured out the bitterness of his tortured nerves. For a long time he was unable to stop, like a man speeding downhill in a car without brakes, and then the spasm was over. He felt nothing but weak and frightened and anxious to be comforted. Humbly, imploringly, he stepped toward her, but now her eyes glowed with the anger of which he no longer felt a trace. She pushed him from her.

"Having called me every name you can think of," she said scornfully, "you now want to kiss me, is that it?"

Rising from his memory, this scene blotted out all the rustling world around him, it gleamed brighter than reality for he had lived in the past so long. Then into the closed precinct of his mind there came a voice, her voice, the same voice that had been speaking in his memory, but calling from the world now, and not in anger, rather with the half-sad, half-mocking intonation that was one of its most delightful moods. "I know you Englishmen fancy yourselves as strong, silent men, yet you might say something. After all, we haven't seen each other for two years."

Startled, he looked up and there she was sitting beside him in the little bar where they had sat so many times. He studied with amazement the large brown eyes and softly curling hair that had been part of his dream. Staring, he watched her expression change into a kind a fear.

"What's the matter?" she asked. "You look at me as if I were a ghost."

He sat motionless, unable to say anything or take his eyes from her face. She looked down to avoid his glance. "I suppose we're both ghosts," she said. Her face was hidden from him but he saw her gentle hair, and the tenseness of her shoulders was tight within his own body too. A waiter brushed by them, insubstantial, impossible because he was outside their mood.

Her shoulders loosened under the compulsion of her mind and she lifted her face. Although her mouth was curved into a smile, the corners trembled. "Haven't you got enough ruined wings to haunt in your decrepit English castles without coming here to rattle chains over my head? I don't want to be haunted!" The trembling captured all her mouth, but again she forced her lips to smile. "Don't you know that American efficiency has abolished all this haunting business; what's the dollar-and-cents value of creaking wainscots?" she continued, growing more fluent. "We don't have them here."

His mind was a thick forgotten lump in the top of his head through which he burrowed in search of speech. "A wainscot is wooden paneling around a room," he said.

He saw her look wildly round the café as if trying to find something to distract her mind, but inevitably her eyes became tangled with his. He asked, "Have you been happy?"

She pulled her eyes away. "Of course. Why shouldn't I have been? I married a man I love very much." She brooded for a moment. "How many times have you fallen in love since—since then?"

"Not once," he said, and felt his eyes drawing hers upward as the sun draws water. Holding her eyes, he saw fear there, but gradually fear vanished until she looked at him with the yielding stare he remembered from many passionate hours. And then he realized that she could not look away even if she so desired, that he swayed her by a power stronger than her will.

They stared at each other as if for the first time, as if during the half hour they had been together they had not seen each other at all, and now his heart knew as well as his eyes that she had not really changed. If anything, she was more lovely.

"You're more beautiful even than I remember you," he said out loud, hardly conscious that he was speaking.

She smiled happily, softly. "You Englishmen usually tell your ladies they're beautiful, don't you?"

Always she had parried his compliments thus. As her voice awakened a thousand echoes in his mind, a tension melted from his limbs. "What do you know about Englishmen?" he asked teasingly. "I'm the only one you've ever seen."

"No, I met another last year. And he was much more like an Englishman than you are. He said 'bally' and 'bloke' and 'right ho' just the way they do on stage. Why don't you ever say 'right ho'?" she asked him like a wistful child. Then she laughed. "You aren't very English. You're a cosmopolitan sort of guy."

"I suppose that's a compliment coming from an American. My dear young lady, I don't believe you appreciate—"

Some gesture he made must have startled her for she interrupted, her face alive with excitement. "Oh, darling," she cried, "you haven't changed a bit." And reaching across the table, she took his hand.

Her palm lay tightly against his palm. "No," he said. "We haven't changed, either of us. Only you're more beautiful, I insist on that."

Her brow wrinkled in thought. "It's always frightened me a little to have you call me beautiful. I know I'm not, but if you think I am that's very important. And beauty's a terrible gift. It's like knowing that you're able to paint a beautiful picture. Wouldn't you be afraid if you knew that?"

"No, I'd be happy."

"Yes, I should have guessed. It used to worry me sometimes, I used to think how defeated you'd feel if you didn't do great things, but I never worried long because I always knew that in the end you'd get what you wanted."

And miraculously, after two years of black discouragement, he felt that he knew it too. The world spread out before him again, waiting to be conquered; she gave him back the world. And suddenly he could not bear being so far away from her. "Darling," he said, "Let's get out of here. You haven't seen my flat. It's such a silly little room."

"Do you remember Mrs. Grundy," she answered, "that ridiculous china dog we had on Sixtieth Street? I still laugh sometimes to think how disapproving she looked."

He beckoned to the waiter, paid his bill, and in an instant they were walking up Lexington Avenue toward his house. Her arm lay yieldingly, reminiscently against his side; her gentle arm restored triumphant years. Round them the city's million demons howled and shouted, drawing up for lights with a scream of brakes, cursing each other with the ribald ululations of a thousand horns; he loved the din that seemed to promise battle and felt he could silence it with a movement of his hand.

Suddenly he felt her arm stiffen against his side. Glancing down quickly, he saw her over-large mouth drawn inward as with pain. "What's the matter?" he cried.

She did not look at him. "Why did you have to come back? Everything had seemed so simple—and sure."

"Do you wish I hadn't?" he asked while the howling city around them seemed in its unending movement to want to tear her from him.

"I don't know; I don't know anything. But I should wish it." She smiled wanly at the grey pavement that pased rhythmically beneath her feet.

Not knowing what to answer, he tightened his hold on her arm.

"I love my husband," she protested. "Really, I do." He only quickened his pace. Her eyes on the pavement, she allowed herself to be led, but she was his no longer; she was another man's wife whom he was dragging furtively through a wilderness of shrieking streets.

He was sure that having remembered her husband she would leave him now. Six more blocks to go, he counted; could he possibly get her over these? A traffic light flashed red in his face, and the cars leapt forward with malicious quickness to block them behind a moving murderous wall. For the half-minute they stood there he gripped her to him, expecting every instant she would try to break away. He even attempted conversation to distract her mind. Holding his lips rigid to get the words out, he asked her the name of a red, pseudo-Gothic building that towered to their right. Motionless, with her eyes on the pavement, she did not seem to hear. Indeed, she might have been a doll, dead and made of porcelain—the arm that bruised his side was as unresponsive as porcelain.

When they arrived at the door of his house, he tightened his sinews for the final issue, but she made no issue. She stood without movement while he unlocked the door; she preceded him into the dark hall. He put his arm round her to help her up the stairs, but the embrace did not bring her closer to him. Quickly he withdrew his arm.

The stairs were mahogany-stained with dusty rubber treads. As she preceded him through dingy zones of radio noise, mounting docilely, despairingly, without joy, his memory fled to the first time she had visited his rooms. She had run before him eagerly then, anxious to see the place in which he lived. He remembered that when his door was closed behind them, without even taking off their coats they had dropped into each other's arms. And in that first embrace was written the whole history that followed.

But now, although she preceded him without rebellion, they seemed further apart than they had ever been, even in anger. She waited inanimate while he unlocked the door, and once inside with the door shut behind her she cowered a little, her eyes on the floor. He reached out to take her coat but she did not seem to understand; she stood there waiting like a condemned woman for what was sure to follow; she stood there waiting for his embrace.

Although a sudden desire overtook him to run away, he had no choice. He stared at her, and when motion came to him at last it seemed to be outside his body—he found her in his arms. Then he pressed his lips against her lips. He felt her body shudder at the contact and stiffen against his arms that strained her to him, but her lips might have been any woman's lips. Unable to believe his senses' verdict, he cramped her against his chest and bruised her face with kisses. Finally he let her go, and she sank weak on the bed behind him. Then he knew that he loved her no longer, and suddenly terror gripped him that he would never be able to feel again. He was cold now, dead, forever cold.

How long he sat bent in despair he did not know. Finally she spoke. "Darling," she said, "don't be sad." He looked up amazed, for he had been so drowned in introspection he had forgotten she was in the room. She stood where he had left her, but she had come to life again; she stared at him tenderly from deep brown eyes. Only then did he wonder what her reaction had been. Supposing she had not felt as he, supposing she loved him still? The thought was too frightening; he attempted to drive it from his mind but remembered that she had just called him "darling." Supposing she loved him still? In an agony of apprehension, he tried to read the meaning on her face.

"We should be happy," she cried. "Can't you see that it's all turned out for the best? Sweetheart, there's no reason to look sad." He winced, but she went on boldly. "Think, we won't have to be scared anymore."

Unable to stand the certainty of her gaze, he dropped his eyes. For a moment she was silent, then she said, "Can you really be sorry that we know now that it's all over? I've been afraid for so long of your coming back."

He should have felt relief, but relief did not come. The most terrible loneliness swept down upon him—they loved each other no longer.

"Now I can return to my husband with a freer heart than I have ever given him. We plan to have a child next year; you know how I have always wanted children. And you too will be free, free to live your life apart from memory."

Yes, he thought to himself, memory is dead indeed. You go back to your husband and the child you will have and to the full meaning of the life from which at last my shadow is excluded. But I, where shall I go? The past has been taken from me.

RETURN

She had a heart-shaped face under golden red hair. Although her features belonged to a woman of thirty-five, they still expressed the eagerness, the breathless sensitivity of a girl. Perhaps her clothes were a little too youthful, too costly, too extremely in the latest mode, yet she carried with her that fragrance of breeding which, although subtle as an expensive perfume, immediately sets a woman apart. She was as out of place in the lobby of that second-class hotel as a kingfisher would be on Broadway, yet she seemed to have urgent business there. Her face was pulled with straining anxiety as she walked with consciously imposed slowness through the mahogany colored lobby, staring anxiously at each of the traveling men who lounged in their leather chairs and followed her trim figure with unanimous turn of eyeball.

As she looked around, the traveling men all seemed to have jowled faces and bodies bulging in the middle. Fat, manicured fingers were stretched out on knees like unhealthy sausages and Elk's teeth rocked on shapeless vests to the rhythm of nasal voices. As she stared nervously into their reiterated face, she received many a wink and leer to which her body responded with a slight stiffening of disgust. However, she kept on, circling the large room again and again.

Finally, an old man got up and walked after her. He was tall but stooping, with a heavy sagging face although the nose that jutted from sallow cheeks was strong and fine. Cut in the nattiest manner of a small-town tailor, his suit of tawny brown matched the necktie from which shone a diamond. He gathered his lips together for speech.

When the woman looked at him with accumulated disgust, his lips turned flabby and he tried to pretend he had not approached her. Yet he stood in the middle of the floor, his lips twitching a little, and watched her as she took another turn round the room and then sat down beside a potted palm. With anxiety plainly written on her face, she studied the people who swung through the revolving door that led to Lexington Avenue. Irresolute, he continued to watch her for a while, and then, with a sudden painful intake of breath, walked up to her again.

"What do you want?" the woman asked, not hiding her loathing. His eyes cringed. "Excuse me, but aren't you Mrs. Nichols?" She went white. "Yes," she said.

His gray face broke into a gray smile that pushed furrows into his cheeks. "You didn't know me, did you, Dora?"

"Are you my father?" she cried. For a moment, while his smile died, she paused, with an effort controlling her face. "Father," she said in a voice more smooth yet strained, "it does my eyes good to see you. I'm sorry I didn't recognize you, but you've changed a lot." He frowned, and she added quickly, "You've gotten older. It's been twenty years, you know. Neither of us is as young as we used to be."

His smile came back, but a little warily. "My God," he said, "you've turned into a beauty." Frank admiration came into his glance.

She dropped her eyes and then with an effort raised them. "It was clever of you to recognize me; I was only twelve when you last saw me. How did you manage it?"

He laughed loudly, checked himself for an instant, and then laughed on. As people turned to see, her face that had been too white became burning red. Suddenly his laugh was gone and his features held a tremulous, pleading look. "When you were married," he said, "I cut your picture from the paper." He drew a fraying wallet from his pocket, fingered among odds and ends, and finally handed her a piece of newspaper. She flattened it out to reveal, staring through a network of creases, her wistful, childish head in a wedding veil. "You see," he cried, "I always carry it with me." As he looked at her sentimentally, she stretched out her hand that was still in its glove, quickly touched his wrist, and then withdrew her hand.

A heavy man with protruding, bloodshot eyes walked up to where they stood. He slapped her father on the back. "Hello, Bill," he shouted, "How's old fish-face this afternoon? Still boiled?" A lid slid over his protruding eye and he laughed in the same raucous key her father had used a minute before, but now her father was embarrassed. Curtly, he got rid of his acquaintance. "Just a man I met on the train," he apologized. "I hardly know him."

"Let's get out of the lobby," she said. "There must be some place where we can be alone."

As he led the way up a short flight of stairs to the dining room, she asked, "You're staying here?" and he answered, "Yes." They might have been strangers were it not for the constraint under which they both moved. They examined the menus with great care, took a long time to order tea, as if anxious to delay as long as possible the moment when the waiter would leave them alone. When he had gone, they both stared silently at the rows of white-covered tables, each with its rack of condiments. They were alone in the overly ornate dining room; obviously tea was not a usual meal here.

Finally her father said, "Just like old times, isn't it, Dora?"

For the first time that afternoon she really looked at him; always before she had dropped her eyes when they met his. For all the smile on her lips, the expression of her face was deeply sad. "Yes," she said, "I can recognize you. I was so silly I expected you would not have changed much. Perhaps because I remembered you so vividly as you were. But that was twenty years ago, wasn't it?"

For an instant there was pain on his face, and then he said with false heartiness, "You must have been surprised when you got my letter after all these years."

"Yes," she said, "and glad. It was awful that you should have vanished from my life so completely, for you know I loved you more than anybody when I was a child. And then one day you were gone; it was impossible to believe. Did you really think when you asked to meet me here that perhaps I might not come? That part of your letter hurt me a little."

"I'm sorry, but the world is a queer place as I've found out to my cost." He shook his head. "Tell your old daddy all about yourself. Have you been happy?"

"Yes, I've been happy."

"It's strange, but I don't even know how many grandchildren you've given me."

"I never had a child."

"I saw in the paper that your husband died a few years ago. Tell me about him. What kind of a fellow was he anyway?"

"He was very kind. I loved him very much. But don't let's talk about him. Tell me about yourself. That's more interesting. Have you been happy in South America?"

"Of course, I've been happy." He began to laugh. "Finding me the kind of person I am was quite a shock to you, wasn't it? You imagined your father more of a gentleman, didn't you?"

She flushed. "Whatever gave you that ridiculous idea?"

"I'm not blind. But why should I be a gentleman? I know all about that. I was a gentleman once, and where did it land me? If you have good manners, it only means you know all the better how to be a hypo-

crite. You know not to make pretty speeches to the people you've betrayed, and to smile and smile at the man you're about to ruin." He was
talking very loud, with violent gestures. "Roberts was a gentleman and
so was Carl Simmons—I suppose they're still gentlemen—but that
didn't keep them from selling me down the river. It only made it all the
easier. They were cordial and acted like good friends. By God, they had
to; I'd made them. Roberts would never have been anything but a bond
salesman and Simmons would hardly have been that if I hadn't helped
them. I said to myself, 'I don't have to worry about them. They're
gentlemen and my good friends,' I said. But when the time came for
them to help me, when I needed only a few more weeks to get my
accounts straight, what did they do?" He paused. "They betrayed me.
And you may be sure they were very polite about it; always gentlemen
they were. They shook hands with me and made nice speeches and
offered me drinks. They told me how much they regretted that circumstances forced them into so unpleasant a task as making me bankrupt.
Just because I'd altered the books a little to tide the company over a bad
place, they let the whole world think I was a criminal. And they wanted
me to be sorry for them. They ruined me, the sons of bitches!"

Dora started.

"I see you don't like my language. If I were a gentleman, I'd say nice
things about them, wouldn't I? But I'm not a fourflusher; I say what I
mean. I'd rather shoot my sons than have them gentlemen."

"Your sons?"

Her father looked shamefaced for a moment, then forced a laugh.
"Yes, my sons. I suppose you and your mother thought I was going to
spend the rest of my life regretting what I had lost. I wouldn't be alive
today if I had. I started out that way, and it almost killed me." He
thought for a minute and with his rising tide of sadness an amazing
change came over his face; his features softened until, vague as a face on
a mist, one could see the man he must once have been. No longer was
he a defiant vulgarian, the sureness was gone and the forced gaiety, he
was a broken man, an exile, a border-haunter. Dora's breath caught in
her throat and for the first time she looked at him as if she really believed
he was her father, for the first time she looked at him with love.

"Do you hate me," he asked, "because I did my best to build something out of what life was left me? Do you hate me because I married
again?"

"No. I admire you. You never were a quitter."

"You wouldn't hate me if you understood what I went through. It wasn't that I didn't love you and your mother, but that I loved you too much. You've got to understand! For the first years I thought of you all the time; I thought how I had brought you disgrace and poverty. I used to risk being recognized in order to get Philadelphia newspapers to find out what had happened to you. When there was any news, it just made things worse, but I couldn't stop. At first, of course, the newspapers were full of my disgrace. I read how your mother was bullied by the police in their attempt to find me. I read how she had to resign from all her clubs. Then there was the week of the auction when everything was sold. And all the time, remember, I was afraid to go out in the street in the daytime for fear someone would know me. But that wasn't as bad as thinking how I had hurt you both. I knew that if I had any guts I'd shoot myself. Eventually, of course, the papers carried no more news of you. That was worse. I imagined horrible things. I saw you begging on the streets. Then I realized I would go mad if I didn't try to forget. Would you have rather I had gone mad?"

"I'm sure you did the right thing. But tell me about your second wife. Naturally you didn't marry her before mother died."

His face hardened. "There speaks the true lady for you. You would like me to have my children illegitimate just because of a stupid convention, wouldn't you?"

Dora hid her face in her cup. Then she looked at him. "God knows," she said, "I'm no believer in conventions."

"What do you mean?" he cried. He stared at her with bright, startled eyes.

"Oh, nothing." She laughed embarrassedly.

"During all my years of exile, I have thought of you as white and pure in a world that is white and pure no longer. I felt that because of you something beautiful still belonged to me; it was partly that belief that gave me courage to go on. You have been a good girl, haven't you, Dora?" he pleaded.

"That's my affair."

"You should answer me. After all, I'm your father."

"All right. I've been good enough."

"What do you mean, good enough?"

"If you don't look out, I'll get angry. And that would be too bad, seeing you again after all these years."

He stared at her without relaxing his face. "Why didn't you have any children. You were married six years, weren't you, before your husband died?"

"Seven."

"Why didn't you have any children?" When she did not answer, indignation ebbed out of his face, leaving him again defeated and tremulous. "I'm sorry, "he said.

The change in him erased the anger from her face. "No, it is I who should be sorry. But tell me about your wife. She must be sweet if you love her."

"I'll show you her picture." He fumbled in his wallet, finally handing Dora a snapshot of a dark woman with a vast bosom and a round peasant face. Although well past middle age, she wore the gingham housedress of a girl. For the benefit of the camera, she had assumed a self-conscious smile that revealed broad, uneven teeth. She stood, heavy and earthy, before one of those cozy and undistinguished white houses that grow like weeds in the suburbs.

Dora had reached out for the picture with a polite smile, but, as she studied it, her eyes, over her mouth that still curved tactfully, assumed an expression of startled disgust.

"Of course," he mumbled, "she is nothing like your mother, but—" He got no further.

Dora controlled her face. "She looks very lovable, very kind. What's her name?"

"Concha."

"A pretty name." There was a pause. "How many children have you got?"

"Five. Three boys and two girls."

"They're all my half-brothers and -sisters, aren't they?"

"Yes."

"Have you told them about mother and me?"

"No. They think I've been a tractor salesman always."

"Haven't you even told your wife?"

He avoided Dora's eyes. "I couldn't while your mother was alive. She would never have married me if she'd known I had another wife. After your mother died, it was too late."

"But she must have known there was something queer in your past?"

He did not look up. "I imagine she did. But peasant women have inherited the wisdom of the ages. They are wise enough to accept what they have without questioning." He beckoned to a waiter. "My bill, please."

"You are in town on business?"

"The offices of my tractor company are in New York. I have to come down every year or so."

"You have been in New York before?"

"Yes."

"And you didn't look me up?"

"At first I didn't know where you were. And then I was afraid you would feel I was beneath you now." He looked at her angrily. "Just as you do feel."

"How can you say that?" Suddenly tears appeared in her eyes. "You know I have loved you more than I have ever loved anybody."

He was touched. Relaxed, his face was ghastly, the fat sagging in broken, disconsolate lines. "You always were a good girl, Dorie. I knew you wouldn't desert your old father."

She bit her lip to stop it from trembling. "When do you go home?"

"Tomorrow."

"But you will let me see you when you come to town again, won't you?"

"Perhaps," he said, his face still broken.

She managed a smile. "Promise me you will."

"I can't. Don't you understand that seeing you only makes things worse. I have forgotten, I have forced myself to forget, and I am happy in my new life. My family knows nothing of my past and I have almost convinced myself that it was all a dream, one of those proud stories of success you tell yourself when you are young and that are without basis. It is best that way. I am respected by my children and my friends. I am a big frog in a small puddle and I try to forget that I ever knew the sea. I try to forget there is a sea. But when I see you, it brings it all back; you are everything I have lost: beauty and culture and wealth. When I look at you, my heart turns to water, I shall return home sadly, for you have taken me back too far, to a world and a pain I thought were gone forever. But in my little house, with my wife to comfort me and my children to love, I shall manage to forget once more. Don't think I don't love you; I love you and all you stand for, more than anything else in the world. That's the reason I will never see you again." He put his thick fingers with their gold rings to his face, and tears appeared between them.

She hid her weeping in her napkin. When she look up, he was gone.

AMERICAN PAINTING

The publication of my first book on American Art, *America's Old Masters*, in 1939, has been hailed as the opening gun of the explosion of interest in American painting which is still reverberating. My concern continued in eleven books, of which ten are currently in print. I was also drawn into many publications of which a selection is reprinted here.

DIRECTIONS IN THE STUDY OF
AMERICAN PAINTING

After neglecting American artistic creation for many decades, the Metropolitan Museum decided to make amends by staging a three-day seminar. The honor of delivering the "Keynote Address" was given to me.

Although this has been billed as a keynote address, it cannot really be that.* A keynote address tries, as it opens a political convention, to lay down a consensus. We, however, are *not* seeking unity. The object of this symposium is to foster the processes, sometimes heated, by which people learn from each other. I do not flatter myself that the ideas I shall now present will met with universal or even general agreement. If they spark controversy, that may well contribute to this symposium the more.

Certainly, it is possible to open on a happy note. At this time, when after so many dark years our speciality has at last come into its own, we may be forgiven if we pat ourselves on our own backs. We have, as a group, much to be proud of. Yet let us remember what Benjamin West often said to a pupil: "You have done well. You have done very well. Now go away and do better."

Much as I like to think of myself as a dashing young man, I cannot hide the fact that my first book on American painting was published thirty-two years ago. If we assign three generations to a century, *America's Old Masters* appeared a generation ago. What a terrifying thought! I feel like Longfellow's *Skeleton in Armor:* "Speak, speak, thou fearful guest!"

The sponsors of this exibition feel that its most original impact will not be in the field of painting, which is already coming into its own. They hope that the sections on decorative arts will create a wave of interest in an aspect of nineteenth-century American creativity that has

---

*An earlier version of this essay appeared in R. J. Clark, *The Shaping of Art and Architecture in Nineteenth-Century America* (New York: The Metropolitan Museum of Art, 1972), pp. 11–26.

been overlooked. I must confess that it has been overlooked by me. I hope to be educated during this symposium. In the meanwhile, I shall deal primarily with a subject concerning which I have some knowledge: American painting.

May I, my fellow workers, congratulate you on being here at all! When the historiography of American art is written, this meeting will have an important place as being, whatever the results of our mutual education, in itself the demonstration of major developments. This is the largest, the most inclusive, and potentially the most important symposium on the history of American art ever held. More than three centuries after painting and decorative arts began moving in British America, Americans have become concerned enough to hold such a gathering as this!

Very significant are the place where we are meeting and the educational affiliations of many in this hall. Only a few years ago, it would have been inconceivable for a museum of the stature of the Metropolitan to pay the attention to American art it is paying with its nineteenth-century exhibition and this symposium. Most museums regarded early American painting as so vastly inferior to European art that it was only considered necessary to let a few canvases, which had not been cleaned or restored, languish yellowly in some dark corner. Trustees often refused to acquire for pittances pictures that their successors would be glad to buy today for large sums. Disdain for the American tradition in art was the correct sophisticated attitude.

After I had published *America's Old Masters,* I soon got to know just about everyone working in the field. They were few. As is to often the case in a neglected, underpopulated speciality, they were cranky and tended to hate one another. I remember having suggested way back in those dark ages that a society be organized of students of American painting, but I was warned that I would be suborning a murder. Indeed, such a meeting would have been a perfect setting for a detective story, since everyone had a motive. Today, I believe, we are less cranky.

Although Lloyd Goodrich had already published his important works on Eakins and Homer, in the 1930s the main scholarly attention was directed toward the first centuries of American portraiture. The interest had originally spilled over from the pre-Depression collecing fad for eighteenth-century English likenesses. Gilbert Stuart, whose style was defined as more English than it actually was, reigned the hero. Although he had dashed off his portraits of Washington at the rate of two every two hours—he called them his hundred dollar bills—to secure a "Stuart

Washington" was the most impressive coup for a collector. English eighteenth-century decorative arts having also been in vogue, American decorative arts of the same period, viewed in their most elegant and transatlantic manifestations, were being explored in the Metropolitan Museum's American Wing and at the somewhat younger Williamsburg restoration.

Lawrence Park's *Gilbert Stuart*, the first modern checklist to appear of any American painter, had been published in 1926. An excellent book on Copley's American work by Barbara Neville Parker and Anne Bolling Wheeler followed twelve years later. Apart from the great names, the interest in our early painters was still largely genealogical. The possessors of likenesses of their ancestors wanted to know who had painted them. This was regarded as pure antiquarianism. The realization, born of modernistic taste, that crude-seeming portraits could have esthetic quality was just beginning to seep in. Francis Taylor, once director of the Metropolitan, liked to say that he had rescued the portraits of *John Freake* and *Mrs. Freake and Baby Mary*, the great masterpieces of seventeenth-century American painting, on a street in Worcester, Massachusetts, as they waited among ash cans for the garbage collector. Since Taylor, one of the most amusing men alive, was never averse to improving a story, I have never decided whether this anecdote was factual or symbolic. In any case, the Worcester Art Museum published, under the leadership of Louisa Dresser, a catalogue of seventeenth-century New England painting that stood out as a lonely tower among the flimsy studies of our early art.

Research had been immensely complicated by a classic example of good intentions gone astray. Thomas B. Clarke, who had befriended Inness and Homer, decided to put knowledge of the beginnings of American painting on solid feet. He announced that he was in the market for early works, the authenticity of which was attested to be inscriptions on the pictures and by supporting documents. "Key pictures" for a whole squad of seventeenth- and early eighteenth-century artists quickly appeared. Only after this trove had received much scholarly attention was it discovered that in many cases the inscriptions and histories had been applied to provincial European pictures. The inscriptions had withstood chemical analysis because they had been put on the back with paint dissolved from the front. Mysterious operators had found in old legal records the limners' names they signed, and they had examined the genealogies of old families for some authentic member whose descendants the genealogist had failed to trace. Into these gaps the mysterious operators hooked a line of imaginary descendants. In the name of the spurious last of these imaginary descendants they concocted an affidavit of authenticity stating that the picture had never been out of the family. Long after the sad facts had been ascertained, legal technicalities prevented their publication, which meant that writers too far from the centers to be reached by word of mouth continued disastrously to base conclusions on the false as well as the true Clarke Collection pictures.

When sources were incomplete and scattered, when few illustrated publications existed and no real effort at synthesis had been made, our major resource was the Frick Art Reference Library. Here were several thousand unpublished photographs of early American paintings accompanied by summaries of what was known, or thought to be known, about the pictures. Since the genealogists who had done most of the research thus reported were better at reading documents than discriminating between styles, the archives of the Frick revealed prevailing confusion. To take one example: the compiler of the first checklist of many an early painter had a simple technique. He listed as the work of an artist every picture that he could discover had ever been attributed to that artist. I never made out whether it was unconsciousness of the fact or indifference to it that permitted him to list without comment the same picture as the work of several different painters.

Into this welter there had marched as a savior one of the most improbable figures you can imagine. William Sawitzky was a Latvian ornithologist who had forgotten his birds to become fascinated with the beginnings of American art. The most self-demanding of scholars, he set a salutary example. However, he was too great a perfectionist to bring, before his death in 1947, much work to publication. It was left to me to publish, also in 1947, the first comprehensive history of American painting before the Revolution.

The spread of interest from Colonial and Federal portraiture to nineteenth-century painting was not so much due to the pursuit of new subjects for specialization as to an encyclopedic concern with defining the whole line of development in our art. Pioneering museums, particularly Brooklyn under the leadership of John I. H. Baur and Detroit under E. P. Richardson, started comprehensive collections; and various exhibitions were staged, one of the most important being "Life in America," which Hyatt Mayor organized at the Metropolitan Museum as far back as 1939. Three excellent general histories were published: by Oliver Larkin in 1949, by Virgil Barker in 1950, and by Richardson in 1956. I extended my own studies with a brief general history in 1950 and two further detailed volumes, one of the generations of West and Allston and the other on the painting of the high nineteenth century. An occasional good book or monograph appeared on some specific aspect of our nineteenth-century art that caught someone's attention. The most sensational of these labors was Alfred Frankenstein's *After the Hunt* (1953), in which, by discovering Peto, he split into two the work attributed to Harnett.

Our mid-nineteenth-century painting was first surveyed as a unit in two pioneering exhibitions. "Romantic Painting in America" was staged during 1943 at the Museum of Modern Art by James T. Soby and Dorothy Miller. Next came "The Hudson River School," put together in 1945 by Frederick A. Sweet for the Chicago Art Institute and the Whitney.

By this time another character as unlikely as William Sawitzky had stepped on the scene. Maxim Karolik was, like Sawitzky—was it pure coincidence?—a Russian. He had been an opera singer. Having fled the Russian Revolution to the United States, he married a wealthy Boston blue blood and became fascinated by her background. In 1949, he donated to the Museum of Fine Arts his collection of American paintings from 1815 to 1865. Highly publicized and highly persuasive, accompanied by a masterly catalogue in which every picture was sumptuously reproduced, the Karolik Collection has had a great influence on the study of the period. In his published letter of gift, Mr. Karolik stated that his primary interest had been in discovering "unknown and the little-known" artists. His approach to his collection placed a spotlight on various painters hitherto undervalued or ignored, particularly two whom we today greatly admire, Martin Johnson Heade and Fitz Hugh Lane. The rediscovery of these artists was a major gain for our understanding of the American tradition. However, a misunderstanding also arose. Some scholars, ignoring the purpose of the collection, interpreted it as a representative survey of nineteenth-century American painting. They felt encouraged to downgrade men like Church, Kensett, and Gifford in whom Karolik had been uninterested, because they had in their own time been acknowledged leaders. If this unjustified prejudice lingers in some minds, it will, I think, be exorcized by a careful examination of American nineteenth-century painting as a whole.

Even before the Karolik Collection began its impressive career, there appeared a movement in the colleges to teach American art. This was due not to any new interest in the paintings, but to the popularity of a major called American Studies. The programs were usually steered by the one faculty dealing with American creativity that had any standing, literature. But for the sake of completeness, some kind of course had to be given in the visual arts. The professors to whom this task was assigned commonly felt that they were being sent across the esthetic railroad tracks into an artistic slum; and like old-fashioned social workers, they considered it their mission to uplift. Each set out to reconstruct the existing study of American art according to the methodology he had been in the habit of applying to whatever aspect of Old World art had been his actual speciality. How far such methodologies are actually applicable to American esthetic developments remains a vexed problem.

I know from my own experience the tensions this question can raise on the level of institutional administration. When the universities were beginning to wonder about American painting, Craig Smyth, the director of the extremely influential New York University Institute of Fine Arts, which had been a haven for distinguished scholars fleeing Hitler, asked me whether I would be willing to give a course in American painting and to lead graduate students. I, being wedded to my typewriter, hesitated, and he went back to his faculty. They proved to be broad-minded. They were willing to overlook the fact that my education as a student of American art had not been conventional; they were willing to forget that American art was not an established discipline. But it was clear that I would have to teach American painting exactly according to the methodology that they applied to the study of European painting.

One can see their point of view. A doctorate is not awarded by a single professor but by an institution, and they practiced techniques of which they were justly proud. But I had to refuse because I believe that the study of American art presents its own problems, which must be dealt with in their own way.

We should not forget that one of the excitements felt by the Hudson River School landscapists was caused by their realization that they had an unhackneyed realm of nature to explore and express. Thomas Cole believed that the painter of American scenery had privileges superior to any other since all nature here was new to art. How fortunate we are to be able to share, in our own field of endeavor, the same pioneering excitement felt by the Hudson River School. Much of the painting it is our privilege to explore is new to art history. What a feast lies before us! From any position we care to take, we have only to look around us to see unexplored esthetic peaks and glades. Our task thus requires more pioneering than is called for in the pursuit of established European art history. We cannot proceed along highly cultivated ground sustained by a host of able predecessors in whose footsteps we can walk. We must blaze our own trails.

When Worthington Whittredge returned from years of study in Düsseldorf and Italy, he concluded sadly that to try to paint American landscape altogether according to the techniques he had learned in Europe would result in blemishing distortion. To learn to paint American nature, he isolated himself for months in Catskill glades. Fellow scholars, we cannot study American art altogether in terms of the European! We, too, have a need for Catskill glades.

Two factors that have been determining in the United States have only partial parallels in any major European school. One is that to a much greater extent than was likely in Europe, American artists, including many of the very best, were self-taught. The other is the unique relationship that has existed between our native culture and the more sophisticated, and also different, parent culture overseas.

The results of this relationship—to what extent artists accepted, refused, or exerted influence—lie within the scope of the most conventional methodology. Yet hazards exist. There is the *a priori* assumption that if anything admirable appears in American art, it *must* have been due to direct European influence, an assumption that has been used to justify some truly amazing bendings and stretching of the most slender evidence. An almost opposite assumption also has its devotees. They believe that any manifest results of European influence on an American artist is such an unworthy betrayal by the artist of his native roots that his pictures must be by definition altogether derivative and bad. If the proponents of these two fallacies happen to get together, they can assassinate a reputation. This has to some extent been done in the case of George Inness. The Europeanophiles explain Inness as a slavish imitator of the Barbizon School. The eagle-screamers say, "In that case, to hell with him!" But, of course, the Barbison School was only one of many influences, native and foreign, that Inness mingled with his own vision and his own temperament to produce a great personal style.

To go beyond results to define the basic causes for relationships between American and European art, we must examine environmental matters not considered by the strict academic view as relevant to esthetic studies. Beneath the reaction to Europe of every American painter lay the need of mediation between the society in which he was born—that way of life experienced in its totality—and civilizations abroad. This dilemma has been met in many different ways, yet in its essence it has remained constant from the beginnings of American art to today.

Profound differences between the American artist and the European are likely to begin as soon as a baby can waddle out-of-doors. The European baby enters an environment that often contains man-made objects of true beauty. At the very least, it contains objects that are old, and time is an excellent repainter, softening contours, meliorating colors. And, always, the European is immersed in an atmosphere of tradition, of culture viewed as a quality that accretes down the years.

The American child is urged by his environment not to take tradition seriously. The world in which he finds himself is exciting, pulsing with change and growth, but new. The chances that he will find close to his home any man-made object of real beauty are small, and time has not yet started its process of toning down. If, as the American gets older, he is to see a monument of art, he must search it out, find it usually in a spot separated from his normal environment. He steps into a museum.

The European who wishes to be an artist is presented with established directions and institutions that give him a solid base to build on or react against. But usually the American must either accept exterior artistic conventions separated from the dynamism around him, or he must proceed from hand to mouth.

It is axiomatic that to be a great artist a man must express his deepest feelings. These deepest feelings are profoundly and inevitably shaped by the environment in which he was raised. If the environment does not offer cultural maturity, how is he to achieve it? By reaching out for flowers growing in another environment, he risks ending up with a cut bouquet that quickly withers. But if he does not reach out, he risks ending up with crudeness. How and in what proportion is he to achieve a viable synthesis?

Down the years American painting has tended to swing between the poles. When our nineteenth century opened, the dominant school, which dated back to the time when America was actually a colonial possession of Europe, had managed to achieve, under the leadership of Benjamin West, a synthesis that functioned. The next generation— Allston, Morse, Vanderlyn—came home from Europe with elegant accomplishments that quickly gave way to sterility. Then there was a period when the painters, fearing too great European influence, sought to grow as exclusively as possible on American roots. As the second half of the century unrolled, the painting scene became complicated enough to contain several beaten paths. Homer and Ryder continued to eschew

European techniques; Inness and Eakins found abroad techniques that they applied to home-grown conceptions; Chase and Duveneck dazzled American audiences with European tricks; J. Alden Weir and Twachtman moved slowly but in the end impressively toward French impressionism; Cassatt and Whistler flourished as expatriates.

Whatever may have been the taste of a generation ago, whatever it may be a generation hence, today opinion prefers among our nineteenth-century painters those who were the less eclectic. This gives a particular significance to the phenomenon of artistic invention.

Although there was once a time when it was believed that every mechanical or scientific invention had a single inventor, it is now generally recognized in the history of science that when the necessary ingredients are available in the general environment, a number of individuals, completely isolated from each other, will make the same creative combinations. That this phenomenon occurs also in art is not sufficiently recognized.

"Methodology" usually assumes that a similarity between esthetic forms must result from some specific link that can be defined in esthetic terms. Even in Europe, I suspect, parallel invention was more rife than is generally admitted. However, in modern Europe the possibility and necessity for such invention has been, because of the presence of strong traditions and close artistic contacts, less great than in the United States. Only too often an American painter could not, however hard he searched, find esthetic sources adequate to help him achieve his ends. So he had to improvise. If he wished to show a man throwing an object, he might easily evolve a form that had been used by a Renaissance artist or ancient sculptor to express a man throwing an object. The body, after all, can engage in only a limited number of contortions, and when you have no pictures to look at, you are likely to look at the people around you. Gilbert Stuart pontificated that in Europe pictures grew from other pictures, while in America they grew from life.

During the nineteenth century, the major esthetic sources available in this country were engravings and at a later date photographs. These contributed to resemblances between American and European conceptions, yet the contribution had to be limited. It is hardly necessary to point out that the translation of printed forms into oil paintings calls for much greater originality than do studies under a teacher or in a gallery of art.

As they develop their styles, all artists make choices among available alternatives. If artists have worked in cultural centers in an atmosphere of strong traditions, explanations for these choices may justifiably be sought in cultural terms. One can proceed along a methodological road, at least seemingly solid, paved with ideas gleaned from books, with the sights and associations of studios, and with memories of past art. But in the study of American painting, if one tries to follow that road any distance, it soon shrinks to a footpath and then vanishes in a tangle of wilderness, trees, and second growth.

There was no effective art school in the United States, let us remember, until the Art Students League was formed in the 1870s. The choices made by artists who began their labors before they went to Europe were commonly decided by two factors not primarily cultural: their individual personalities and the conceptions they derived from their total environment. Most significantly, the only coherent school developed in the United States during the nineteenth century, the Hudson River School, preached as doctrine the avoidance of cultural and artistic influences. A beginner, Asher B. Durand wrote in his "Letters on Landscape Painting" (*The Crayon*, 1855), should not worry about theory or look at the other men's pictures until he had developed a style of his own in personal contact with nature.

The fact that so many aspects of American art grew spontaneously from the interaction of personality and environment makes particularly unfortunate the fissure that sometimes threatens to divide the study of our esthetic development between academic specialities. The art historian, rigidly avoiding what I am told is sometimes called "the sociological fallacy," writes about paintings as if they were miraculously conceived by disembodied cultural machines. The sociologist, not wishing to stray into the preserve of the art historian, heroically turns his back on all pictures while he writes about the climate of taste or the economics of selling. Such doctrinaire limitations of scope set writers on both sides of the divide to barking up the wrong trees.

Speaking of trees, their role in the iconography of American painting in another indication of peculiarity. To have read every work of literature that was available to Durand and looked at every picture he might have seen will not help us so much to explain the specific content of his landscapes as to have a knowledge of forestry. Durand was a farmboy painting for other farmboys. Henry T. Tuckerman tells us in his *Book of the Artists* (1867) that Durand could, in depicting "a group of forest trees standing in their individuality," leave out "the devices usually used to set off so exclusive a scene" because he made each tree so characteristic of its species "that the senses and the mind are filled and satisfied." Tuckerman urged the viewer to "mark the spreading boughs of that black birch, the gnarled trunk of that oak, the drooping sprays of the hemlock" and so on throughout a long panegyric.

A very valuable contribution of American Studies to the elucidation of American painting has been an emphasis on comparison among the various arts. This method has given us many stimulating insights, but within it lurk pitfalls. There has been a tendency, since chains of influence are often sought, to stress similarities to the extent of ignoring differences. And when similarities are found they are often defined, without further examination, as the result of direct cross-fertilization. The simultaneous invention, mentioned earlier, is often ignored.

Let us consider an often-cited example. In his famous lecture "The American Scholar" Emerson supported intellectual concern among Americans with their own environment. How often we have read statements running something like this: "Following the lead given by Emerson's 'The American Scholar,' the Hudson River school painters depicted the American land."

This postulated order of events reflects the long-held primacy of the literature faculties in American Studies. A simple check of chornology reveals that Emerson delivered "The American Scholar" twelve years after Cole's native American landscapes set off a major artistic explosion. Furthermore, the Hudson River School esthetic preached a much more exclusive concern with American experience than the Transcendentalists ever supported. Emerson and his followers felt no kinship for the Hudson River School. Emerson, as he wrote, found himself unresponsive to visual art until he went to Italy; Boston bought from Cole not views of the Catskills but views on the Arno; Boston remained the port of entry for European art; Winslow Homer fled the New England atmosphere to New York; Boston's favorite American painters were not Durand or Kensett or Church or Heade but Washington Allston, William Page, whom Boston considered "the American Titian," and that disciple of the Barbizon School, William Morris Hunt. When Hunt exhibited at the stronghold of the Hudson River school, the National Academy, his work was so hooted at that his attitude toward New York became that of the young lady to the Bowery: "They do such things and and they say such things! . . . I'll never go there anymore."

The often-marked resemblances of "The American Scholar" and indeed most Transcendentalist writings to the Hudson River School were not necessarily the results of direct cross-ferilization, since both movements reflected the same broad environmental imperatives. American cultural independence was preached to all by historical fact. After the War of 1812, the United States had turned her back on Europe; our society was going its own way. We had no Metternich system, no Revolutions of 1830 and 1848; Europe had no herculean expansion across a continent.

Another link between the Transcendentalists and the painters was the general acceptance of an optimistic pantheism well suited to the happy, prosperous, and rural situation of the United States before the tragedy of the Civil War and the subsequent rise of industrialism. Emerson clothed this pantheism in great prose and brilliant intellectual reasoning, but it was also sounded by illiterate preachers baptizing yokels by total immersion in streams of which the New England philosopher had never heard.

The different arts and sometimes various schools within the same art tended to reflect different aspects of American life. The Transcendentalists were intellectual; the Hudson River School was non-intellectual. Emerson saw painting as a step in the ladder to a philosophical understanding of Nature. Once you had climbed high enough into the intellect, you needed this imperfect visual approach no longer. For their part, the painters were much less concerned with ideas than with the emotions raised through the senses by the fact of Nature. They did not sit in libraries, but climbed mountains. They were almost without exception not formally educated. And their public shared their conceptions. Indeed, a basic aspect of the Hudson River School revolution was a shift in patronage from educated gentlemen to self-made merchants, who had not been students but farmhands and clerks in country stores.

In thus discussing Emerson and the Transcendentalists, I have, of course, referred to only one aspect of nineteenth-century literature among many. Literature was the most protean of the American arts. Just to mention a few names—Bryant, Poe, Hawthorne, Mark Twain, Howells, Whitman, Emily Dickinson, Henry James—is to call to mind innumerable possible comparisons—resemblances and differences—with American paintings. But this is too large a subject to be pursued here.

Nor can I, in discussing the relationship between painting and architecture, do more than pursue briefly the theme I have set myself of differences between the arts. A man who is securing a building engages in a much more public and generalized social act than when he is securing a painting. Partly because a house is so expensive, partly because a building protrudes as a conspicuous symbol visible to the whole community—friend and foe alike—partly because public buildings are cooperative ventures and private ones are entangled with the ancient mystique of the hearth, there is greater pressure toward conservatism in architecture than in any of the other arts. During our nineteenth century, conservatism (in art as well as life) looked to Europe, was derivative, eclectic, cosmopolitan. Thus American architecture became enamored of foreign labels. While our most original painters tried to deny what European instruction and influence showed in their work, our most original architects enclosed their spaces in shells that carried such names as Greek revival, Gothic, or Romanesque. Even the wild, vernacular exuberance of the shingle style masqueraded under the pseudonym of Queen Anne—what would that royal lady have thought of the didos cut, for better or worse, by this clearly nineteenth-century style?

As far as promulgated theory and active cooperation went, architecture and painting traveled hand in hand only when painting was in fact at its most eclectic. It was toward the end of the century that the architects pursuaded the super rich that they should, like Renaissance princes, embellish their churches and homes with painted decorations. This movement left the painters we now consider the strongest to one side. Can you imagine Thomas Eakins making an embellishment for the Vanderbilts at "The Breakers"?

Comparisons between architecture and painting exemplify the divergences created between the various arts by different types and levels of intervention through technology. Technology—the balloon frame, cast-iron fronts, the elevator, steel framing, and so forth—sprang up in the very center of architectural practice, like Jack's beanstalk rising explosively to tower over an ancient grove. In painting, technological inventions altered actual physical practice only by minor variations in long-established methods: colors created by chemistry, metal tubes that simplified carrying oil paints from the studio into the landscape. Technology's main influence on painting can be compared to the appearance of a new planet, which, without actually colliding with its predecessor, shifts, by gravitations and repulsions, surfaces on the old planet. I speak, of course, of the influence on painting of an alternate means of recording images: the camera.

In the mid-century, painting cooperated with the decorative arts in the sense that pictures by leading painters were, to an extent not unique but very unusual in the history of art, created not to hang in churches or aristocratic halls or museums or mansions or tax-exempt collections, but in the living quarters of the ordinarily prosperous. In this phase, which was the phase of the Hudson River School, painting was at its most aggressively concerned with native subject matter and home-grown technique. However, the furniture over which the pictures hung responded to almost opposite pressures. In his most informative catalogue of the Metropolitan's exhibition "Nineteenth-Century America," Berry Tracy writes: "The period of the late forties to the Philadelphia Centennial of 1876 was particularly characterized by the emergence of a range of styles, labeled variously as Grecian, modern, Gothic, rococo, Elizabethan, Louis XIV, Louis XV, Renaissance, Louis XVI, and 'neo grec.' "

Throughout the nineteenth century, the decorative arts echoed and even magnified the eclecticism of architecture. It was by no means considered essential to stick to one style in one piece of furniture. The nineteenth-century artifacts could, indeed, be said to resemble collages, in which seemingly disparate elements are combined in ways that would have amazed their original designers. The results could be exciting original creations, yet it is hard to find close parallels for this approach among important painters. The eclecticism of such a late nineteenth-century artist as Chase was different, partly because Chase avoided any conspicuous mixture of styles in a single picture, partly because *his* eclectism concerned itself primarily with contemporary European sources. He did not go back to the ancients or the Middle Ages or even the old masters, unless we include in that category Velázquez and Hals. One of the few important painters who was eclectic in the manner of the furniture makers was John La Farge. Perhaps it was no coincidence that La Farge was—I refer to his stained glass—the only important painter to play an active role in the decorative arts.

The course of sculpture was greatly influenced by two factors, neither of which had any reference to painting. One of these factors seems today reasonable, the other wild. The rational consideration was that the availability of marble and of craftsmen skilled at shaping stone induced the majority of the American sculptors to work, even if for sale to their compatriots, in Italy. The wild factor descended from the vagaries of sexual taboo.

The physical female body was never more covered up and thus never more a subject of interest. Painting could deal with the nude only charily because of its verisimilitude of color and texture. But naked sculpture had the auspices of the ancients; the color of marble suggested but did not duplicate flesh; textures could be kept hard (indeed to do anything else was beyond the skill of most sculptors); and iconographical tricks were developed to bring in respectability. If, for instance, a sculptured naked lady were chained, as in Powers's *Greek Slave,* this made her—whatever other ideas we might have today—an elevating rather than a degrading symbol. Her shackles demonstrated, so the nineteenth century rationalized, that she was not a hussy engaged in exhibitionism but a pure woman forced to exposure against her will. The monopoly the sculptors enjoyed of subject matter so seductive to themselves and so salable contributed perhaps more than any esthetic consideration to giving to partially or completely unclothed females primacy as sculptural figure subjects well into the twentieth century.

As I get toward the end of this discussion, the time has surely come to take up the question, so relevant to contemporary times, of relevance. To phrase it another way: how far are dead men to be indulged by forgiving them for living in their own time, not ours? This matter has two facets: one esthetic, the other environmental.

Writers sometimes insist that in our judgments of past art we should apply what they call modern insights. I will confess that, after all I have lived through, I am still flabbergasted that some men familiar with art history can apply to esthetic evolution the conception of progress. They should have observed that in art what follows is by no means necessarily better than what went before. They should know that the only constant is change: the position any generation occupies will be soon deserted. yet there is no lack of presumably rational and educated human beings who feel that the movement of taste has come to a halt in their own times and, more specifically, in themselves. If a painter of the past does not fall in their preconceptions, the worse for him!

Far more pervasive is the issue as to whether an artist of another era has the right to have had social ideas different from those we have today. To be relevant and thus worthy of attention, an artist, so it is copiously argued, must have done not *his* thing but *our* thing. Take, for instance, the matter of being a gentleman. Throughout the nineteenth century, you could hardly have insulted an artist more than by accusing him of not being a gentleman. Today many an artist, if you called him a gentleman, would feel an urge to punch you in the nose. Does this mean that the past artists were snobs whom we must, from our exalted social consciousness, despise?

These seem vexed matters, and they are at the moment throwing up much spray. But perhaps if viewed rationally the solution lies obviously at hand. The need is, of course, for the present to achieve as much pleasure, inspiration, and understanding as possible from the achievements of the past. What is involved is a mediation between two points of view; both must be represented at the conference table. The present is automatically there in the form of the critic who, however much he may reach out in a desire for sympathetic understanding, is still rooted in his own times. The past is there in the integrity of the object being examined. Let the two parties by all means get together as wholeheartedly and as intimately as it is possible for them to do. The result will of necessity be contemporary because of the age in which the critic lives. But it will not be so superficial and one-sided as if the critic beats on the conference table, berating the poor nineteenth-century artifact for not being up to the present date, for not being relevant.

Relevance, indeed, often sneaks in the back door while social consciousness calls for it vainly from the front. It is easy to attack the nineteenth-century painters for being escapist, unconcerned with modern social issues. But why, if these pictures are so abysmally irrelevant, is a sudden rampant concern with them one of the major developments of contemporary American taste? Perhaps we can find an answer in the fact that those critics who most vigorously attack nineteenth-century American painting are also those who most self-enchantedly cast themselves as members of a cultural elite. They view with alarm what they consider a wave of popularism that dares to presume that a man who was not especially educated in taste would have authentic esthetic insight. But such popularism is an important aspect of contemporary thought. And the central line of artistic achievement that moved from Thomas Cole through Windslow Homer was popularist in inspiration and patronage. It was launched in the teeth of an angry elite, won for a while almost universal aceptance in the United States, and gradually faded away under the sneers of a new self-appointed elite.

Ever since I was honored by the invitation to open this symposium, I have pondered on what should be my *envoi,* a statement to end with, like the moral of an old fable. I felt required to try to work into a single sentence my most fundamental beliefs concerning the study of American art. I finally reached this phrase: *Let no arbitrarily imposed limitations block our search for understanding.*

But no sooner had I set the phrase down than I realized that it required expansion; and it occurred to me that we are too impressed with ancient sphinxes and soothsayers for their ability to produce cryptic sentences capable of many interpretations. Almost any statement that is very brief can carry various meanings.

In suggesting that in our search for understanding we should transcend arbitrarily imposed limitations, I have not forgotten that every individual study must seek a finite objective. My meaning is that, whatever methods we establish to assist us in reaching specific ends, we should remember that our techniques were established for methodological reasons and need not constitute the only road to truth.

Such a study as we are undertaking resembles a great watershed in which all the components are interrelated and important. Investigation starts with rills that flow between narrow banks, bubbling past flat fields or rushing down declivities. But the forward current would be stopped if the rill did not flow into a stream—the banks now more distant—and then into a river. Augmented as it advances by a continual influx of more streams, each fed by its own ganglia of rills, the river joins with other rivers until a swelling flood flows majestically into an ocean that is also refreshed by still more waterways. Any mariner who ventures out on that ocean should realize that he is sustained by the waters from the inland rills; and any navigator of a river, however beautiful the prospect that he sees around him, must be considered provincial if he insists that no responsible historian will frequent seas where the limitation is the lack of obvious boundaries, where the shores may be out of sight, and he must, to reach the finite harbor he seeks, sometimes takes his reckonings from the stars.

Each of us may well navigate at different times in different types of vessels on various waterways. Even if some prefer to remain more specialized, let us *all* respect the courses sailed by others if they are well and truly sailed.

Our labor is a united one to which all limitations must be means, not ends. The other day I heard Father Robert I. Gannon, the retired president of Fordham University, ask: "What has happened to the humanists?" I trust that, if he were in attendance here, he would find many of them present, men and women who realize that art is only secondarily a subject for study, primarily one of the glories and joys of life.

Archibald MacLeish stated in an address to the Century Association: "The true definition of a civilized society, whether primitive or technologically advanced, is a society which understands the place of the arts: which knows that the arts are not decorations at the fringes of life, or objects collected in museums or exhibited in theatres or concert halls or published in books, but activities essential to humanity because it is through the arts and only through the arts that what is human in humanity can be conceived."

SPIRITUAL VALUES REFLECTED IN EARLY AMERICAN ART

Any examination of spiritual influence on early American art in the English-speaking Colonies must be based on the realization that in exact proportion to the strength of their religious faith most of these early Americans believed that the visual arts should be excluded from worship.* This is a phenomenon which it would take many such conferences as this to plumb, but fortunately we are here exonerated from needing to do so because the phenomenon was not in any way an American creation. It was brought to our shores by immigrants, religious sectarians from the Old World.

The taboo was for painting a crippling one, since the most coherent groups of early Americans poured out their emotional, their imaginative, their esthetic selves in their revolutionary worship of God. The sermon was the favorite art form, so passionately enjoyed that some communities needed, in order to have necessary work done, to limit by legislation the number of sermons delivered in a week. "Eloquence," wrote an eighteenth-century American divine, "gives new luster and beauty, new strength, new vigor, new life to truth; presenting it in such variety as refresheth, actuating it with such hidden powerful energy that a few languid sparks are blown into a shining flame." This could describe the effect of great religious painting. When the Rev. John Cotton preached, so an admirer wrote,

> Rocks rent before him, blind received their sight,
> Souls leveled to the dung hill stood upright.

This could be the subject for a great religious painting. But the painters were not allowed to lift their brushes.

---

*An earlier version of this essay appeared in *The Influence of Spiritual Inspiration on American Art*, ed. Mario Ferrazza and Patrizia Pitnatti (Vatican City: The Smithsonian Institution, 1977), pp. 102–17.

However, the taboo against religious art had one loophole. The Protestant sectarians were preoccupied with death as both the finis and apotheosis of human endeavor. Grave stonecutters were allowed religious expression forbidden painters. Seventeenth-century artisans, carrying on by inheritance and apprenticeship traditions older than American settlement, made the symbols on the gravestones they cut rich in the extreme. Mermaids rise before us, indicating that Christ was half-man, half-deity. Peacocks strut, representing immortality. The world spins in its sphere, surrounded by the sun, moon, and stars. Arrows, pick-axes, and spades demonstrate the inevitability of death. The decorative borders running down the sides of the stones combine pomegranates, promising eternal life, with figs denoting prosperity and happiness. A grapevine shows that the deceased has labored in the biblical vineyard.

It is permissible for scholars on occasions like this to quote other scholars, and thus I may be permitted to repeat what an historian of American art published more than thirty years ago. It is true that he bore my name, but the years that have extinguished his red hair have made me in many ways a different man.

"The spirit of early New England," the youth wrote, "still reigns undisturbed in many a crumbling graveyard. A few steps from the highroad through rank grass carry us to the intellectual world of our distant forebears. Louder than the shrilling of the crickets and the song of birds, lank skeleton jaws shout 'Memento mori! Fugit hora!' But every skull is tipped with living wings and many a bony forehead wears a crown. All those hollow eyes and lipless mouths brings not terror but majesty. We stand in the world of Raleigh and Burton; this is the shrine of Elizabethan death. Calmly and regally, he calls his subjects home. The merchant and artisan lie side by side. Soon there is a stirring in the soil; grass raises little spears that speak of resurrection; it is spring on earth as in heaven, and the sun of God's grace shines warm on the blossoming New England hill."

All of Colonial America was not New England, and, although there were many religious sectarians elsewhere—my mother's devoutly Quaker ancestors lived in Maryland—much of the population was only partially involved, or not at all, with the Protestant objection to religious art. There was a sizable minority of Catholics and they did commission pictures. Thus in Philadelphia, St. Mary's Roman Catholic Church commissioned what John Adams, when years later he was attending the Continental Congress, described as "The Crucifixion by Hesselius, with the bloodstains trickling down, the mob of Roman soldiers, the darkness." That picture is lost, but we do have a *Holy Family* attributed to Gustavus Hesselius. A Swedish immigrant who arrived in 1712, Hesselius was a relation of the immensely influential Protestant philosopher Emanuel Swedenborg.

Not here in the Vatican—not, indeed, anywhere—could Hesselius's *Holy Family* be considered a masterpiece. Religious painting could not truly blossom from seventeenth- and eighteenth-century American soil.

In addition to doctrinal prejudices which forced religious pictures to be rare exceptions, a whole series of phenomena prevented the development on American shores of any complicated painting style. There existed no coherent tradition, not only for religious art, but for any type of painting. The thirteen British colonies and even areas within a single colony were separated by wide reaches of wild nature. The principal trade routes did not link American centers with each other but went from each across the ocean. However, very little knowledge of European art moved in ships. The first American painter of any importance to reach Europe was Benjamin West, who arrived in Italy during 1760. There being no substantial lure, the European artists who visited or settled in America were workmen too incompetent to succeed at home. Their points of origin and thus the style they practiced were extremely various. The non-artistic American immigrants almost never belonged to a social class that would permit them to bring along good pictures, and the quality of what European canvases subsequently purchased by collectors was dictated by the meagerness of American purses. Their acceptance was justified by the ignorance of the American buyers and the general tendency in those days to make little distinction between a copy and an original. The Americans secured bad copies attributed to great names, dreadful daubs.

Add that in no American center were there facilities to develop that knowledge of the nude body which was essential to figure painting. There were none of the casts from the antique which European art students sketched. Life classes did not exist. If you asked your wife to pose, she would go home to mother. America's first art school, the Columbian Academy, opened in 1795 and closed almost immediately. Among the contretemps: the baker who had been hired to pose in the nude lost at the last minute his courage. The organizer of the academy, the painter Charles Willson Peale, tried to remedy matters by taking off his own clothes, but his elderly, rotund figure revealed, alas, little anatomical structure.

All the impediments to sophisticated style and knowledgable renditions of the figure would not have blocked the road to religious painting had those settlers of British America who lacked doctrinal objections been willing to forge ahead while ignoring European precedent. The English-speaking Americans, until the Revolution broke the colonial net, cared desperately about European precedent. They had no intention, particularly when it came to cultural matters like painting, of showing crudeness by violating prevailing European canons.

As colonials, the Americans were convinced that the variant culture being fostered by their own experience should be hidden and then re-formed rather than expressed and gloried in. This inhibited the various arts in exact proportion to the practicability of importing models from abroad. Only naïve artists—schoolgirls, sign painters—who considered their production too lowly for comparison with serious European art, felt free to paint according to their own ideas. But there was one type of professional printing that had to be created, without adequate European models, on American soil.

To have your portrait painted had long been in England an indication that you were successful and would have a posterity that would be proud to remember you. Americans rapidly became successful, the possessors of wide acres, the founders, presumably, of dynasties. Although an occasional extreme Protestant minister refused to sit for his own likeness lest he practice the sin of pride, there was no deep religious objection to portrait painting. And the form seemed a necessity to the creators of a new world who, however culturally modest, were not unconscious that the society and its prosperity were the achievements of their own brains and hands.

Efforts were made to procure portraits by sending written descriptions across the ocean, but what came back was, however socially elegant, not personally acceptable. There was no way to get around it: portraits had to be painted in the presence of sitters—and in those days few American men and almost no American women made the very expensive and very time-consuming trip abroad in a square rigger. The problem thus raised would have been simpler if there had been important European portraits in America to serve as models. But almost without exception the American settlers had come from too simple European backgrounds to bring with them any such heirlooms. American portraitists and sitters were forced to set out on their own, and in so doing they created the first important and indigenous American art.

Since we are concerned here with spirituality, with moral values, it must be emphasized that portraiture is an art which enables us to look, more directly than is the case with many more imaginative forms, into the ideals and social structures of a time and place. Portraiture is—or was, at least until very modern times—a social art. It was not, in the time and place of which I am speaking, an individual staring by himself in his mirror or soliloquizing in his diary. It was not an artist expressing his personality through private and perhaps highly individualistic interpretations of his neighbors. It was two individuals cooperating on an image which not only would be satisfactory to themselves and their immediate companions, but would key in, when sent out into the world, with the then accepted conceptions concerning what was admirable in human character, would express favorably the role of the individual in his preferred place in the structure of society. We can thus trace through the portraits the change in spiritual values that led to the American Revolution. In the old textbooks, the American Revolution was attributed to American outrage against injustices legislated in England. But many an intelligent schoolchild must have felt a disproportion between these pinpricks and the great explosion. It is now becoming more and more realized that there had developed on the new continent a type of human being who served different social and moral imperatives from those accepted by Englishmen. Only a few examples can here be cited of the forces that created the change. To begin with, the hazards, both physical and psychological, of a trip to a wild new continent established natural selections: the immigrants were all persons who preferred danger to being trapped in old modes. They moved from a cramped world to a world of boundless space, a world that presented no reason for poverty and where upward mobility was so great that no aristocracy could stay in the saddle long enough firmly to seat itself. A world in which novel problems defied conventional solution and demanded improvisation. A world in which men, not carried along by cultural or social currents that could be made relevant to their situation, had to swim for themselves. A world in which a man must strike out for himself and also be dependent on his neighbors. Americans required the moral principles of self-reliance, tolerance, equality. The importance of the individual became the basic principle of early America.

The paradox was that before the American Revolution this principle was not consciously recognized or ever identified in intellectual terms. The change took place inconspicuously and everywhere, in fields, along streets, indeed, wherever Americans dealt with the world around them. The American Man went into the Revolution still clothed to a considerable extent in the borrowed clothes of colonialism. He came out of the

Revolution knowing himself and determined to establish—as he did—the modern world's first great democracy. We can trace this development in portrait art.

Borrowed clothes! For the American colonial portraitists there was only one easily available type of European model. Before technology had developed cheaper forms for reproducing pictures, the likenesses of important people were brought to a large public by engravers who reproduced, in small, and in black and white, and on paper, painted likenesses by major portraitists. The first American painter who can be demonstrated by documents to have been born on these shores, Nathaniel Emmons (1704), was so naïve that he hardly recognized the difference between an engraving and a handmade picture. This is revealed by a comparison between his *Portrait of Andrew Oliver*, a leading Bostonian, and *The Right Honorable Charles Montague*, originally painted by the British court painter Sir Godfrey Kneller, and translated into a mezzotint engraving by J. Smith.

Emmons's portrait is done like his model in black and white and is hardly larger than the print. He imitated the lettered legend universal in engravings but unknown in European painting, and, having no printing press, made by hand several examples of the picture. Montague's body, in its elegant costume and posture, reappeared in Emmons's picture as did the conventional background, but the face Emmons was forced to study from life. Had its possessor tried to frequent the luxurious haunts of the Hon. Charles Montague, that face would have given him away at once as not being a graceful gentleman but the dour, down-to-earth middle-class inhabitant of a different world.

The moral, the spiritual issue was that the engraved sources represented an entirely different attitude toward man and his place in the world from the attitudes which grew naturally from American conditions. Kneller and his English colleagues worked for a society in which a man's class was so important that his individual personality could be slighted. Artists concentrated on rich settings, elaborate costumes, and graceful poses. Gestures and faces became semi-impersonal symbols of rank.

During 1754, Laurence Kilburn advertised in New York that he was certain he could please the Colonials by, as he put it, "taking a true likeness, and finishing the drapery in a proper manner, and also in the choice of attitudes suitable to each person's age and sex." But where in his pattern book was the gesture suitable for a merchant who had just bought prime beaver skins from a naked Indian?

Emmons's practice could not, of course, for long satisfy anyone. Americans wanted life-size figures, done not in black and white but in color. The need to enlarge and to paint with oils—the engravings gave, of course, no hint as to color or brush strokes—forced the artists to set out to a considerable extent on their own. The better painters solved their technical problems by simplifying the engraved forms until, with their inadequate techniques, they could handle them. In the process, they often changed the mood, as a New York artist active in the 1720s whom I have called the Peyster limner did when he adapted a high court picture, *Lord Buckhurst and Lady Sackville,* and again an engraving after Kneller, for his own portrait *De Peyster Boy with Deer.* The English print expressed the grandeur of a great noble garden from which a tame gazelle has appeared to be patted; but, the American picture breathes an air of wild innocence. The deer seems to have stepped out of the forest.

The master depictor of American colonial mores was Robert Feke, who was active from Boston to Philadelphia in the 1740s and 1750s. He showed American aristocratic pretentions as what they were: a dream, a happy dream, the play-acting of people to whom the world had been very kind. Out of a frowning coast and a dark forest had come a pot of gold; the rainbow's end rested permanently on the Colonies. Wealth, position, ample living. These were the gifts of America. How could you be crabbed and sad? You had to sing.

The first great artist in any field produced by America was John Singleton Copley. Born in 1738, he was of the high Revolutionary generation, and his art expressed exactly the dichotomy with which Americans went into the Revolution, insisting that they were loyal Englishmen fighting for the British Constitution, but about to throw that constitution and its king out of the window. Copley made much use of imported engravings. His renderings of European costumes is meticulous, yet the stance of the bodies underneath has been changed to accord with shrewdly depicted, unadorned, unflattering American heads. Where in paintings by Feke such as *Mrs. William Bowdoin*, the high-spirited aristocratic aura was the soul of the pictures, in Copley's art the essence was always the likeness.

Copley's *Portrait of Paul Revere*, for which, of course, there is no engraved source, was as much a revolutionary cry as David's *Tennis Court Oath*. Although silversmiths were the aristocrats of American artisans, Revere is presented to posterity not as a gentleman, but wearing his work clothes with his tools and creations before him.

In the heat of the Revolutionary conflict, colonial thinking melted away, revealing in its nakedness the American idealism which had been evolving since white men had settled British America. The quintessential document could be said to be the most popular of American portraits: Gilbert Stuart's Vaughan and Athenaeum portraits of George Washington, painted in the 1790s. What strange portraits of an eighteenth-century ruler! There is nothing about the heads quietly shown against plain backgrounds to tell us that we are looking at the President of a nation, one of the greatest men in the history of the world. If we are impressed, it is by the character of the individual shown.

A curious aspect of the American Revolutionary period was that the favorite painter of George III, the leader of British art who succeeded Sir Joshua Reynolds as President of the Royal Academy, was an American who never denied his enthusiasm for the Revolutionary cause.

He was to play a key role in the development of British religious painting.

West had been born in Pennsylvania in a Quaker community opposed to religious art. His burial in that shrine for British heroes, Saint Paul's, was for a time blocked because there was no record that he had been baptized. During his student years in Italy (1760-1763) as the first American artist to study abroad, he had become a pioneer in the dissemination of a new Protestant neo-classicism devoted to expressing, through painted tableaux known as "historical paintings" the virtues most admired by the rising middle class: altruism, filial piety, honesty, bravery, patriotism to name a few. This was to be done through reconstructing on large canvases elevating scenes from the antique. After he settled in London, West electrified taste and earned the passionate admiration of the king with such pictures as *Regulus Leaving Rome* and *Agrippina with the Ashes of Germanicus* (1768).

But West, having received in Pennsylvania no formal education, had no basic feeling for the classics and, being of the American Revolutionary generation, he had a highly innovative turn of mind. He painted, as a scene from the American French and Indian War, the first important modern battle picture, *The Death of Wolfe* (1770), in which he dared show soldiers not in togas but in the uniforms they actually wore. He brought scenes from the Middle Ages into neo-classical history painting. And, because of his alliance with that head of the church, the king, he forced the Anglican bishops to receive into their churches, reluctantly and with much grumbling, paintings which expressed the true obsession of his childhood environment: religion. This was a revolution in official English religious life.

The paintings keyed in to Protestant preconceptions by being in fact huge illustrations to the Bible. His huge canvas *Death on a Pale Horse* came from the Book of Revelation. Painted in 1817, it reveals that West, ever open to ideas, was, at an early date, moving esthetically into the Romantic movement. The first important French Romantic painting, Géricault's *The Raft of the Medusa*, was exhibited two years later.

West's American pupil Washington Allston, who was to do similar pictures, wrote concerning *Death on a Pale Horse*, "It is impossible to conceive anything more terrible. I am certain no painter has exceeded West in the fury, horror, and despair." Such pictures presaged the nineteenth-century artistic habit, best known to us now through the illustrations of Gustave Doré, of finding in the multifaceted Bible scenes capable of highly dramatic expression.

Another influence on religious painting was exerted by tremendous pictures done during West's extreme old age—his *Christ Rejected* was painted when he was seventy-seven—which prosed out biblical events in such sober detail that they can be read like a book. Such pictures, which appealed to what might be called the "Sunday School taste," had a great run in the nineteenth century.

The brand new United States was enchanted to claim West—although he never came home he cherished his American connections—an artist who then had such great international influence and reputation. When West gave his *Christ Healing the Sick* to the Pennsylvania Hospital, viewers paid admission fees that were almost an endowment. The Pennsylvania Academy mortgaged its building to buy *Dead Man Revived by Touching the Bones of the Prophet Elisha* painted in England by West's South Carolina-born pupil Allston. Ten Boston gentlemen subscribed the then huge sum of $10,000 for Allston's unfinished *Belshazzar's Feast*. Yet the style did not flourish in America. The Church of England might be forced to open its doors to art, but not so the Protestant sectarians. The pictures were too big for American rooms—the Pennsylvania Hospital had to erect a special building for *Christ Healing the Sick*—and the necessary skill for figure painting was still unachievable in America. In any case a new school of painting was getting under way, which was to be the most spiritually inspired school in all American history.

My listeners may have noticed that in stating that only portraits were of necessity painted on the American continent I made no mention of views of American scenery. This was because there was no demand for such pictures. Eighteenth-century colonials accepted the European dictum that, since the proper study of mankind was man, landscape painting was a low form of art which achieved what respectability it had in direct proportion to how much the vista had been created by the hand of man. It followed that the scenery of a wild new land was the least paintable of all.

But the Romantic movement and parallel developments in American religious thought found spirituality less in the accumulated wisdom of religious thinkers than in the prattling of an innocent child. The conviction that the hand of God was visible in unedited Nature completely turned the table concerning landscape painting. Now the most inspiring vista was that least shaped by the hand of man. American scenery, newly and very sparsely inhabited as compared to that of Europe, was the most inspiring of all.

It was an indication of on-hanging provincialism that Thomas Cole, whose example set going what is known as the Hudson River School, was an immigrant escaped from what Blake called the "dark Satanic mills" of nascent English industrialism. But after Cole had, during 1825, exhibited in the window of a New York City frame shop four idyllic views of Hudson River scenery, taste for such pictures mounted in the United States with the velocity of an explosion.

Although he can be considered the father of the Hudson River School, Cole was not a true member—every true member was American-born—because he could not accept wholeheartedly the conception that Nature's inspiration was, without exterior strenghthening, a powerful spiritual force. He painted alternately with his pure landscapes moral allegories of a type better suited to literature. Take, for instance, *Youth*, the first canvas in a four-picture series called *The Voyage of Life*. The youth's guardian angel, who has guided his boat in the previous episode, *Childhood*, has stepped ashore, and the young man sees in the sky vapory domes, symbolizing the glorious hopes of youth, which be intends to reach. However, if you look closely, you will see that the river on which he floats turns away from the vision. He will never reach it. He will, in the remaining episodes, face currents and storms from which only the return of the guardian angel will rescue him. Such pictures resemble much what Romantic painters in Europe were doing to great applause, but, to Cole's chagrin, American collectors preferred his naturalistic views.

Asher B. Durand, the true leader of the Hudson River School, denounced this conception, stating that a landscape was "great in proportion as it declares the glory of God and not the works of man." The conception that Nature is itself so good that man does not need the intervention of a guardian angel was an expression of American optimism: Nature had indeed, in supplying a small population with an unspoiled huge continent, showered prosperity on the self-reliant; beauty on those with eyes to see. Yet, however much it was also encouraged by their environment, the belief in Nature's God was for the Hudson River School painters a deep religious faith.

Far from seeking, as did so much of the world's religious art, the refining influences of religious and humanistic precedent, the Hudson River School believed that Nature in its purity "is," as Durand put it, "fraught with high and holy meaning, only surpassed by the light of Revelation." A painting that evoked the same feelings and emotions that we experience in the presence of reality was a visual sermon, an active force urging man, as Nature herself did, to a nobler life. This doctrine overcame a fear that had long worried American democrats: the fear that art was a useless luxury, a toy for the idle that could not be afforded by a nation that had its way to make. Even the most pragmatic minds were drawn to pictures that brought to the people God's tangible world. A painting over the fireplace was as much a necessity as a Bible on the table.

Even as a theologian would be blasphemous if he rewrote Scripture, painters should not distort natural phenomena that were, as Durand put it, "types of divine attributes." Yet the Hudson River School esthetic did not seek what we should today call photographic reproduction. Durand considered "servile" imitation "in every way unworthy." Although a painted landscape should be "true," the viewer should get more from it than from an unassisted ramble through nature. "The artist as a poet will have seen much more than the mere matter of fact but no more than is there and than another may see if it is pointed out to him."

The Austrian scholar Fritz Novotny tells us that the great struggle of nineteenth-century European art was to achieve a synthesis between naturalism and idealism. The Hudson River School did not suffer from this dichotomy. Living in a happy world, used to expressing ideas through things, Americans insisted that the ideal was not opposed to the real, but its perfection. The painter carried man closer to the divine by presenting exactly those aspects of nature which he recognized as perfect and which elevated his own emotions that were conceived of as being more sensitive than the emotions of persons not artistically gifted, yet in essence the same. The artists sought such communion as a Quaker preacher engaged in when he rose in Meeting to share with his less spiritually endowed fellows the words which God, operating within his own breast, had inspired him to say.

Out of the artists' religious base grew the characteristic that most separates the Hudson River School—and, indeed the Native School as a whole—from almost all European art. It is thus the greatest block against the appreciation of nineteenth-century American painting by eyes trained to conventional esthetics. Even as a preacher, who heard God speaking in his breast, should not distort the expression of his inner light with his own idiosyncrasies and temperament, so the painters wished to give, as far as possible, the impression that their pictures were not objects made by individual men but actual segments of nature. Skill should be used not to impress the viewer with an artist's virtuosity or his temperament but so to subordinate means to ends that the means disappear and only the ends are perceived. A landscape should make the viewer feel as if he were actually in the presence of Nature at her most sublime. Even the mood of the picture should be revealed as not the artist's but the landscape's own.

The artists knew that their practice was different from the European and were proud of their originality. Their theology dictated that Nature, a visible embodiment of God, was the fundamental art school. As self-reliant Americans, convinced of the priesthood of all believers, the Hudson River School artists were opposed to beginners' visiting exhibitions, to their looking at the works of accomplished artists, either European or American, either old or new. A beginner would be "in danger of losing his individuality." Seeking instruction, except in the rudiments of mixing paint and putting it on canvas, might seem to beginners a saving of time, but was, so Durand wrote, "pernicious." A beginner should "go first to nature to learn to paint landscape"; only after he had learned to "imitate nature" could he "study the picture of great artists with benefit." However experienced he became, so Hudson River School practice dictated, a painter should spend every summer walking under the sky, reviving his inspiration with new vistas, new beauties.

The Hudson River School emphasis on dealing charily with already existing art could be interpreted as a response to non-spiritual conditions. It was surely in part a reaction to America's still existent, still stultifying colonial obsequiousness to European culture. Avoidance of art exhibitions and art schools made good sense in a land where European painting was still represented by disfigured daubs bearing great names; where what art schools that existed were rudimentary and almost useless. But yet the doctrine was practiced where the practice was not dictated. The painters became prosperous enough to go abroad should they have wished to go. Several of the best painters stayed determinedly in the United States or crossed the ocean only toward the very end of their careers. Most went when, although already professional artists, they were still at an impressionable age. They were not overwhelmed. Carrying in their hearts that "earlier, wilder image" of American nature, they did not wish to be led away into mazes, however resplendent, of other traditions. The object of their studies was to acquire only what technical skills would enable them to express with more telling effect their visions of nature's gospel.

Worthington Whittredge, who came from Ohio and studied in Germany and Italy before he had any direct contact with the Hudson River School, felt it necessary to modify what he had learned abroad by engaging in postgraduate study at home. After his return to the United States he sketched for months in the Catskills, the mountain range by the Hudson whose natural beauties constituted the university of the Hudson River School.

The Hudson River School shared the democratic idealism of American political thought. In the school's most persuasive statement, his *Letters of a Landscape Painter*, Durand called for "an original school of art worthy to share the tribute of universal respect paid to our condition of political advancement." The artists wished to paint not for a few, not for an elite, but for the many. The applauding historian, George Bancroft, wrote that this pointed the way to "the sublimest success" since, by learning to appeal to the common man, the artist would penetrate to "the universal sense of the beautiful . . . that lies deep in the human soul."

The Hudson River School dominated a half-century or more of American painting, from 1825 to 1875 and beyond. It included many painters, greatly admired in the United States, whose works are unfortunately hardly known in Europe. The major painters were, in addition to Cole, Durand, and Whittredge, Frederic E. Church, John F. Kensett, Martin Johnson Heade, Sanford B. Gifford, and Fitz Hugh Lane. The style of the internationally known Winslow Homer, who lived well into the twentieth century, was nurtured in the Hudson River School.

When the style first appeared, the wealthy and well-educated group of connoisseurs who were familiar with and subservient to European fashion derided the Hudson River School landscapes as crude works of uneducated men. But the connoisseurs were soon won over. At no other time in American history has a school of American painters been so popular with every facet of American society, from the Atlantic seaboard to the edge of settlement, from the rich collector to the humble purchaser of an engraved reproduction. It is no coincidence that this most national of American schools was also the most religiously inspired. Nineteenth-century Americans were deeply concerned, according to their own lights, with spiritual values.

A Speech Given on the Occasion of the Exhibition of Colonial and Federal Portraits at Bowdoin College

When I was invited to speak on this occasion, it seemed clear to me in very general terms what ought to be said.* The occasion being the visit to my native city of one of the very old American art collections, a collection that goes back to important eighteenth-century beginnings in American art, my theme should obviously be Bowdoin's connection with the long span of esthetic creation in America. But how to make the point was another matter.

I am sure that you have all agreed to deliver speeches at one time or another, and thus you are familiar with the psychological steps that follow. You write the date down in your engagement book and observe with a certain relief that your notation is pages and pages ahead of the part of the book in which you are writing your current engagements. The speech is clearly scheduled for some future time that may never come. In any case, months lie ahead, so why worry?

But the months pass, and one night you wake up unhappily from a dream in which you were back at college and suddenly faced with taking a final examination for a course you had forgotten you had enrolled in. After a few minutes of wakefulness the reference finally comes clear: That speech: it is now only a few weeks away. Panic!

I am old enough in the verbal game to feel confident that if you can only get started, you can continue and finish a speech—but how was I to get started? A Harvard man, how was I to speak to Bowdoin graduates about treasures they have always cherished?

My panic concerning this speech sailed in over the darkened fields of

---

*Bowdoin College Museum of Art published an earlier version of this essay in pamphlet form in 1967.

West Cornwall, Connecticut, where I spend the summers. We have learned in West Cornwall to rely for everything on the general store, but I did not expect Yutzler's Country Store to come to my rescue in this dilemma. However, it did by supplying me with a copy of *The New York Times*.

There was an article headed: "Art Chiefs Study Their Jobs Here; 38 Administrators Attend a Culture Game Seminar." The story explained that New York University was holding a seminar for administrators of community art councils and centers, "one of the newest specialties," as the paper pointed out, "in a specialized age." William R. Taylor, identified as Professor of American History at the University of Wisconsin, had been imported to give the fledgling art administrators an historical background. "It was a gloomy view," the *Times* reported. "He spoke of the way Americans have sustained hostility to the arts over a good part of their history."

Professor Taylor's gloomy view is refuted by this exhibition that we shall all visit as soon as I am happily silent and this dinner is adjourned.

That it does supply a refutation is to my mind one of the very important contributions of the Bowdoin College Museum of Art. It is not one of the largest collections in the United States, although in one major particular—as I shall point out in a moment—it is incontrovertibly the greatest. However, it is an important collection that goes far back in the history of American culture, back beyond the founding of Bowdoin College itself, back before the American Revolution and the birth of the United States. The collection has grown charmingly, naturally, and effectively with the growth of America to this moment, more than two centuries after a happy beginning in our culture which—as I shall again point out—is exemplified in the collection itself. And, gathering here tonight, we can feel confident that the collection will continue to grow far into the lifetime of our descendants, to be an inspiration to them as it should be to us.

I have quoted with some asperity the gloomy view of Professor Taylor that Americans have almost always been hostile to art. The statement, although far from correct, is of considerable cultural significance because it has so often been made, not only in the present day but also down through the generations to the very beginnings of self-conscious American culture. The statement is usually accompanied by the contention that this opposition to art has recently evaporated. To use the term most commonly employed, American art has finally "come of age." Every generation contends that it has at long last seen American culture come of age.

We hear the contention today. There has just been a cultural explosion. For the first time, Americans have become concerned with culture; for the first time, American painters have reached a stature that makes them admired abroad. It has been utterly forgotten that at the time of the American Revolution we sent painters to England who led in the evolution of European art and were admired across the European continent. And almost all the subsequent glories of American art are almost unknown to our self-appointed esthetes. Convinced that in their own generation our art is belatedly coming of age despite a continuing American hostility to art, the average cultured American refuses even to look at what has been done before in his own world.

This perpetual wall is in itself a demonstration of America's lack of hostility to art, of eagerness even if it takes a frustrated form. Why it has taken this form is a matter too complicated for us to consider this evening although I might point out that it is a strange phenomenon. The inhabitants of most nations gain a sense of self-satisfaction from boasting, often to an exaggerated extent, of the cultural traditions they exemplify. Esthetically minded Americans, however, too often get their sense of satisfaction by insisting that they personally are more cultured than their nation and their neighbors; that they are, indeed, esthetic missionaries bringing artistic light to a people up to that moment benighted.

This is a free country, and every man has a right to play, without criticism, every harmless cultural game he pleases. But this cultural game has not been harmless. It has, indeed, done much to encourage such esthetic weaknesses as the attitude deplores.

The tendency of every generation to start over again, as if there had never previously been any American art, has been to esthetic creation on these shores a major handicap. We need only compare our cultural attitudes to those of the French to realize what a great disservice we are doing to ourselves. A Frenchman emerges from the cradle in the belief that he inhabits clime which is Arcadia itself, the natural habitat of art. If he recalls a school of French painting not currently admired—like those overinflated nineteenth-century figure pieces which he derisively dismisses as "style pompier"—if he comes on such a school, he pushes it aside as untypical of the French. What is most typical of France is what is most beautiful. This attitude encourages Frenchmen to make and keep France beautiful.

On the contrary, the attitude of American cultural snobs encourages ugliness in America. The student of our Wisconsin professor, being told—with however many crocodile tears—that Americans have always been hostile to art, that they live, willy-nilly in an esthetic jungle, is not encouraged to go out and do something about the ribbon building and the filling stations that destroy the beauty of our countryside. It is hard to get him interested in preserving the great architectural achievements of the American past—he has been assured that they are not worth preserving. I was told only the other day that the French quarter of New Orleans is about to be overtopped by a two-story highway that will send trucks roaring through the air between the old houses and the Mississippi. There are some immediate economic advantages. Why not give in to them when one is assured that America never had any culture worth bothering about?

The collection we are going to visit this evening is a visible argument for the age of American culture. It goes back indeed to the very event that was, until recently, believed to mark the beginnings of the fine arts in America.

Modern researches have carried the history of American painting back to the 1660s and even exhumed some really beautiful pictures painted on these shores in the seventeenth century. However, it was once thought that the opening impetus was given to American painting by the arrival in New England during 1729 of a well-known and accomplished painter from old England, John Smibert. Even if we can now carry American painting further back, Smibert's arrival remains a key development. After a brilliant start in the seventeenth century, New England painting had lagged, particularly behind that of New York where there was in the 1720s a powerful school which I named, some years ago, the Patroon Painters. Smibert's influence revivified New England painting, making it the most powerlful school on the continent, a leadership it held into the nineteenth century. Smibert's contributions to American art were indeed double: he was a painter himself and an importer of European models for painters. Both of these directions are represented in the Bowdoin collections.

We shall find in the exhibition we shall visit in a moment two portraits by Smibert. They are sensitive, sober, unflamboyant. Evidence exists that Smibert left a successful career in England for the American colonies because of the perpetual pressure there was on him in an aristocratic society to paint glittering, flattering images. Amusingly enough, he encountered a similar pressure in Boston, where a successful merchant rather liked to be painted as if he were a lord. But in New England it was a pressure that could often be evaded—and he did successfully evade it in the two portraits which Bowdoin owns. Although prose rather than poetry, the pictures are technically accomplished works presenting a solid base for the development of a democratic portrait art.

More exciting to the modern imagination is the studio Smibert established in Boston which can be considered the first museum of European art on this continent. It remained more or less intact for many years after Smibert's death in 1751, becoming an adjunct to a paint shop kept by his nephew.

Let us imagine ourselves in the shoes of a young saddler from Maryland who had some ambitions to be a painter and whom the tides of life had landed in 1765 on the streets of Boston. The young man's name is Charles Willson Peale; he is to become one of the leading painters in America—and he will eventually write an autobiography. He tells us that he happened in Boston on a color shop which "had some figures with ornamental signs upon it. . . . Becoming a little acquainted with the owner of the shop, he told me that a relation of his had been a painter, and said he would give me a feast. Leading me upstairs, he introduced me into a painter's room, an appropriate apartment lined with green cloth or baize, where there were a number of pictures unfinished."[1] There were also copies of European masterpieces, old master drawings, and many prints.

Peale stared about him thunderstruck, for he had never known that the world of art was as rich as this. He stammered for a moment before he succeeded in asking the color dealer what had been the name of his wonderful uncle. Smibert, the man replied, John Smibert. Peale then mourned that Smibert was dead, and wondered whether any painters still lived who could equal him. The dealer told him about a man who resided down the street, a man called Copley.

That Copley was kind to Peale when he called, showed the young saddler his work, and lent him a painting to copy, is less germane to our subject than that many an American painter, including Copley himself, found inspiration in the Smibert collection of European art which Peale considered such a "feast." Today, some dishes from that feast are almost certainly in Bowdoin's possession and a few may well await your tasting around the corner.

There is a cloud of evidence, which Mr. Sadik has in his catalogue of

---

[1] I have translated Peale's autobiographical statement from the third person to the first person.

Colonial and Federal Portraits analyzed with an admirable conservatism, that when the Smibert collection was sold, parts of it were bought by James Bowdoin III and bequeathed by him to the college that bears his father's name. At the head of the list according to eighteenth-century ideas was a copy of Poussin's *The Continence of Scipio*, a canvas described and praised in many documents of the time. Two other copies of European masterpieces in Bowdoin's possession also seem to have come from Smibert's studio. Today we take copies less seriously than did the eighteenth century—we have other ways of becoming familiar with the great art of the past—and thus Smibert's copies did not make the trip down from Maine to New York.

However, examples from Bowdoin's fine collection of old master drawings did make the trip. You will notice that many of them, and some of the very best, came to Bowdoin College in 1811 through the bequest of James Bowdoin III. That this benefactor bought drawings from Smibert's collection is made clear by inscriptions on some of them. Exactly how many came from the source we do not know. It is agreeable to imagine that the great drawing by Breughel, which is the star of the collection, passed under Peale's eyes way back in 1765 when the young saddler yearned for art. In any case, the presence of this drawing and many others in the Bowdoin collection as part of that first gift reveals that they have been cherished on these shores for more than 150 years.

Smibert had an American pupil—or, perhaps, I should say an American follower—who was a more charming painter than he, and was, indeed, our greatest artist of the first half of the eighteenth century. This artist's name was, as you know, Robert Feke, and of his best work Bowdoin owns a disproportionate share: five canvases out of the very small remaining oeuvre of an artist whose mature career lasted less than a decade. Most museums—the Metropolitan and the National Gallery are examples—do not own a great Feke. Bowdoin owns—I repeat—five including his most elaborate picture and only full-length, General Samuel Waldo.

When most under Smibert's influence, Feke painted, as his master liked to do, shrewd character studies, but when he hit his mature stride he preferred—as the Bowdoin portraits show—a more lyrical view.

Looked at from the standards of the Old World, where class evolution was slow, so slow, the Colonial aristocrats were characters in a fairy tale. Cinderella rode down the streets of Boston in her pumpkin carriage, but she did not have to fear the chimes of midnight; her horses would never change back to mice. Sitting behind a ledger heavy with the records of prosperity, Dick Whittington knew that he had been his own puss in boots. Out of a frowning coast and a dark forest had come a pot of gold; the rainbow's end rested permanently on New York. Wealth, position, grace, ample living; these were the gifts of America. How could you be crabbed and sad; you had to sing.

Feke's Bowdoin pictures are lyrical in mood, naïve in conception, simple in technique, bright in color (although some of the flesh tones seem to have faded). To these attributes, Feke added plasticity. He went further than any previous American-born painter into the third dimension, giving shape in addition to outline, adding weight to flat forms. He did this in a very simple manner. His men's figures are stylized into cones; his women's into a contrast between a few tight and expansive forms.

After 1750, the drift toward the Declaration of Independence expressed itself in portraiture by a rise to dominance of a prime concern with personal idiosyncrasy which had always been present as an undertone in American art. Significantly, once Feke had struck his elegant stride, low church ministers no longer sat to him. In a few decades these men of God were to be called by Tory orators "the black regiment," for they incited the Colonists to Civil War. Now they expressed, perhaps unconsciously, their disapproval of Colonial aristocratic dependence by shunning the accomplished Feke and leading their congregations to a humble man of the people who painted houses as well as portraits. His name was Joseph Badger and Bowdoin owns an excellent pickle-faced portrait from his brush.

I must confess that I have now begun to dip into a lecture on American Colonial painting in general that I have given on many other occasions. That I can do this so easily is an indication that the Bowdoin collection exemplifies extremely well the development of American portraiture in what was its great era: from Smibert through Stuart. You have a first-class Copley and a whole galaxy of Stuarts. Sully is well represented and Rembrandt Peale. But now that I am mentioning names the realization comes over me that what is being exhibited in New York is only a small part of the holdings of the Bowdoin College Museum of Art. I have just been working on a book about Winslow Homer and know that, through the activity of Professor Philip Beam and Marvin Sadik, you have just acquired the memorabilia from his Prout's Neck studio to add to fine pictures you already own. And, of course, if I allowed my feet to stray from my own path of American art, I would find myself confronted with a whole series of vistas where the Bowdoin collections shine. In the meanwhile the pictures wait and the moment has surely come for me to sit down. Congratulations and thank you.

INTRODUCTION TO WILLIAM
DUNLAP'S *HISTORY OF THE RISE AND
PROGRESS OF THE ARTS OF DESIGN
IN THE UNITED STATES*

If, as in neo-classical (or sentimental) moods I like to imagine, there
exists an American Muse, surely that then very young lady intervened
actively in two opening events of American culture: the creation of the
portrait *Mrs. Freake and Baby Mary*, and the writing of Dunlap's *History*.*
Limned by an anonymous hand in the first decade of known American
painting—the 1660s—the Freake portrait set our art off with a brilliant
beginning. It was a work of such touching beauty that almost a century
was to pass before there appeared on these shores another picture of
equivalent charm. And Dunlap's book, in 1834 the first published history of American art, demonstrated, for later generations to ponder, the
many delights that can spring from a felicitous marriage between art
history and literary skill.

Dunlap was himself a painter, who had shared in the excitements
about which he wrote, and who was personally acquainted, often intimately, with many of the men whose careers he so evocatively described. However, his greater gift was as a writer. An author-producer,
he composed some fifty plays, many of which found permanence in
print. He had also completed a history of the American theater and
various biographies when, at the age of sixty-six, he set to work on his
history of the arts of design.

That he is sometimes styled "the American Vasari" is apposite
enough, since Dunlap worked in the manner which was practiced by
that sixteenth-century Italian chronicler and which was continued by

---

*An earlier version of this essay appeared in William Dunlap, *History of the Rise and
Progress of the Arts of Design in the United States*, repr. ed. (New York: Dover, 1964),
pp. vii–xvi.

many a subsequent writer. Dunlap identified himself most closely with
an English "Vasari," George Vertue. An engraver by profession, Vertue
had, for some twenty years before his death in 1756, gathered material
for a history of English art. His notes were bought from his widow by
the aristocratic dilettante and writer Horace Walpole. During Dunlap's
boyhood, there appeared *Anecdotes of Painting in England, with some Account of the Principal Artists and Incidental Notes on other Arts, Collected by
the late George Vertue, and now Digested and Published from his Original
Manuscript by Horace Walpole.*

Dunlap was following Vasari and Walpole when he organized his
book as a series of Biographies, some long and some short, each independent of the others except insofar as the lives of the different characters had in actuality crossed. This traditional form slighted most of the
shibboleths of twentieth-century academic art history. Far from regarding personal character and the happen-chances of his daily life as of secondary importance in the understanding of an artist's esthetic
achievement, Dunlap was, like his predecessors, frankly and gleefully
concerned with evoking personality. He recorded the minutiae of a creator's life: how a painter made and spent his money, how much he ate
and drank.

The influences of artists on each other are mentioned if they come
naturally into the narrative—as in the case of teacher and pupil—but
Dunlap did not seek out and emphasize chains of influence as a modern
scholar would. Individual artifacts are named and brought into the story
when and where the author considered them of importance, but are
rarely given the attention and space reserved for anecdotes of the artists'
lives. Criticism circles primarily around subject matter: what was the
artist trying to show, was it worth depicting, and did the artist carry out
his intention effectively? The "formal" considerations modern scholar
analyze are, if mentioned at all, passed quickly over. Even the critical
summaries of artists' careers are, however evocative, brief and general:
what was a man's rank beside his fellows, what were his principal
strengths and defects?

Dunlap was, indeed, within the modern scholarly meaning of the
term, not much of a "connoisseur," but this creates no serious lack in
the usefulness of the book. Creations by the artists he discussed are, due
to such modern conveniences as museums, cameras, and art libraries,
more widely available to us than they were to him. We may make our
own analyses of form and color, may juxtapose photographs and draw
complicated lines of influence. But what Dunlap preserved—the charac-

ters and the careers and the environments of the creators—would, in many cases, but for him have vanished into the vagrant dust.

Even if out of key with modern scholarly practice (where lackluster writing is so admired and, alas, so often achieved), the sprightliness of Dunlap's style falls into a long and noble tradition. It dates back to the centuries before the invention of fiction, when what we today call "non-fiction" was the accepted vehicle of prose literature. Vasari wrote with exhilarating dash, and so did the best of his followers, including William Dunlap.

As every tyro in the field knows, Dunlap's history is crowded with facts valuable for today's students. Particularly as the publishers of this edition have added a comprehensive index, this information may be mined without bothering with any of the surrounding passages, as a prospector may dig for gold, even in the most beautiful landscape, with his face forever aimed at the ground. Although such restricted digging is often required by the exigencies of research, I should like to urge that the reader find enjoyment by using the book another way.

To begin with, you must get yourself quiet, for this is not a narrative that moves rapidly to any objective like a superhighway which burrows under all umbrageous country lanes. Put on your slippers, place a drink by your elbow, and resolve to ramble imaginatively with the author through vanished times. His avowed object is to make you acquainted with a great many people. He himself finds them all interesting because he is eternally amused and excited by the human race. With some men to whom he introduces you he is barely acquainted; after nods are exchanged, he will express curiosity to know more about them. Concerning others, he will pull you aside for a whisper of gossip. But if he meets one of his cronies or a man whom he greatly admires, then the session will be long, extending late into the night, and there will be much laughter. For this William Dunlap, when he has the right material and gets going, is a very funny man. Here is such an anecdote as he will tell:

In the early period of [Gilbert] Stuart's career as an independent portrait-painter, he had for his attendant a wild boy, the son of a poor widow, whose time was full as much taken up by play, with another of the paint-er's household, a fine Newfoundland dog, as by attendance upon his mas-ter. The Boy and dog were inseparable; and when Tom went an errand Towzer must accompany him. Tom was a terrible truant, and played so many tricks that Stuart again and again threatened to turn him off, but as often Tom found some way to keep his hold on his eccentric master. One day, as story-tellers say, Tom staid when sent of an errand until Stuart, out of patience, posted off to the boy's mother, determined to dismiss him; but on his entering the old woman *began first.*

"Oh, Mr. Stuart, Tom has been here."

"So I supposed."

"Oh, Mr. Stuart, the dog!"

"He has been here, too: well, well, he shall not come again; but Tom must come home to you. I will not keep him!"

"Oh, Mr. Stuart, it was the dog did it."

"Did what?"

"Look sir! look there! the dog overset my mutton pie—broke the dish—greased the floor, and eat the mutton!"

"I'm glad of it! you encourage the boy to come here, and here I will send him!"

"It was the dog, sir, eat the mutton!"

"Well, the boy may come and eat your mutton, I dismiss him! I'll have no more to do with him!"

The mother entreated—insisted that it was the dog's fault—told over and again the story of the pie, until Stuart, no longer hearing her, conceived the plan of a trick upon Tom, with a prospect of a joke, founded upon the dog's dinner of mutton-pie.

"Well, well, say no more: here's something for the pie, and to buy a dish. I will try Tom again, provided you never let him know that I came here to-day, or that I learned from you any thing of the dog and the pie."

The promise was given of course, and Stuart hastened home as full of his anticipated trick to try Tom, as any child with a new rattle. Tom found his master at his easel where he had left him, and was prepared with a story to account for his delay, in which neither his mother, nor Towzer, nor the mutton made parts.

"Very well, sir," said the painter, "bring in dinner; I shall know all about it by-and-by."

Stuart sat down to his mutton, and Towzer took his place by his side, as usual; while Tom, as usual, stood in attendance.

"Well, Towzer, you mouth don't water for your share. Where have you been? Whisper."

And he put his ear to Towzer's mouth, who wagged his tail in reply. "I thought so. With Tom to his mother's?"

"Bow-wow."

"And have you had your dinner?"

"Bow-wow."

"I thought so. What have you been eating? Put your mouth nearer, sir."

"Bow-wow!"

"Mutton-pie—very pretty—you and Tom have eat Mrs. Jenkins's
mutton-pie, Ha?"

"Bow-wow."

"He lies, sir, I didn't touch it; he broke mother's dish and eat all the
mutton!"

From the moment Tom thought if he wished to deceive his master he
must leave Towzer at home, but rather on the whole concluded that with
the dog, the devil, and the painter, he had no chance for successful lying.

As we have seen, Walpole called his edition of Vertue *Anecdotes of
Painting in England*: the anecdote always played an important role in the
Vasari tradition of art history. The authors preferred not to prose out
their points as would the writers of modern monographs, but to exemplify their conclusions in scenes. Here is an example of how Dunlap
compares the styles of Benjamin West and Stuart:

I will mention the following circumstance which took place about 1786,
on occasion of a visit [by Stuart] to his old master's [West's] house and
gallery, in Newman-street. Trumbull was painting on a portrait and the
writer *literally lending him a hand*, by sitting for it. Stuart came in and his
opinion was asked, as to the colouring, which he gave very much in these
words, "Pretty well, pretty well; but more like our master's flesh than
Nature's. When Benny teaches the boys, he says, 'yellow and white
there,' and he makes a streak, 'red and white there,' another streak, 'blue-
black and white there,' another streak, 'brown and red there, for a warm
shadow,' another streak, 'red and yellow there,' another streak. But Nature does not colour in streaks. Look at my hand; see how the colours
are mottled and mingled, yet all is clear as silver."

Unless charmed out of his critical sense by such passages, the modern
reader will point with horror to the fact that Dunlap interlards non-
fiction with conversations. In this practice, one feels strongly the influence of Boswell's *Life of Johnson*; neither Vasari nor Vertue went in for
much dialogue. Boswell, as far as the modern reader is concerned, gets
away with his endless quotations on the assumption that he is giving
verbatim reports of what he has listened to—but, of course, stenographic
notations would read very differently from the passages Boswell has
shaped into parts of a work of art. Dunlap, too, usually claims to be
quoting what he heard. Even the story of Stuart, the boy, and the dog,
although much of it is in the third person, is presented in the way Stuart
would have told it. That the wild portraitist's particular idiom was in-

deed accurately caught is revealed by the similarity in his talk as reported by Dunlap and his other friends.

To the little dramatizations that gleam on his pages, Dunlap brought skills he had developed in writing for the theater. He was a master in the phrasing of dialogue. Having established succinctly the place and the characters, he ignited a flash of action which illuminated exactly the point he wished to convey. If an artist is quoted, we are almost always told to whom he made the statement and where. This contributes to our sense that we are not in a scholar's study but experiencing life as it was actually lived. And, almost by paradox, the technique contributes to those ends of scholarship which are most often served by that most unliterary of devices, the footnote. Seeking always artistic verisimilitude, Dunlap hooks every statement into the body of fact by embedding the source in the narrative.

Although his anecdotes crackle, Dunlap's chapters tend to wander. This can sometimes be an irritation—even the most charming and informed guide can, if garrulous, be a bore—but, on the whole, we are given a rich sense not only of artistic life but of the broad environments through which the artists moved. General historians would do well to read Dunlap. Where, for instance, is there a better picture of the English army as it appeared during the Revolution to the American inhabitants than in the following paragraph from the account of his own career that Dunlap included in his *History*?

The time is early 1777, shortly after Washington's victories at Trenton and Princeton had made the British draw their front line back. The place is Perth Amboy, now their principal remaining post in New Jersey:

> Here were centered, in addition to those cantoned at the place, all those drawn in from the Delaware, Princeton and Brunswick; and the flower and pick of the army, English, Scotch, and German, who had at this time been brought in from Rhode Island. Here was to be seen a party of the 42d Highlanders, in national costume, and there a regiment of Hessians, their dress and arms a perfect contrast to the first. The slaves of Anspach and Waldeck were there—the first sombre as night, the second gaudy as noon. Here dashed by a party of the 17th Dragoons, and there scampered a party of *Yagers*. The trim, neat and graceful English grenadier, the careless and half savage Highlander, with his flowing robes and naked knees, and the immovably stiff German, could hardly be taken for parts of one army.

As his published diaries[1] reveal, Dunlap started his active researches for his *History of the Arts of Design* on November 17, 1832, by writing Washington Allston and two other artists to ask the aid. More correspondence followed, and also many interviews, as increasing information led him from one informant to another. The old gentleman must have operated with the most awe-inspiring energy since the manuscript was not only completed but printed within two years.

Although his definition of "the art of design" included sculpture, architecture, and engraving, Dunlap's primary concern was with the art he himself practiced, with painting. An elderly man possessing a long memory, a file of diaries, much industry, and a wide acquaintance, he managed to grasp a wide chronological span: from artists who had worked in the second quarter of the eighteenth century to the emergence of the Hudson River School which was to remain active until late in the nineteenth.

Concerning what might be called the introductory period of American art, the some hundred years of activity before West and Copley bestrode the scene, Dunlap, it is true, was very sketchy. Quite good on Smibert, he had heard of Feke, Theus, and Blackburn, but was utterly ignorant of Bridges, Greenwood, Pelham, and Badger. The earliest artist he discussed, John Watson, had come to his attention because Watson had worked at his own birthplace, Perth Amboy. Dunlap speculated that, although they had left "no traces that we can discover," many other painters had undoubtedly preceded Watson. It was both an indication of Dunlap's great influence and of how much more careful a scholar he was than his successors, that for years his passage was misread and Watson categorically described as the very first artist to have painted in America.

To deal with the great painting outburst that slightly preceded and for some time followed the Revolution, Dunlap was perfectly placed in space and time. Although twenty-eight years younger than Benjamin West and John Singleton Copley, eleven than Gilbert Stuart, and ten than John Trumbull, he had studied in London when these artists were converged there. He had been, like all the important American painters of the time—with the partial exception of Copley—a pupil of West's. His accounts of the painters he had known in West's studio, and of others of that generation whom he later met, are as fascinating as they are numerous, and add up to by far the most important source that exists on this very important school.

---

[1]William Dunlap, *Diary*, 3 vols. (New York: New-York Historical Society, 1930).

Dunlap concluded—an opinion shared by many in England and on the Continent as well as in America—that West was one of the greatest painters in the world. In that paragon's studio, he imbibed the conventional neo-classical esthetic of the time: Art should appeal to the rational rather than the sensuous faculties. The highest form of art was that depiction of the acts of religious or secular heroes which had been commonly practiced by the Old Masters and which was known as "historical painting." Subject matter was of the first importance and should always be clearly presented. Since the object of art was to teach virtue, a good artist had to be a good man.

These conceptions Dunlap often stated in his *History*, but his was not a theoretical mind. He was much more concerned with understanding and appreciating whatever he saw around him. His moralizing, for instance, did not go very deep. He could, it is true, be stuffy about the naked bodies of prostitutes presented to the public as embodiments of our common mother, Eve, but he was a frank and uncensorious biographer. Gleefully grasping the opportunities presented by Stuart's vagaries to create a dashing picture of a far from moral man, he nonetheless acknowledged the profligate's tremendous artistic skill. As for younger artists who strayed away from the Westian esthetic: he complained, but gave them their due.

The early romantic Allston was thirteen years younger than Dunlap and forty-one than West. He responded to Dunlap's urgings with autobiographical letters, from which the chronicler quoted this description of Allston's first visit to the Louvre:

"Titian, Tintoret, and Paul Veronese, abstolutely enchanted me, for they took away all sense of subject. . . . It was the poetry of colour which I felt; procreative in its nature, giving birth to a thousand things which the eye cannot see, and distinct from their cause. I did not, however, stop to analyze my feelings. . . . But I now understand it, and think I understand *why* so many great colourists, especially Tintoret and Paul Veronese gave so little heed to the ostensible *stories* of their compositions. In some of them, the Marriage of Cana for instance, there is not the slightest clue given by which the spectator can guess at the subject. They addressed themselves not to the senses merely, as some have supposed, but rather through them to that region (if I may so speak) of the imagination which is supposed to be under the exclusive dominion of music, and which, by similar excitement, they caused to teem with visions that 'lap the soul in Elysium.' In other words, they leave the subject to be made by the spectator, provided he posseses the imaginative faculty—otherwise they will have little more meaning to him that a calico counterpane."

The denial of the primacy of subject matter, this insistence not on rational reactions to form but emotional reactions to color, was heresy within the neo-classical esthetic Dunlap had accepted in West's studio. But Dunlap does not denounce; he mediates:

> The reader will perceive that Mr. Allston is far from being devoid of the imaginative faculty which he here speaks of, and that he saw objects with a poet's as well as a painter's eye—indeed they are the same. His own pictures are replete with this magic of colour, at the same time that he is strictly attentive to the story in all its parts, character, actions, and costume. It certainly is not fair to leave the spectator to make out the story of a picture, and to be puzzled by finding Pope Gregory alongside of Saint Peter, and both dressed in costume as far from truth as they were similarity of opinion. All the charm of colour may be attained without sacrificing truth.

Dunlap was even willing to put Allston on a par with West, "to whom, if inferior in facility of composition, he is superior in colour and equal in drawing."

Allston, who had been among West's pupils, represented no more than a turn, if a significant one, in the same esthetic flow. The true explosion in American art took place when Dunlap was almost sixty. Then Thomas Cole, thirty-five years his junior, led an entirely new beginning, initiating (among other styles) the Hudson River School which was dedicated to realistic painting of the American landscape. Dunlap helped discover Cole when the revolutionary was a complete unknown. In his *History*, he quoted the young man's wildly revolutionary arguments, the very antithesis of neo-classical theory:

> "Will you allow me here to say a word or two on landscape? It is usual to rank it as a lower branch of the art, below the historical. Why so? Is there a better reason, than that the vanity of man makes him delight most in his own image? In its difficulty (though perhaps it may come ill from me, although I have dabbled a little in history) it is equal at least to the historical. There are certainly fewer good landscape pictures in the world, in proportion to their number, than of historical. In landscapes there is a greater variety of objects, textures, and phenomena to imitate. It has expression also; not of passion, to be sure, but of sentiment—whether it shall be tranquil or spirit-stirring. Its seasons—sun-rise, sun-set, the storm,

the calm—various kinds of trees, herbage, waters, mountains, skies. And whatever scene is chosen, one spirit pervades the whole—light and darkness tremble in the atmosphere, and each change transmutes. . . .

"I mean to say, that if the talent of Raphael had been applied to landscape, his productions would have been as great as those he really did produce."

Dunlap soothed his conscience by demurring politely, and then showered Cole (as we still do today) with praise.

In giving all artists, as best he could, their due, Dunlap allowed them, whenever he could, to speak for themselves, quoting page after page from the autobiographical letters they had written him. This adds to the authenticity and also the variety of a book which, I hope, will afford new readers not only instruction but also the pleasure it has consistently given me since I first made its acquaintance.

PAINTING AND SCULPTURE, 1820–1865

Henry T. Tuckerman, whose *Book of the Artists* (1867) was the most inclusive and representative work on what was then contemporary American creation, expressed little surprise that artists should emerge from the Ohio Valley or from even more recently settled parts of the West.* But Maine was another matter! That the sculptor Paul Akers had been born at Saccarappa and raised at Salmon Falls (only a few miles from Portland) made Tuckerman marvel at "the obscure and isolated unfolding" of a "gifted soul" in such a "scene of primitive toil."

Akers's concern with working in the round was encouraged by his father's "toil": the parent was a wood turner, and the lad executed on the family lathe "original designs," "beautiful toys." However, the sculpture of his mature years was not a further outgrowth of his environment but rather the most promising of successive efforts to escape. While still young, he had substituted Paul for his given name, Benjamin, in acceptance of the jeers of his contemporaries who, angered by his criticism of their games and their profanity, had mocked him as "St. Paul."

Sculpture was then the most exotic of American arts: its practitioners commonly resided in Italy, where marble and assistants skilled at fashioning it were easily available. Although Akers modeled many portrait heads in Washington, D.C., he carried the clays to Florence to be "finished in marble." His ambitious works—*Una and the Lion, Diana and Endymion, Lost Pearl-Diver*—were completely executed abroad in the cold, meticulous neo-classical idiom then internationally rampant. Akers returned to Maine only when, too sick for further expatriation, he was slipping toward his early demise. His *Reuel Williams* seems to date from this final phase of his career.

The other Maine-born sculptor to achieve distinction between 1820 and 1865, Edward Augustus Brackett, was less addicted to Italy than

---

*An earlier version of this essay appeared in A. Hyatt Mayor and Mark Davis, *American Art at the Century* (New York: The Century Association, 1977), pp. xv–xxvi.

Akers was, but no more addicted to the region of his birth. Brackett began his professional career in the Ohio Valley, at Cincinnati, and settled eventually in Boston. It was too much to expect that sophisticated sculpture, then in the United States no more than an emerging art, should take its baby steps in the new, northeasternmost state.

Among American arts, painting had been the first to achieve true stature. The dominant mode had been portraiture, and the greatest portraitists of all had worked in Boston, the capital of Maine as long as that future state remained part of Massachusetts. Thus, as Miss Dresser has revealed in the chapter on portraits, there hung on northeastern walls major American works from the days of Smibert through the long career of Stuart.

The 1820s, the decade that opened with the granting of separate statehood for Maine, witnessed other important changes that were to affect art in the new political entity. Stuart's death in 1828 was symbolic: he had been the last leading American painter to specialize gleefully in portraiture, and he left behind him no important artist who was enjoying a productive career in Maine's neighbor, Boston. With dramatic suddenness the artistic spotlight was swinging away from Maine, to the banks of the Hudson. The Erie Canal had just begun disgorging into that river a direct flow from the Great Lakes which carried to New York City the produce of the West, creating the permanent national metropolis on lines of trade that passed New England by. And in 1825, the year that the canal opened, Thomas Cole showed in the window of a New York frame shop three views painted along the Hudson in the Catskill Mountains. These electrifying canvases presaged a green tide of landscape painting that was to sweep across the nation. New York had replaced Boston as the artistic capital of the United States. The portrait was ailing: long live the Hudson River School!

At its most typical, that school sought extreme naturalism, wished to depict as exactly as possible the specific characteristics of each local American prospect. This was radical practice in the early nineteenth century, when accepted theory both here and in Europe preached that landscape must be heightened and generalized to be worth painting.

The old taste which the Hudson River School superseded is exemplified by two pictures reproduced on pages 62 and 63. Philadelphia-trained Thomas Birch shows us a coast scene which, although identified as Maine, might have been painted anywhere in the Western world, since the rocks, the waves, and the boats are not rendered from direct observation but are rather the clichés of an international romantic marine tradition. The contribution of Boston's own Alvan Fisher is fresher, and indeed, delightful, but no more realistic. Fisher has used Camden Harbor as little more than a theme around which to improvise gracious shapes.

Thomas Doughty played a transitional role in American landscape development. He had done much to set the Hudson River school rolling, through his influence on Cole, but once the new esthetic was in full motion he could no longer compete. He eventually retired to that sinking art center, Boston, which remained faithful to "idealized" pictures while naturalism conquered elsewhere. From there he made trips to nearby Maine. Doughty's *Desert Rock Lighthouse* is one of the most realistic of his paintings, yet the composition, mounting in such calculated steps to the lighthouse past rocks and figures, is more clearly contrived than the Hudson River esthetic preferred.

Although the Hudson River School became the national landscape manner, practiced by artists from all over the nation even if resident in New York City, it specialized in depicting a restricted area. Maine was outside the usual beat. Asher B. Durand spoke for most of his colleagues when he expressed disapproval of those important exceptions who, as he put it, "make long journeys in search of the picturesque in order to gain attention and win applause, when by the common roadside . . . nature has furnished elements . . . more essentially beautiful." It was the exceptions who painted Maine.

Cole, although the founder of the school, was not completely of it, as he was never altogether convinced that nature was in its essence beneficent, a moral force reflecting the face of God. Cole was always searching for something nobler than "the common roadside." He painted philosophical and historical allegories which were entirely beyond the school's usual repertory, and in 1844 he made a trip to Maine. Fascinated by an abandoned log cabin in a new clearing, he applied to this pristine world in his *Deserted House on Mount Desert Island* that elegiac mood, that romantic melancholy at the passing of time and the mutability of man which he had applied to Old World grandeur in his five-part series, *The Course of Empire.*

Cole's one personal pupil of importance was Frederic E. Church. Like his master, Church differed from the run of the Hudson River School in not being a pantheist. However, he sought to bring meaning to nature not through Cole's allegories but with the facts of the scientist. He reproduced natural details with almost trompe l'oeil exactitude and combined them into compositions completely accurate for the regions painted, even if light and form were often caught at their most extreme. Being at heart an explorer, he preferred to find his subjects away from beaten paths. He hunted volcanos in South America and icebergs in far northern seas; he was the first leading landscapist to make many trips to Maine.

Church, a painter of many more strengths and skills than is commonly recognized, was the most accomplished artist to depict Maine before the arrival of Winslow Homer, but he was not as closely identified with the state as Fitz Hugh Lane, a far less accomplished technician of less power but possessed of great charm. Lane usually worked out of his birthplace, Gloucester, Massachusetts. One may postulate that he would have become a full-fledged (and leading) member of the Hudson River School had he not from childhood been a cripple, tied to crutches or wheelchair. He did not, with the other most gifted landscapists, migrate to New York City; the long tramps through the Catskills that were obligatory for the school were outside his possibilities—but on the deck of a boat he moved with delightful freedom. He haunted the coast of Maine.

The seeds of Lane's style were old-fashioned and lowly. Trained as a lithographer, he continued to practice that trade simultaneously with painting, and he concentrated on what had long been for printmakers a salable staple: harbor views containing boats and showing in the foreground recognizable landmarks, often towns embellished with human action. This vernacular mode Lane glorified with a clear, breathless poetry, with subtle renditions of light and air that certainly grew out of his own temperament, and probably also from the example of such Hudson River School leaders as John F. Kensett, who painted many coast scenes although rarely northeast of Rhode Island.

Next to landscape in the hearts of mid-century Americans were those depictions of ordinary life known as "genre." A leading practitioner, Eastman Johnson, was born in Maine during 1824, but, as he did not do much work there until after 1865, his career is reserved for a succeeding chapter. In the present chapter, genre is represented only by a Maine picnic, the achievement of Massachusetts-born and New York-based Jerome B. Thompson. Thompson's style both profits and suffers from extremely emphatic draftsmanship which invests individual figures with simplified effectiveness but destroys unity of composition. His *Pic Nick* breathes the rural warmth, the agreeable high spirits—notice how pretty are the girls—which made his paintings of sentimental genre subjects from popular poetry—"The Old Oaken Bucket," "Home, Sweet

Home," "Woodman Spare That Tree"—major best-sellers when circulated in chromos.

On a professional level above purely artisan achievement, Maine had as yet developed no more than provincial painters. Her leading resident landscapist was Charles Codman, who had been trained as a decorator of clock faces, and now produced signs, fire buckets, and banners, as well as easel pictures in two styles. One style, which has already been discussed as artisan work by Nina Fletcher Little in the preceding pages, revealed the meticulous literalism of the topographical craftsman. The other was a mixture of the facile decoration which ornamental painters emblazoned on walls and tea trays with deeper conceptions based on the more romantic works of the Hudson River School. In "The Moose Hunter," we feel the influence of early works by Cole.

Although Codman largely avoided it, the likeness trade was in pre-Civil War times the financial backbone of Maine's more ambitious resident artists. They had, it is true, to vie with outsiders, such as Boston's Thomas Badger, who made painting trips to Maine. However, the competition, in the portrait doldrums which followed the death of Stuart, was not too hard to meet.

Portland's own portraitists were the brothers Charles Octavius Cole and Joseph Greenleaf Cole, the sons of a Massachusetts painter-craftsman. Charles, as his portrait *A Young Lady of Portland* shows, had the warmer response to personality, even if his forms tended to be buttery. Joseph's style is colder, but more effective pictorially. In his *Mrs. Mellon and Son* he treated his subject as if it were a still life, arranging faces, bodies, and clothes in a spare, handsome, abstract design.

A poignant reminder that talent can, like a wild rose in a hedgerow, grow and wither unperceived is given in the portrait of the Reverend Silas Ilsley which hangs at Colby College, a work of semi-naïve freshness and considerable beauty, which scholars have not yet connected with any other picture, or any identified hand.

Maine's mid-century little master was Jeremiah Pearson Hardy, for some sixty years painter in ordinary to the region around Bangor, where he had been born. He painted fecund bulls and pet dogs, town nabobs and town characters, and experimental pictures of his family, whom he loved to pose by lamplight or firelight, and also in silhouette. Hardy had worked as an engraver in Boston; he had studied in New York with the president of the National Academy and future inventor of the telegraph, Samuel F. B. Morse; but once he returned to his native ground he cultivated his "modesty" and seems never again to have carried his paints farther afield than other Maine communities. Ingenious, gay, gentle, possessed of an agreeable color sense, finding true poetry in the matter-of-fact, Hardy was one of the most engaging of the provincial American artists who in the mid-century practiced away from the centers a style balancing delightfully between the sophisticated and the naïve.

From its attainment of statehood until after the Civil War, Maine was at its most isolated from the principal streams of American art. But all was soon to change, The extension of vacationland northward brought an influx of creators from New York City and other centers: Eastman Johnson returned for the summers to the state where he had been born; Winslow Homer's family helped establish a vacation settlement at Prout's Neck. Thus was the stage set for exciting developments to follow.

THE YANKEE INVENTOR PAINTERS

Robert Fulton and Samuel F. B. Morse, the inventors of the steamboat and the telegraph, began their careers as professional painters.* For both, the scientific pursuits that made them world-famous were a second choice, turned to only after art had failed them. This reveals how far we must travel from the twentieth century, when painters yearn to express space in abstractions, if we are to understand the days when America's first two major inventors dreamed of becoming Raphaels.

Colonial Americans were likely to characterize their culture as a whole in comparison with the very different society of the Indians. In writings on this subject, the word "science" rarely figured. The white man's secular philosophies and all his skills ere summarized as "the arts." "The arts" included not only what we today call the fine arts, but the arts of law and government, the art of husbandry, the art of housewifery, and all the multitudinous activities of artisans.

It was the artisans who in Colonial America practiced the applied sciences, and they saw little distinction between working with paint and working with metal. Robert Fulton wrote that no mechanical invention could be complete until "the artist knows the necessary proportions."

Specialization was open only to a few men in a few large cities, but jacks-of-all-trades sprang up everywhere. The New World was large and hard to travel; and on every seacoast, up every river, against every mountain problems arose that could not be solved by any traditional know-how. And as pressing as the problems were the needs: all the needs of civilized men entangled in wilderness or isolated in provincial towns. If a craftsman had an ingenious mind and competent hands, he was called on to practice a wide variety of "the arts," making, as he went along, little inventions to suit the old to the new. Watchmakers fashioned fire engines and astronomical instruments, painters built church organs, blacksmiths designed mills.

---

*An earlier version of this essay appeared in *Art News Annual*, 27 (1958), 46–63, 182–86.

The wide-ranging ingenuity fostered by those early days is epitomized by the career of Charles Willson Peale, who preceded both Fulton and Morse as a painter-scientist. Born in Annapolis, Maryland, during 1741, Peale served his apprenticeship to a saddler, and then taught himself upholstering, chaisemaking, watchmaking, brass founding, and silversmithing. When he saw an opportunity to make money by painting portraits, he took the money. Like many other craftsmen who drifted into the fine arts, Peale was surprised that this new activity brought him increased admiration from his better-educated neighbors.

It cannot be said that early America was unsympathetic to painting. For one thing, in a society of self-made men and women, portraits aimed at glorifying and immortalizing the individual were a necessary expression of deep-seated social aspirations. Wherever ingenious craftsmen and enough moderately prosperous families were thrown together, a portrait painter was likely to appear, by spontaneous generation.

For almost a century, skill flared and waned and then in 1738 two American cradles received gifts to the future world of art: John Singleton Copley was born in Boston, Benjamin West near Philadelphia. They were hardly in their teens before their unfolding talents were hailed with jubilation by Americans eager to nurture in the New World such esthetic flowers as had long grown in the Old.

West was at twenty-three an experienced portraitist when a group of Philadelphia merchants subscribed to send him to Europe for polishing. Rarely has a move to bolster Colonial pride been more successful. Although West settled in London, he was always considered an American, even after he was chosen to succeed Sir Joshua Reynolds as president of the Royal Academy. His fame extended throughout Europe because with the self-reliance of a frontier craftsman he again and again questioned traditional European artistic forms, and, with naïve ingenuity, redesigned them. There can be inventors in art as well as in science, who need not in themselves be great painters. West was such an inventor. His pictures do not overwhelm us seen today, but in their own day they opened up channels down which soon flowed the torrents of European art.

Catching on his arrival in Europe the first echoes of a changing archeological and moralistic attitude toward Greece and Rome, West gave celebrity to the Neo-classical style that was to become, under Jacques-Louis David, the official art of Revolutionary and Napoleonic France. As Paris was reaching out for this manner, West turned his brush to contemporary happenings, inventing the heroic news picture which flourished until the advent of the camera and still staggers down aisles of official art. Before 1800 West was building, on the example of Rubens, an early romantic manner; and in his old age he laid down the line that has, for better or worse, been followed ever since by Protestant biblical painters.

That this artistic inventiveness was not altogether a personal gift was revealed when John Singleton Copley arrived in Europe at the age of thirty-six, after having painted in his self-taught American style the intense portrait that proved him a superbly gifted artist. He had hardly touched upon European art before he, too, began tinkering with its canons. In 1775, when he had been abroad less than two years, he struck, in his *Brook Watson and the Shark*, the note of macabre sensationalism that inaugurated Romantic realism in French painting when it was struck again by Géricault in *The Raft of the Medusa*.

So the success of the subscription to send West abroad made such subscriptions an American habit. In 1766, a group of Maryland gentlemen sent Charles Willson Peale, at the age of twenty-five, to study with West. This self-graduated saddler, who had practiced so many trades at home, found it stultifying to concentrate during two whole years in London, on nothing but painting. He mended clocks and bells, dabbled in sculpture and mezzotint scraping, and took home with him only enough European stylistic convention to soften his old vernacular portrait style.

A gallery of portraits of American heroes he painted in post-Revolutionary Philadelphia apprenticed him to showmanship, and his universal curiosity fascinated him with the natural wonders of the half-explored New World. Heralded by a preserved paddle-fish, specimens—animal, vegetable and mineral—appeared in his studio and spread out until quite naturally the painter had invented the popular museum of natural history.

In the twentieth century, great institutions have rediscovered such of Peale's devices as the habitat groups in which preserved animals and plants were arranged together to simulate a natural environment. Peale's intention was in equal parts scientific and esthetic. Using painting, sculpture, archeology, taxidermy, botanical classification, controlled lighting, "deceptions," paleontology, and even background music on an organ, he recruited all "the arts" to create the gigantic composition he called "the world in miniature." The greatest adventure of Peale's life was his exhuming from a swamp in Ulster County, New York, in 1801, of the first mastodon skeleton seen anywhere in the world since the Stone Age.

In his painting of this event, he shows himself in the foreground, holding one end of a huge drawing. In the background a large wheel reveals that the scientist-painter was also a precursor of Sawyer: not wishing to pay for the power that would move his endless chain of buckets, he made the inside of the wheel so broad that children could run within it and thus turn it around.

Robert Fulton was twenty-three years younger than Peale, but like him educated as an artisan. Born in 1765 at the frontier metropolis of Lancaster, Pennsylvania, Fulton imbibed from the first influences both esthetic and mechanical. The prodigal Benjamin West had painted in Lancaster during the 1750s, and his canvases in the American vernacular style had hung on local walls for Fulton to see. These early works of a painter now "the companion of kings and emperors" were food for young dreams.

But louder in Lancaster was the hammering that accompanied mechanical invention and production. In many workshops, craftsmen were responding to a command of the wilderness that was relayed to them by clients in buckskin. Since European muskets, designed for warfare in open fields, could not steer a ball to its mark through the tangled branches of an American forest, the Lancaster gunsmiths were, as a group, developing the most accurate firearm in the world: the "Kentucky rifle" that, during the Revolution, barked out in the hands of frontier sharpshooters the knell of that conspicuous target, the hero on horseback.

Choice of a profession was forced early on Fulton since his father died bankrupt when he was ten. The future inventor turned his back on the gunsmiths' shops, became an apprentice to a Philadelphia jeweler. And the metalworking aspects of his new trade interested him less than its esthetic possibilities. The jeweler made lockets; Fulton specialized in plaiting the intricate designs out of a beloved's hair, in painting the little portraits on ivory which were to be placed in lockets. First from his master's shop and then, when he was twenty-one, on his own, he advertised as "miniature painter and hair worker."

Fulton's little likenesses of Mr. and Mrs. John Wilkes Kittera reveal the bright colors, the high spirits, and the naïve knack for catching a likeness that brought him local admiration. Local admiration was now naturally followed by a subscription to send him abroad to Benjamin West.

For seven years Fulton labored to imitate his triumphant master, but, unlike the older painter, he was unable to join in a creative whole the

artisan ingenuity that came naturally to him with European esthetic sophistication. His portraits of Lord Stanhope and Joel Barlow show that
he learned to paint a tolerably realistic likeness, but when he undertook
imaginative figure painting, he turned out the sentimentalities indicated
in an engraving after his *Lady Jane Grey the Night before Her Execution.*
Fulton, West wrote, "came to England with an intention to study painting, but, doubting his success, turned his attention to mechanics."

This change unleashed the inventor's imagination. His first major
project was, indeed, less a practical plan than a prophetic vision: he
dreamed out a system of small canals that was a preview of modern
railroading. Not like ordinary canals obeying the commands of geography, his shallow, water-filled ditches were to tunnel through mountains,
cross rivers on bridges, climb hills on inclined planes, thus taking the
shortest route between cities. On his uniform system, groups of identical
freight and passenger barges were to advance in trains, pulled, of course,
by the prime movers of the time, horses. His mechanical devices were
crude, and the whole thing came to no real practical result, but the
drawings he made of his ideas were infinitely freer and more eloquent
than the pictures he made as a professional painter.

Fulton's second engineering scheme, which remained the darling of
his heart, was equally grandiose but less original. Its basic conception
was taken, without apparent credit, from the most amazing of all Yankee
tinkerers, David Bushnell, who during the American Revolution had
built in the Connecticut River the first submarine in the world's history
to move underwater. Bushnell's effort to sink the British fleet in New
York harbor had failed for reasons which Fulton felt he could remedy.
He enlarged Bushnell's submarine—which had been shaped like an up-
ended turtle—to resemble, when not submerged, a small sailboat. Fulton
tried to sell it as the deadliest of weapons to Napoleon, then to Napoleon's prime English enemy, Pitt, and then to Russia, Holland, and the
United States. But the inability of the device to do any damage under
actual conditions of warfare, which had tripped up Bushnell, remained
to trip up Fulton.

When in 1802 Fulton was induced by the New York statesman-mil-
lionaire, Robert R. Livingston, to give his most serious attention to
the steamboat, he was a mechanic who had twice been tricked by his
imagination into heroic schemes that had failed. Now he unhooked his
Icarus wings and got to work on a purely practical level. He viewed his
problem as a series of small problems—water resistance, the best shape
for paddle wheels, engine proportions, gears, hull design, measure-

ments—that had to be solved one by one and then brought into harmony. Combining at last the ingenuity particularly fostered by America with European sophistication and skill, he sent the *Claremont* on its historic voyage in 1807.

Now, as a prosperous steamboat inventor, Fulton collected art and painted as an amateur. Yet the candy-box-like refinement flaunted by his miniature of Mrs. Oliver Hazard Perry reveals that his imagination was still incapable of fully expressing itself in the fine arts.

Although the gap in ages between Robert Fulton and Samuel Finley Breese Morse—twenty-six years—was hardly more than the gap between Peale and Fulton, the cultural break was immeasurably greater. Peale and Fulton had grown up during those creative decades that had built the United States and sent off to Europe American painters who had pioneered in the development of Old World styles. Morse was born in 1791 into an established nation, self-conscious about its newness and less eager for excitement than stability. Furthermore, Morse was not a birthright inheritor of the American artisan tradition; his father, Jedediah Morse, a New England minister, had written famous geography but had never worked with his hands.

At an age when West and Copley, Peale and Fulton were painting salable pictures, Morse was in the toils of formal education, painting strictly as an amateur on the side. When, at the age of twenty-one, he received parental permission to become a professional painter, he rushed off at once to London.

Before he had put a truly purposeful brush to canvas, Morse already held a basic conviction that was never to leave him. Since the United States could contribute nothing to the development of a painter, it was the duty of a patriotic American painter to imbibe in Europe skill and beauty which he would bring back, exactly as he had received it, for the elevation of his uncultured fellow citizens.

Although Morse's craftsman-trained American predecessors had carried with them across the ocean self-taught painting techniques and ideas, Morse went as a cultural beggar. That an American could be an inventor in the fine arts was an idea foreign to his philosophy. He intended to find out what kind of painting was most admired by the most admirable Europeans and to learn to paint in that way. To his father he communicated the results of his researches: "I cannot be happy unless I am pursuing the intellectual branch of the art. Portraits have none of it; landscape has some of it; but history has it wholly."

By "history" Morse meant the direction in which West had pioneered but which by then had become stale and academic. West's concern with the contemporary world had been forgotten in favor of an effort to reconstruct the long-past events that lay at the headsprings of Europe's religion and culture. To depict, as West had done, aspects of the upstart American civilization would now be considered pure barbarism by the critics Morse followed. The grand style consisted of reconstructing—the larger the better—events from the Bible or Greek or Roman antiquity. The son of so fierce a Protestant could not bring himself to paint the Bible; Morse prosed out a larger-than-life Hercules writhing in death agonies.

The canvas was painted to express not what he was but what he wished to pretend to be. A small statue of Hercules he made as a sketch from which to paint was more successful. The murky painting created no excitement, but the sculpture won a gold medal. However, a serious concern with sculpture had not been part of Morse's plan. Essential to his plan was a long stay in Europe—he regarded his *Dying Hercules* as no more than a student exercise—but unlike the American artisan-painters who had preceded him, he was unwilling to earn his living as he went along. "I will not degrade myself by making a trade of a profession."

Rather than starve, he came home in 1814; after four years his father would no longer pay for his English studies. but he did not feel himself yet prepared to create great pictures and he was sure that he could do nothing to prepare himself in the United States. He was forced to the humiliating recourse of trying to earn by painting portraits money to carry him back to Europe.

That Morse considered his portraits hack-work advanced as well as impeded the result. Since he felt the critical conceptions he had learnt by rote in Europe did not apply to such ignoble labor, he could paint without affectation renderings of objective reality which were suited to his talents and temperament. But he made little effort to excel as a portraitist. Although he produced excellent Romantic likenesses: fluent, gracious, virile, sometimes "tastefully" tricked up, they were at best perceptive records of personality. These portraits, like that of Professor Silliman, are as effective as any produced in Morse's American generation; had he never invented anything they would keep his reputation alive.

Landscapes, Morse had written his father, had more of the intellectual in them than portraits—but, of course, he meant only renditions of tradition-soaked Europe. When he painted such raw American phenomena as Niagara Falls, he was careful to explain that he was only amusing himself. Indeed, he depicted America in a much more direct style than he used for such Old World scenes as *The Wayside Shrine of the Virgin at Nettuno*. His attitude toward landscape is typified by his painting of the pseudo-Gothic building that contained his New York studio; to elevate his subject, he expunged New York's Washington Square and substituted a lagoon under a becastled mountain.

As for the grand style of historical painting, which he had alone considered worthy of a great artist, Morse made no attempt in that direction for fourteen long years.

Morse's sterile eagerness to improve America by importing ready-made art from Europe, even if unrealized, seemed to raise him above less self-conscious painters. He became the founder and perpetual president of the National Academy of Design. For years, Morse had argued that he could not practice the grand style until he had visited Italy. In 1829, when he was thirty-eight years old, he won his way at long last to the land of Raphael and Michelangelo. However, Italy did not, as he had expected, quicken in him his esthetic sensibilities; it reawakened the prejudices of his father's Puritan rectory. Seeing the masterpieces he had hoped to admire hanging in Catholic churches, adding to what he considered bigotry, he concluded that "man is led astray by his imagination more than any other faculty," and decided that painting could do no more than be "one of the greatest correctors of grossness and promoters of refinement." From this conclusion no inspiration for original masterpieces sprang. As the showpiece of his European tour, he painted a handy guide to culture, his *Gallery of the Louvre*, containing miniature copies of thirty-seven of the most famed old masters there.

Morse came to realize that he could never create powerfully in a purely European style, but he could see no sources of inspiration in his own culture. His cultural compass had lost all deviation. As he sailed home from his disastrous European trip, he yearned for a new lodestar, and conceived the idea of the telegraph.

But Morse did not abandon all to follow his invention. He continued to paint, though with increasing discouragement; he experimented with the newly invented camera, not for itself, but as a possible aid to his hesitating brush; he became a professor of art at New York University and a lecturer on culture everywhere; he sublimated his frustrations into hatred of the Catholics that led him to run for mayor of New York City on a bigoted anti-immigrant ticket; he dreamed of entering the ministry, and essayed other inventions than the telegraph. Thus he echoed the

versatility of the old artisan jacks-of-all trades—but not with their buoy-
ant ingeniousness. His movements were the gyrations of despair.

But all the while, like a lagging spirit of romance, the telegraph sham-
bled along toward the rescue. The project ran exactly counter to all
Morse's theories of great painting and was ideally suited to his abilities.
As a painter, he had sought to uplift his fellow men; as an inventor, he
served them, As a painter, he had valued theoretical conceptions because
they were not practical; as inventor, he labored to harness the visions of
abstract scientists to the most practical of ends. By finally giving scope
to his natural, hard-headed realism, to the unconventional ingenuity that
was part of his American heritage, Morse completed the invention of
the telegraph in 1844; he became rich and famous.

Although he had gone much farther as a painter than Fulton, his
drawings of machines had much less flair. They seem aggressively anti-
esthetic, while Fulton clearly gave an artistic quality to his rendition of
a machine. the explanation for this is not far to seek.

Fulton, like Peale who also mingled esthetic and scientific pursuits,
subscribed to the old conception of "the arts" as the pantheon of all
men's skills. Considering himself "the artist" whether engaged in painting or scientific invention, he saw his life as a single piece and quite
naturally labored to make visually satisfying his drawings of canals, and
model houses, and submarines, and steamboats.

On the other hand, after the invention of the telegraph was a reality,
Morse wrote, "The very name of pictures produces a sadness of heart I
cannot describe. Painting has been a smiling mistress to many, but she
has been a cruel jilt to me. I did not abandon her; she abandoned me. I
have scarcely taken any interest in painting for many years. Will you
believe it? When last in Paris in 1845, I did not go into the Louvre, nor
did I visit a single picture gallery. I sometimes indulge in a vague dream
that I may paint again. It is rather the memory of past pleasures, when
hope was enticing me onward to deceive me at last. Except for some
family portraits, valuable to me for their likenesses only, I could wish
that every picture I ever painted was destroyed. I have no wish to be
remembered as a painter, for I never was a painter. My ideal for the
profession was perhaps too exalted—I may say is too exalted. I leave it
to others more worthy to fill the nitches of art."

These words reveal that in mid-nineteenth-century America science
had, like an unruly son, broken away from art, but it had not yet overwhelmed its parent. Morse, the greatest American inventor until then,
felt that his life would have been worthier had he been a great painter.

ASHER B. DURAND: AN ENGRAVER'S AND A FARMER'S ART

Asher B. Durand was the founder and, for a generation, the leading figure in the Hudson River School.* The first half of this statement will appear to many readers as obviously false. Did not Thomas Cole create a sensation with views of the Hudson River in 1825, while Durand did not specialize in landscape for at least another ten years? Did not Cole's example, by breaking down imported esthetic canons, open American scenery to enthusiastic acceptance as preferred subject matter for American painters? And, although Durand was an accomplished creator of many landscapes worthy of admiration and even love, was not Cole a greater painter? The answer to all these three queries is "of course," yet Cole was a precursor, not a true member of the Hudson River School.

Every important Hudson River School painter was American-born,[1] while Cole's family had fled to the United States, as refugees from the English industrial midlands, when he was seventeen. He was never fully to accept the optimism, based on American experience, of the Hudson River School artists whose basic tenet was that Nature was good. Seeing much evil in man and his world, Cole painted menacing and violent landscapes, in addition to quiet and sunny scenes, and created moralistic multi-canvas epics like *The Voyage of Life*. His painting technique was very different from Hudson River practice. One of the most tactile of landscape painters—which is a secret of his greatness—he rendered with

---

*An earlier version of this essay appeared in *Asher B. Durand* (Yonkers, N.Y.: Hudson River Museum, 1983).

[1]This statement relies on the distinction between the Hudson River School and what I have called the Rocky Mountain School which painted tremendous canvases related to the sensational scenery of the Far West. The leader of that school, Albert Bierstadt, was born and trained in Dusseldorf. The perspicacious critic James Jackson Jarves considered Bierstadt a "Dusseldorf artist," and the contemporary chronicler of mid-nineteenth-century century art, Henry T. Tuckerman, added "to this fact may be ascribed both his merits and [his] defects." Significantly, all Bierstadt's most important followers were, in sharp contradiction to the Hudson River School, foreign-born. They heightened their observations of Nature into studio-stunners.

great power the shape and position of objects, rather than the continuity of nature in America's deep vistas, walled with mountains, which the Hudson River School artists painted as typical of their land.

Although Durand did not specialize in landscape until the mid-1830s, he served from 1845 to 1861 as the president of that powerful artists' organization, the National Academy of Design, and in 1855 and 1856, he published *Letters on Landscape Painting*, the most basic and influential description of the Hudson River style. His landscapes achieved great acclaim.

Durand was born to parents long settled in America in an area of New Jersey still bucolic. (The community, then called Jefferson Village, is now that affluent suburb of New York City, Maplewood.) From the front door of his childhood home he saw a deep vista of cultivated fields; beyond the back door rose a small, wooded mountain. The family supported themselves by farming. Although trained in silversmithing and watchmaking, the father could not resist wasting his skills as an impractical "universal mechanic." The whole Durand tribe—Asher was the sixth of eight children—carried Yankee ingenuity into horseplay and mad invention. A brother combined gears and mirrors into a machine that could worst a New England schoolmaster at grammar. Little Asher got hold of a bit of copper, hammered it out flat, worked out his own graving tools, and, to the cheers of his relations, created an image that would print. Naturally, he was apprenticed to an engraver.

As an apprentice to an engraver, Durand learned what was to be the fundamental technical expedient of the Hudson River School. Modern art historians, determined to find what seems to them more suitably elevated sources for the landscapists' style and achievements, have overlooked the significance of the fact that a large majority of the painters began their careers and received their basic training in the workshops of commercial engravers.

The pictures produced in those shops were too little—usually measurable only in inches—for effective use of lines of perspective. Since the prints were altogether in black and white, color could not be used to push some forms forward and others back. Of course, the artists showed distant objects as smaller than foreground objects, but this could give little sense of the continuity of space or indicate any air in between overlapped forms. But the engravers did have an effective tool: black-and-white values. Durand stated that gray was the most important hue to landscape painters. Although not allowed to be visible, it modified all colors, "without dissipating them" according to distance. As the eye went back into the picture, the darks became lighter, the lights softer and weaker until at last the mingling of dark and light resolved into comparative conformity.

The basic progression of values is created by the accumulation of atmosphere through distance. But in different parts of the picture the values are modified by variations in the consistency of the air itself: rain, mist, complete clarity. Further changes are produced by varying intensities and qualities of light as it penetrates the air, or is held in it, or reflected back from surfaces: soil of different sheen and color, trees, water. Since, in the Hudson River School landscapes, all this and more was expressed by variations in an invisible but pervasive black-and-white pattern, the aerial effects were built into the structure of the picture, conveying a consciousness of all-pervading atmosphere. Atmosphere, Durand wrote, "carries us into a picture rather than allowing us to be detained before it."

The method learned in engravers' workshops was particularly suited to the needs of the artists who typically indicated a consciousness of the size of their continent. Not for them the restricted views that were the subject matter of the French Barbizon painters from Corot onward. Hudson River School landscapes revel in space, often being panoramic views.

Fundamental reliance on values did create limitations. It was impossible to catch within the overall consistency such tactile rendition of forms, dependent on strong contrasts of light and shadow, as Cole achieved. Neither could Hudson River artists depict, with Constable, the evanescent effects of quickly moving cloud and shadow that typify the English climate. Fortunately, the American climate is much more stable: long periods of consistent weather. As for the one uneasy aerial spirit of the northeastern United States, the thunderstorm, the Hudson River Artists learned to hold it motionless as it approached—a menace in a frozen moment.

When the Hudson River School continued into its second generation, luminosity was more emphasized, particularly when artists turned from mountain scenes to the glittering seashore. The resulting change sparked almost a hundred years later, at the end of the 1940s, a theory that spread among the art historians like wildfire. Although there is not a shred of documentary evidence for such a dichotomy, it was postulated that there existed beside the Hudson River School a dissident group for whom the name "luminist" was then invented. The major characteristics of the "luminists" were defined as a lyrical, charmed, silent depiction of atmospheric light, with an absence of visible brushstrokes. Further consideration has much damaged the theory through the realization that "luminism" was not actually a style apart, but one aspect of general Hudson River School practice. Thus such leaders of the school as John F. Kensett practiced "luminism" upon occasion in response to special visual effects of light, atmosphere, and, particularly, reflecting water. All the fuss could have been avoided had there been a recognition of the influence on the "luminists" as on the other Hudson River School painters of the engraver's craft. At their greatest variation, the "luminists" did no more than speed up or slow down, for heightened effect, the natural progression of black-and-white values.[2]

Downgrading the engravers' craft, as it was practiced by the young Durand and so many of his colleagues, has been made feasible today only by the nineteenth-century development of photography and photoengraving. Nowadays, to disseminate widely any work of art it is only necessary to plop a camera before it and hand the result over to an anonymous worker adjusting a machine. But across the Western world for century after century (and during Durand's period as an engraver) any general knowledge of the visual arts was dependent on the achievements of engravers.

The importance of engravers to their knowledge, reputations, and prosperity was recognized by professional painters, who elected them to their honorary academies. If they wished to look beyond the art locally around them, artists had to study printed plates. And, although an artist would often paint several versions of a successful picture for various patrons, and would exhibit such of his works which were not altogether out of his hands as widely as he could, any large reputation particularly across national boundaries depended no more on his own skill than on the skill with which his work was presented by the engraver. Furthermore, in societies becoming increasingly middle-class, an artist could often make more money from multiple sales of engravings for small

---

[2]The effect of engravers' values (although not mentioned here) is thus described by the high priest of luminism, Barbara Novak: "In luminist landscapes measure confines natural elements within an abstract of ideational order. This order operates across the surface or in depth. As in classic art, mathematical and geometric correlations predominate over organic irregularities. Luminist measure, imposing an absolute order on reality, also gives specificity to the ideal. Thus the categories of the real and ideational are tempered. Qualification affects every aspect of luminist art: form, tone, light are all subject to the subtlest discretion of calculated control. These minute and economic discriminations release poetic rather than cerebral effects.

sums than from extracting large prices from the well-to-do for original paintings.

Reproducing or painting on a printable metal plate required of an engraver much more skill and esthetic insight than is needed to translate a book from one language to another. The translator is operating in the same artistic medium with his original, and at the same length. The engraver must reduce the size of the image, not uncommonly on a scale of more than one hundred to one. He must communicate the effects of color altogether in black and white. And practical demands are made by the technology of printing that have no relation to the technique of painting (and, for that matter, sculpture or architecture).

The great reduction of scale forced an intuitive determination of what were the most important aspects of the picture and how to combine them in order to communicate both the meaning and the effect of the whole. "Through the cunning of a technical process," wrote Durand's son John, "a line engraving displays the principal elements of a painting—composition, drawing, form, gradations of light and shade, and subtleties of effect—everything but color. In competent hands, the mechanical processes employed, like delicate sculpture, become a fine art, and the engraver a genuine artist. Sometimes his art equals, occasionally surpasses, that of the painter whose work he copies."

In the United States, it was much easier for engravers to study their art than for painters since ably executed prints were imported in quantity from Europe while equivalent paintings, being too expensive for American purses, were not. The painter had to make what use he could of engraved translations, while the models the engravers studied were in the language of their own art.

The future landscapists flocked to the engravers' workshops not because they foresaw the use they would eventually make of what they would learn, but because engravers, having the widest market, were the most prosperous of American artists. There were jobs galore for young beginners who wanted to learn a profitable trade.

Typically Durand was an an apprentice asked to do no original work. For trade cards, letterheads, lottery tickets, diplomas, tickets to balls or horse-races, illustrations and title pages for books, commercial portraits of distinguished persons, ancient or modern, Durand copied usually European models. Each task was a lesson and a test of the skill he had achieved up to that point. It went out into the world for general praise or blame. When Durand's six years of apprenticeship were over, his master took him into partnership.

Gradually Durand began making original engraved renditions of oil portraits by America's best painters. He became intimate with the artists and profited from their criticism of his work. When Trumbull called him in to do the huge plate of his *Declaration of Independence*, he was assigned such a task as made the reputations of the very greatest English engravers who by their superior skill were conquering the European market. Durand's signal success, after three years of labor on the plate, demonstrated him to be the greatest engraver in America. There are those competent in such matters who regard him as one of the greatest in all the history of this art.

After President Jackson had as a populist gesture closed the Bank of the United States, local banks had the right to establish their own paper currency and all the bills had to be designed and printed in engraving shops. Forgers helped business along by duplicating any bank notes that were not executed with truly professional skill. One of the Durand family tinkerers, Asher's brother Cyrus, went further. He invented a mechanical lathe which ruled on the plates lines that no counterfeiter could match. And Asher set out to draw and cut vignettes which were to have an amusing effect on the iconography of American mural painting into my own young manhood.

The conception that the classical connoted solidity—nineteenth-century bank buildings were made to look like Roman temples—gave Durand, who of course knew no Latin or Greek, a chance to rampage around in classic symbolism. Archimedes, Neptune, Hercules are given local meaning by being shown in the company of American cogwheels, canal locks, cargo boats, cows, or mountains. It was particularly delightful to Durand that a classical reference made acceptable revealing the female body somewhat or even altogether naked above the waist. Renditions of semi-nudes that would have made well-bred girls faint had the lower parts of the bodies been shown in modern dress, were, if it was a toga that had been thrown open, acceptable on currency. The assumption was that the figures were cultural as representing classical marbles, not indecent as they would have been had they represented flesh and blood. Durand was particularly given to exemplifying patriotism by showing a semi-clad female figure offering from an amphora a drink to the American eagle. The Chemical Bank specified that the eagle thus shown on its currency be no namby-pamby bird but present "a ferocious, spirited aspect."

After such designs had vanished from currency, they continued to embellish stock certificates and, until the 1929 stock market crash, they were vastly enlarged in murals which symbolized mining or merchandising by a classic nude handling or associating with indicative paraphernalia.

Durand felt a passionate desire to make a large plate, the prints to be sold individually as works of art, of a female nude. His inspiration was, he explained to his family, the technical skill achievable, as revealed by old engravers, in rendering flesh. The problem was to find a model. Nice girls would not pose nor could he outrage his wife by asking her to do so, and bad women, being considered the most evil part of creation, would obviously debase any picture for which they posed.

Every painting school had its privileged nude subjects, purified by the circumstances in which the figures were caught unclothed. Diana and her nymphs seen by the peeking Actaeon who—thank God not the viewer!—is to be suitably punished. Susanna, cringing when surprised by the Elders. The English-speaking world of Durand's time had Musidora, a character from James Thompson's celebrated poem, the *Seasons*. Not only was she "bathing in the flood" with utmost innocence, but the male eyes that saw her (usually, as in Durand's picture, from off the canvas) viewed her with reverence and married her soon thereafter.

Durand created his image from pictorial sources. It is criticized for anatomical inaccuracy, but this writer, who owns two impressions, finds it altogether charming. We moderns are very used to distortion (whether conscious on the part of the artist or not) for emotional effect. Musidora is most charmingly what she was intended to be: a nubile girl, not yet fully conscious of her body in any sexual sense, virginally enjoying a sylvan dip in a secluded glade.

Disturbed by the anatomical criticism—had he not read that the test of an artist was his skill at drawing the naked figure?—Durand sought more information that he could secure from engravings. The only life-sized female nude that had so far been painted by an able American artist was John Vanderlyn's *Ariadne* executed in libertarian Paris. Vanderlyn brought *Ariadne* home in 1815 in the hope that the shock effect would draw the public to a private museum he intended to establish. The museum had not proved a success, and the shock effect made the picture unsalable to any private citizen. Durand bought the painting as a source for an engraving. First he copied *Ariadne* in oils the size of the plate he intended to create, and then picked up his engraver's tools. This became one of the occasions when the engraving was superior to the original.

Twenty years ago, I published a description of Durand's *Ariadne* which I shall venture to quote as I do not think I can improve upon it:

"Vanderlyn, taking over the typical fault of French neoclassicism, failed to establish a true esthetic connection between the firm body and the umbrageous landscape in which it reposed. The fair, naked form—printer's ink communicates soft resilience—is strongly drawn, yet weightless. On her bed of draperies, in her trance-like sleep, full-breasted Ariadne touches the earth but inhabits the air. The landscape that enclosed her but through which she seems majestically to glide, is both real and ghostlike. Gray leaf and bark glimmer against black, heightened in vision. As in Titian's paintings of Venus and the musician, the actual seeming body seems present only in dress." It is widely inprobable that Durand was thinking of Titian; he was unconsciously expressing his own feelings. It was thus shadowy and thus firm, thus haunting and unattainable and strange, that voluptuousness manifested itself in New Jersey's somewhat puritanical son. (When he finally moved completely into the warmer medium of paint, he abandoned the female nude.)

After having made himself into a great engraver entirely by his own efforts in the fourteen years he practiced that art, Durand abandoned the pursuit (according to his son he sacrificed a fortune which he could have made through the banknote business). He had for years been experimenting with oil paints, out in the fields and in his own workshop, accepting no more instruction than he had sought in his first steps as an engraver. Now he determined to give his full time to practicing as a painter. Beginning as a portraitist was the obvious step since he had engraved so many portraits by others.

I have for some years lunched on most weekdays in the presence of Durand portraits, and can testify that, although impressive, they are not convivial companions. Having reduced life-sized likenesses to their basic elements to make them tell in a small black-and-white plate, Durand, when himself depicting at life-size, did not restore the subtleties and graces he had formerly edited out. And not being habituated to color, he allowed it no major role, using it to enhance his forms that are unabashedly dominated by black-and-white values. We see powerful, utterly sincere, grave and intense images. Durand, who had rarely been called on for prints from female portraits—only actresses were then well enough known to create a sale for engravings—rarely attempted oil likenesses of the ladies who would have ruled them stark. But stark, powerful renditions of males suited the times well and pleased.

Durand had been called on to engrave for illustrated periodicals serving female audiences paintings of persons acting out a story that appealed "to domestic sentiment" and were within the scope of the American imagination. Now he enlarged such scenes into paintings in which the figures were about half life-sized. In the manner of the engraved illustrations, he depicted historical events as genre (that is, in personal terms), and in a form resembling theatrical stills. These canvases seem to me his least effective paintings. He lacked the histrionic gift, the sentimentality, or the sense of humor needed to give life to such stilted groupings.

The temperamental restraint, which prevented Durand from becoming a successful genre painter, also prevented him from undertaking until middle age the subject matter that had from his childhood moved him most profoundly: a religious and esthetic passion for Nature. On Sundays, he did not attend church, "the better to indulge reflection unrestrained under the high canopy of heaven. This mode of passing the Sabbath became habitual with me in early life." He found under the skies in God's outdoors "the *intuition* by which every earnest spirit enjoys the assurance of our spiritual nature and scorns the subtlety and logic of positive philosophy."

The task of communicating in paint this "*intuition*" seemed to Durand so high and difficult a task that he had to be pushed into attempting it. A financial depression combined with the premature death of his prime patron, Luman Reed, reduced his portrait commissions, and the death of Reed brought him into the close contact of mutual sorrow with Thomas Cole.

Cole fired and encouraged Durand's landscape efforts. However, his training as an engraver, his religious beliefs that skimped the problem of evil, and his altogether American experience in prosperous land, made it impossible for Durand to follow in Cole's footsteps. Instead, he beat his own trail which was followed by the younger American artists who shared his convictions and joined with him to form the Hudson River School.

It is important to our understanding of the first generation of the Hudson River School to remember that the major actors—painters, purchasers, critics—were graduated farm boys, who had been brought to New York City by the prosperity that had floated there on the Erie Canal. They painted, bought, or wrote about the pictures in terms of childhood memories heightened by nostalgia. They viewed the painted landscapes with eyes of men to whom the fields and forests had been, during their formative years, almost their entire exterior world. They thus brought to what the artists painted a wealth of detailed understanding which modern city-bred viewers do not share. I once wrote that those deeply concerned with the iconography of the Hudson River

School should study forestry. The suggestion elicited considerable irritation, but its validity is amply demonstrated by the high percentage of Durand's preparatory drawings being portraits of trees.

Toward the end of his career, Durand said, "What a relief it is to be able to stand for an hour before some fine tree, in direct sympathy with it. I have done so as a boy on long summer days, and now when a man I had a higher appreciation of it than ever and enjoyed it all the more— the great happiness in standing face to face with nature."

Trees were, of course, the embellishment of sylvan landscape. They seemed to stand taller in those days because no man-made structures, with the exception of church steeples, even approached the great trees in height. Standing in fields, they gave shade to weary tillers of the soil and also to the cattle who congregated beneath them. The condition and species of the forest vegetation told a farmer at a glance the nature of the soil beneath. The worship of trees, mythology reiterates, is as old as mankind.

Durand passionately shared this worship. Wishing to show the goodness of God at its highest, Durand sought perfect examples of every race of trees in his northeastern America, drawing them as he found them in poses that could be fitted into pictures.

Although he could not find within his society models for the human figure, he needed only to walk his landscape to find perfect arboreal models. He urged young painters, "Choose the most beautiful and characteristic. If your subject be a tree, observe wherein it differs from those of other species, whether pointed or rounded, drooping or springing upward; next mark the character of its trunk and branches, the manner in which the latter shoot out from the parent stem, their direction, curves and angles. Every tree has its traits of individuality—some kinds assimilate, others differ widely; with careful attention these peculiarities are easily learned. . . . By this course, you will obtain the knowledge of that natural variety of form so essential to protect you against frequent repetition and monotony."

Tuckerman wrote concerning many of Durand's canvases that "only the great skill and truth of their execution would atone for the paucity of objects in such a landscape. Yet so characteristic is each tree, so natural the bark and foliage, so graphic the combination and foreground that the senses and the mind are filled and satisfied with this purely sylvan landscape. Mark the boughs of that black birch, the gnarled trunk of this oak, the tufts on yonder pine, the drooping sprays of the hemlock, and the relief of the dead tree—is it not such a woodland nook as you have often observed in a tramp through the woods? Not a leaf or flower on the ground, not an opening in the umbrageous canopy, not a mouldering stump beside the pool, but looks like an old friend."

And what of modern city dwellers who lack intimate familiarity with trees and indeed with the entire country world which they visit only as vacationists? Do they lose mightily by lack of informed association with Durand's detail? Do they find a compensating gain in not being distracted by particularities from the artist's deep emotion and reverend purpose? Durand envisioned wide-vistaed landscapes as cathedrals expressing the glory of God, sought "the quiet loveliness of Nature, the subdued and modest aspect, brilliant without glare, like the gentle and most estimable virtues of the moral world." For a simple soul, unconcerned with philosophers' speculation or religious dogma, contact with the infinite brings melancholy as well as comfort. Durand's tone is exactly expressed by William Cullen Bryant, the writer closest to the Hudson River School, in his then famous poem *Thanatopsis*:

> To him who in the love of Nature holds
> Communion with her visible forms, she speaks
> A various language; for gayer hours
> She has a voice of gladness, and a smile
> And eloquence of beauty, and she glides
> Into his darker musings, with a mild and
> Healing sympathy, that steals away
> Their sharpness, ere he is aware.

Thomas Cole's *The Oxbow:* The Romance and Harmony of the American Landscape

When his art burst on the nation in 1825, paintings by Thomas Cole such as *The Oxbow* gave depictions of American landscapes the status of serious and important art. The acceptance as beautiful of a view like this, a bend in a river in the rugged terrain of Massachusetts, indicates a major change in American attitudes and taste.*

Ever since the country's beginnings, it had been taboo for ambitious American artists to paint the uncultivated natural world around them. The Declaration of Independence did not change the situation, because it did not extend beyond politics. Since the United States was a new-comer among nations, it strove to repel charges of crudity by pursuing correct taste as practiced in Europe.

Correct European taste was Neoclassical, and insisted, in the words of the poet Alexander Pope, that "the proper study of mankind is man." It followed that a landscape had esthetic value only insofar as it had been shaped by human minds and hands. The largely untamed countryside of the new continent was thus ruled the least paintable of all.

The artist who smashed the American taboo against painting the American world was, not as paradoxically as it might seem, an immi-grant. Thomas Cole (1801–1848) had, at the age of eighteen, persuaded his parents to flee the smoky skies of English industrialism to what he visualized as a new Eden.

Cole's artistic emergence coincided almost exactly with two historical consummations: the promulgation of the Monroe Doctrine and the opening of the Erie Canal. The doctrine warned European nations away from our hemisphere; the canal made direct trade between the Eastern Seaboard and the expanding West financially practical. It fostered a new

*An earlier version of this essay appeared in *Travel and Leisure* (July 1985), pp. 80–81, 117.

class of merchants who, as they operated within their own continent, displaced the old New York City aristocracy that had become wealthy through overseas trade. The newcomers cared little about Europe. As former farm boys, they were predisposed to like the views of American scenery created by the Hudson River School, which Cole inaugurated.

Cole differed from his followers, whose paintings (like his) are so highly·valued today, because all of them—Durand, Kensett, Church, and the others—were American-born. Raised in a pre-Civil War environment that shed peace and prosperity on the land, these American painters were themselves romantics who repudiated the cold shackles of Neoclassicism and did not feel the break between the real and the ideal that troubled Europe. They saw American nature as the physical manifestation of a benign and benevolent God. Their optimistic paintings were regarded by the broad American public as revealing the glory of divine creation.

But Cole, brought up in England among the dislocations of emergent industrialism, remained haunted by a sense of ingrowing evil—a sense that man and his world were not so wonderful. He painted *The Oxbow* as a temporary escape from laboring month after month on a series of five canvases, *The Course of Empire*, which depicted man building a wicked city and then bloodily destroying it. But in his return to the American land, Cole found himself facing another dichotomy: between untamed nature and the agricultural pursuits of man.

Other artists of the Hudson River School liked to show agriculture in the foreground merging comfortably with wilds in the distance. But in his *Oxbow*, Cole did not gloss over the fact that the encroachments of cultivation would destroy the fierce grandeur of the wilderness. He was determined to show these two opposites as independent entities that never meet, to divide the foreground equally between them, and yet to reveal that the separates could live together in harmony. Thus he faced awesome problems of pictorial composition.

Cole chose as his subject an actual scene just south of Northampton, Massachusetts, that contained "the oxbow," a dramatic bend of the Connecticut River. In his painting, wild nature is on the viewer's left; dark green unbroken foliage rises steeply to a middle distance blocked by angry gray clouds.

Cultivated nature, on the right, stretches back for miles and miles, as is indicated by the shrinking of details. It is tableland, shown as flat as it could be, and colored a grayish tan, in extreme contrast to the mounting wild foliage. A huge paddle-shaped field is cut off by the curving river from the lowland whose surface it exactly duplicates. Presumably, it is joined to the riverbank under the cliff, but the attachment is not visible. A storm in the background concentrates its fury on the wild side, while the lowland and small hills that are an extension of it are quiet in clear sunlight.

On the tableland, the painting is precise: we can see the wheels of a wagon occupying no more than an eighth of an inch of canvas. But the untamed foliage is rendered with broad harsh brushstrokes. The umbrella that belongs to a landscapist's paraphernalia protrudes from the cliff high over the tableland but seems too frail a pin to hold the composition together.

As I have prowled art galleries here and abroad, I have kept an eye out for landscapists who could match Cole's ability to moor firmly painted objects in space by invisible tensions that hold them in opposition as cables hold upright a suspension bridge. Not Claude, Rubens, Constable, Turner, Corot or, of course, any Impressionist. Perhaps Salvator Rosa (sometimes), and probably Poussin, although as a classicist Poussin never attempted anything like *The Oxbow*.

It is a fascinating occupation to identify the many forms in Cole's composition. Each in itself is completely naturalistic, but at the same time it interacts with other forms to fasten together the daring composition. In the end, you cannot imagine moving a single object or conceive of pulling, even with two tractors, *The Oxbow* apart.

That *The Oxbow* is a show stopper is evident in the large gallery of American paintings at the Metropolitan Museum of Art in New York City, where it hangs. No one passes it by. The casual viewer may not understand all its implications or realize what an impossible composition is shown before him. Yet he does feel the relief from tension that great art can bring by manifesting harmony in our diverse and dangerous world.

ART IN YOUR ATTIC

We Americans are so used to thinking of art as something you go far away to find that only too often we are like the fairy-tale hero who combed the world for a magic churn that was right under his nose all the time.* You do not have to sail to Europe in order to secure art worthy of your home; you do not even have to carry your checkbook into the hushed salons of big-city art dealers. Hidden away in some corner of your parents' or grandparents' house, you may well unearth the paintings your great-grandmother selected for her wall. If, like so many of us, you have moved away from your family homestead, you may discover in a little antique shop around the corner the pictures which somebody else's great-grandmother bought and cherished. Sometimes, for the mere labor of carrying a load down the attic stairs—or for a few dollars—you may secure just the spot of color and design that is needed to give your living-room distinction.

When Great-Aunt Harmony wanted a picture to enliven that dark place in the hall, she might make it herself, never doubting that she knew how. Had she not been to the best Ladies' Seminary in the region, where she had been taught "dancing, needlework, and painting in oils"? And when Harmony got married, her groom wanted portraits of them both as parlor pieces. He did not mourn that he lacked the cash to pay some famous member of the National Academy. He hailed a face-painter who came by in a carriage and paid him with three nights' lodging and a bottle of rum.

While Harmony and her husband lived, the pictures hung on their walls, blending perfectly with the furniture and china. However, Harmony's heirs—particularly that fancy daughter-in-law from the city—thought the whole decorative scheme stuffy and out of date. Furniture and pictures went up into the attic together.

Most of us have long since discovered that old American furniture has

*An earlier version of this essay appeared in *Mademoiselle's Living for Spring* (1948), 30–34, 154–55.

charm and value. The corner cupboard the fancy daughter-in-law despised is now the pride of your dining room, and you would not accept five hundred dollars for the old highboy (or maybe you'd jump on it). But, unless you are a very unusual person, you have left up in the attic the pictures that used to hang beside these prized heirlooms.

You probably know quite a bit about American primitives: how this particular kind of picture has become a cult among sophisticated collectors and art critics; how they hang in major museums and bring fancy prices on New York's Fifty-Seventh Street. But do you realize that the pictures that lie forgotten in corners of American attics are also American primitives?

The theme song of this article might well be "Bring those paintings down, babe; bring those paintings down!" Carry Great-Aunt Harmony's pictures from the attic to the parlor. Or, if your family furniture and decorations have, most unjustly, gone to a cousin, search the dark corners of village junk shops; go to country auctions.

Should your picture-hunting carry you out of the home and involve scribbling your signature in a checkbook, be cautious! Only a few American primitives are worth large sums; do not bid high when you see something pretty, on the theory that you are getting a very valuble painting that you could sell for three times what you pay. Priceless pictures, it is true, are sometimes knocked down for a few dollars, but, particularly in the field of painting, you have to be a howling expert before you can be a good judge of values. Pay for a painting only what it is worth to you in the decoration of your home. Then you cannot lose. Should you, in addition, make a killing—that is sheer profit.

If you are anything like me, the first thing you do when you come into possession of an old painting is to carry your treasure out into the sunlight where it can be examined to the best advantage. Undoubtedly, color and design will be obscured by dirt. However, don't rush indoors for a soapy rag. Probably more pictures have been ruined by being washed with soap and water than by any other misfortune. The soap attacks the paint; the water dissolves the glue-like substance which sticks the paint to the canvas. The picture may look better for a short time, but in a few years the colors will flake off.

When your know-it-all neighbor comes by and urges you to clean your painting by rubbing it with a raw potato or onion, just laugh. For although this vegetable cure sounds very sophisticated, it depends on friction, which is bad, and on the water in the vegtable, which is worse.

Superficial dust may be safely removed by brushing the picture lightly—never bear down hard on a painting—with a soft brush, or with absorbent cotton moistened by a gasoline-type cleaning fluid. If you wish, you may gently rub the surface with a high-quality emulsion cream furniture polish. You will be surprised how much brighter your painting will come.

However, neither of these methods will take off the old, discolored varnish that gives the "brown soup" appearance which was once regarded as the hallmark of an old master. Although various chemicals will remove this yellowed varnish, I advise you to leave it alone, since the same chemicals, unless handled with the greatest skill, will also remove the all-important top layer of paint which contains the artist's finishing touch. If you want the picture to look like new—and if you are feeling rich—carry it to a professional restorer recommended by your local museum. Otherwise, be proud that the old canvas looks its age.

A painting is not ruined if it is torn. A very cultured lady of my acquaintance sold a beautiful old family portrait as almost worthless because there was a rip across one of the eyes. What was her horror, on walking into a major museum a few months later, to see the ancestress hanging there serenely, her facing bearing no visible scratch. Rips, of course, must be fixed by professionals, but do not worry about them unless they are conspicuous enough to ruin the effect of the picture. After all, part of the fun of hanging Great-Grandfather's portrait is that it was not painted yesterday.

You may want to put a new frame on your treasure, but do not move too hastily. Even if, at first glance, the frame looks strange and out of fashion, remember that it was selected by the artist or by the person who originally bought the picture. Frame and painting are likely to go together like coffee and cream. Before you throw the frame out, give youself a few days to get used to it. And consider the possibility of painting it a color that would chime better with your décor.

American attics contain many kinds of pictures that fit in with contemporary living. Most obvious, of course, are paintings which have a particular meaning for the owner because of family associations. If you possess a portrait of Grandmother that makes her look handsome and gracious and noble, you have probably already brought it downstairs. If Grandmother is still overhead, associating with dust and spiders, I suspect it is because she is shown with a hatchet face and painted in so literal a manner that the picture seems crude. Bring her down anyway. The very unconventionality of her likeness may make it a prize. American primitives are admired because of their honesty and because of the simplicity with which they were painted. Their emphasis on flat design and geometric patterns approaches modern techinques of painting and is particularly suited to contemporary taste.

Do not fall into the trap which caught a rich New England lady a few years ago. She possessed a large portrait of her great-grandfather, who had been a clergyman. Worried because the picture emphasized the mole on his cheek and the rotundity of his belly, she hired an artist to paint a copy that smoothed out all the details she considered strange or ugly. She hung the copy in her living-room and tossed the original into the attic. One afternoon she invited an official of an important museum in to tea. He examined the rainbow-tinted copy with as straight a face as he could summon, and then asked whether it had not been made from an old original. When she admitted the truth, in his suavest manner he persuaded his hostess to take him up to the attic, and then to give his museum the battered but honest portrait which she had considered too mean for her drawing room. I happened to be present when the portrait arrived at the museum, and I shall never forget the excitement with which we wiped off the dust and cobwebs to reveal one of the greatest early-American pictures I have ever seen.

Portraits are not the only type of painting which has a particular suitability for your rooms because of family association. The old American artists habitually advertised that they made "perspective views of gentlemen's estates." You may well find a watercolor drawing of the house in which an ancestor lived, or—if you are lucky—one of those farmyard scenes which are among the most delightful of American primitives. When a good husbandman paid over money for a picture of his house and barns, he wanted everything in its place: the well sweep where it belonged; the prize rooster crowing on the dung-hill; his cows grazing in their pasture; Great-Grandmother herself is shown pouring a pail of slops into the pigpen. Here is life itself in minature.

When not engaged with slops and pigs, Great-Grandmother may well have been a painter herself. She had started off when, as a mere slip of a girl, she had spent a glorious season or two at boarding school. Many were the styles in which she was taught to paint, and every one of them is suited to your guest-bedroom or parlor.

In those days, young ladies were not supposed to get so interested in life that they forgot about death; it was a routine assignment to paint in watercolor a graveyard, complete with weeping willows and weeping maidens. In the center was a large tomb bearing the names and dates of one or more family casualties. I was fortunate enough to find one such "mourning picture," done on silk, the creator of which had been not only talented but also underpriviledged; her relatives had been so uniformly healthy that, although she painted as large a tombstone as her classmates, she had been forced to leave it bare. Inspired less by active sorrow than the lugubrious romanticism of youth, mourning pictures are not too depressing for your rooms.

The depictions of fruit and flowers which Great-Grandmother drew on velvet are among the most prized of American primitives, although I must confess that I personally find them a little dull. Perhaps because I was born a boy, I prefer the old girl in a more romantic mood. She painted a much-ringleted maiden—could she have been thinking of herself?—finding a very bouncy Moses in the bulrushes. She drew on medieval ruins frowning most awfully down precipitous cliffs. Although she dutifully depicted prim young ladies, good as gold at their knitting, her heart seemed more in her drawings of wild she-creatures riding throught the twilight with demon lovers. I suspect Great-Grandfather had his bad moment bringing this skittish bride to earth.

Passionately interested in the part of the nation where they lived, Americans painted and collected pictures with a regional interests. The face of the continent was preserved in thousands of landscapes. Admiring romantic scenery, the painters depicted sunsets on the Rockies or the White Mountains; they showed thunderstorms roaring down the valley of the Hudson or the Ohio. Yet they had a quieter mood, too, which appreciated the flowers in a lowland field or the quaint charm of a village green. They were fascinated by their fellow citizens, by children playing in a New England barn or boatmen dancing as their barge floated down the river. Indians coursing the plains supplied an ever-exciting subject, as did the glowing smokestacks of Mississippi steamboats pushing through the night. Down south, artists showed the cotton pickers in the fields. Whatever your local habitat, pictures of it were painted.

There is always a chance that, mixed in with the primitives in attic or antique shop, you may find a canvas by a famous fine-arts painter. The artist's signature may enable you to identify him, but, unless the picture has never been out of your family's possession, be wary! Most art dealers are fine, upright men, yet there are bad apples in every barrel and sometimes it is a great temptation to double the price of a picture by the simple act of scrawling a name in the lower left-hand corner. Grandmother, of course, would not have gone for such forgery, although she may have gotten confused and, in making a list of her possessions, attributed a family painting to the wrong artist.

Do not be discouraged if the author of your picture cannot be found on any list. You do not expect every chair in your house to be a museum piece; nor must your dining-room table be worth five thousand dollars. You are delighted with your furniture if it fills its utilitarian purpose and is agreeable to live with. You need ask no more of your paintings. If they brighten your walls, if they help give your house personality, if they bring a smile of pleasure to your guests, you may well be content. Your voyage of exploration through that darkest wilderness, the American attic, will have been a success.

WHICH COMES FIRST:
THE HEAD OR THE BODY?

Members of the American public who know nothing else about American art think they know one thing. They may believe that Copley founded a famous hotel in Boston, or that Winslow Homer wrote the *Iliad*, but they do know one thing. A scholar rash enough to admit that he is writing books on American painting almost fears to meet strangers lest the inevitable story can reappear more than once an evening. It bursts from the mouths of babes, debutantes at cocktail parties, or old crones at historical society meetings. I was even stopped in the street once at midnight by a drunken neighbor who shouted till the skyscrapers rang, "Do you know what an itinerant painter did! He brought a lot of already painted bodies to my grandmother's house, let her pick out the one she liked best, and then added her head."

When I was a young man full of faith in the human race, I believed the demand of prefabricated bodies and superimposed heads that was told me by so many worthy-looking people and was published in so many expensive books. And, furthermore, it can make perfectly good sense. According to the most sophisticated version of the tale, primitive painters, who in the summer scoured the countryside with horses and wagons, were in the winter imprisoned by impassable roads. To while away the heavy hours and to keep from losing too much time, they ran up a store of headless bodies. Because they were working completely from imagination and without models, they created those fine flowing designs of lace and sleeves and and belt and necklaces which certainly are not naturalistic and which some modern critics have called "abstract."

Come spring, so the story contines, when they were knocking again on farmhouse doors, they laid the half-finished canvases out on the lawn and let the rural chatelaine choose the costume and anatomy she most fancied. Wasp wrists and pearls, of course, came higher than unfashionable gown and dumpy figure. One always has to pay for the best.

The pictures themselves seem to give mute testimony for this practice.

Very often the head is painted in a different style from the body: features are somewhat three-dimensional and naturalistic while the torso is stylized and flat. Furthermore, different bodies by the same artist can be amazingly similar. Often ladies in adjoining towns or even adjoining houses are all shown wearing the same dress.

The story, falling from so many tongues, makes on the face of it such good sense that it would seem incontrovertible except for one fact: the lack of even a shred of historical evidence.

For ten years now, since first a horrible doubt crept into my mind, I have been searching for one fact more tangible than Aunt Emma's memory, now that she is in her dotage, of what she was told as a girl. I have read diaries and documents and combed antique shops and historical societies; even asked over national radio hook-ups that anyone get in touch with me who could substantiate the story. So far, I have drawn a complete blank. And even more significant is the fact that no cache of unsold headless bodies has even been found.

For the reverse practice, there is an absolute flood of evidence. In Europe, fashionable portraitists as a regular thing painted heads in the sitter's presence but would not have dared suggest that lords and ladies serve as clothes horses. Often the artists carried home a favorite dress or a complement of medals which were then hung on an apprentice or a wooden lay figure. The master painter often did not touch the canvas once the features were done: in the workshop of the fashionable London portraitist Kneller, lace was added by one specialist, cocked hats by another, marble columns in the background by a third.

Although on a much less elaborate scale, the same practice was carried to the new world. Having painted George Washington's head on full-length canvas, Stuart employed Jeremiah Paul to work on the background; Stuart's more famous portrait of the hero, the Athen port[rait] was never finished: the features are there, but the body and background are lacking.

INHABITED LANDSCAPES

One of the most venerable and widely accepted fallacies concerning the history of American art is the belief, common for more than a century, that landscape painting did not exist on these shores until the appearance, during the 1820s, of the Hudson River School.★ Like most errors, this conclusion contains a grain of truth, but the grain has been enlarged as if seen through a microscope.

The earliest-known American paintings were created in the 1660s. From this date on past the end of the eighteenth century, official thought all over the Western world was concentrated on man in his social aspects. Accepted philosophy did not find God in Nature, but saw Him standing apart, judging nature. To be untamed was synonymous with being evil. Humanity was not admissible into a drawing room or into heaven until it had been made over by correct religious principle, polite breeding, and wise aristocratic government. Nature too needed editing, came to its own when modified into a formal garden.

The highest form of art, it was generally agreed, was "historical painting," the organization on canvas of figure compositions illustrative, according to refined mental principles of human heroism, piety, or grandeur. Although portraiture was also dedicated to the glorification of social man, it was not considered part of the grand tradition because it could go only a short distance toward the "ideal" without loss of that essential factor, likeness. However, it was the most lucrative of modes and thus widely practiced.

Landscape painting lacked official philosophical support, the more so the more it revealed the world uncorrected by human taste. Thus, in his celebrated *Discourses*, Sir Joshua Reynolds attacked Rubens for reproducing "the accidents of nature," preferred Claude for being "convinced that taking nature as he found it seldom produced beauty." Applying the same generalizing principles as the historical painters,

---

★An earlier version of this essay appeared in *Art in America*, 42, No. 2 (May 1954), 106–11.

Claude sought "ideal form," but Reynolds could not help wondering "whether landscape painters have a right to aspire so far." Firmly he classed the mode as a minor one; with this ruling the leading academicians of other nations agreed. Although landscape painting continued to be practiced, it was admired only grudgingly, and then when the naturalism of the Dutch and Flemish painters was subordinated to the more artificial formulas of Claude.

Genre painting that dealt with life as it was actually lived was even lower in the scale, since it showed man not in a reformed state but acting out his natural cussedness. It was, Reynolds explained, "a little style, where petty effects are the sole end." The originals of Hogarth's majestic genre scenes were unsalable to the connoisseurs; Hogarth made his living from engravings sold to a less exalted public, who were glad to see depicted the villainy of a well-bred rake, the virtue of an industrious apprentice.

Revolutionary forces were on the move. Resenting the aristocratic domination, the rising middle classes insisted that they did not need to be molded. Far from being born evil, man had been corrupted by evil social institutions. Man was naturally good and so was the world. God revealed Himself in ordinary human actions in the landscape He had made with His own hands.

Despite official disapproval, activity in landscape and genre painting mounted everywhere to answer an augmenting bourgeois demand. From the first, basically a middle-class nation, America was no exception. In seventeenth century New York, Dr. Jacob de Lange hung in his "great chamber" four genre pieces and ten landscapes; this was only a fraction of his collection. When Nathaniel Emmons, the earliest American painter known to have been native-born, died in 1740, he was praised for his "admirable imitations of nature, both in faces, rivers, banks, and rural scenes." At the first American group exhibition, the Columbianum held at Philadelphia in 1795, almost as many artists showed landscape and genre works as showed portraits. Such examples could be cited indefinitely.

Since this interest arose from the people, it was in America, as elsewhere, intimately associated with the most popular of graphic arts, engraving. Such over-mantles as *The Plantation* were influenced by imported wallpaper designs. Easel landscapes and watercolor views were often made, even by humble painters, to be reproduced; artisan and amateur painters tended to follow the preconceptions of the printmaker. In drawing schools and books of art instruction, the English immigrants who were the most conspicuous of our late eighteenth- and early nine-teenth-century landscape painters disseminated both the iconography and the basic technical approach of aquatint engraving.

There were exceptions, but, from the first, American views that were not decorations painted directly on the walls paid lip-service to accepted doctrines by having as their ostensible subjects aspects of man's remodel-ing of nature—a city or a mansion—but these elements were pushed into the backgrounds. In the foregrounds, no sharp line was drawn be-tween the two aspects of the new piety: interest in nature and interest in ordinary human life. Pictures were alive with genre: workmen at their tasks or the proprietors of the private houses depicted strolling at their ease. All was embedded in landscape, and increasingly the artists sought to render nature as she appeared to their eyes. Toward the end of the eighteenth century, an interest in the wilder aspects of scenery became manifest. Thus the legend accompanying an engraving of Jacob Hoff-man's *View on the Mushanon River* (1797) stated, "No quarter of the world, however celebrated, affords more novel and sublime scenes than are to be met with among the romantic wilds of America."

When, as the nineteenth century unrolled, romanticism triumphed in America as elsewhere, many pure landscapes, entirely devoid of genre elements, were painted at the higher professional levels. However, pop-ular engravers, and their close allies, the artisan and amateur painters, continued to prefer the old mixture of the two modes. This is exempli-fied, as far as paintings are concerned, by the tremendously successful lithographs of Currier and Ives as far as paintings are concerned and by the pictures in the Garbisch collection. Having won their artistic revolution, the people saw no reason why they should not pile on their plates all the spoils, and even ape the aristocrats they had overthrown by glorying in their own remodelings of nature. Certainly a depiction of an almshouse in all its glory was an act of piety to the common man.

JOHN FREDERICK KENSETT

John Frederick Kensett is a remarkable artist whose work forces us to reassess an era, revealing again how much the painter can contribute to the general historian, if only the general historian has eyes to see.* For the period during which Kensett worked, straddling (as it does) the Civil War, is generally described as rough, violent, vulgar, dedicated to crude expansion. The terms Mr. Howat uses, in his perceptive catalogue, to describe Kensett's pictures—"subtle," "elegant," "delicate," "simple"—would seem to denote virtues alien to that American environment.

The assumption would naturally be that Kensett would have been ignored by his contemporaries, "a violet by a mossy stone, half hidden from the eye." But in fact he was greatly admired in his own time, and not only by a narrow elite cowering from the boisterous environment. He was popular and well paid, a civic as well as an artistic leader, widely considered a major ornament to American life.

These hushed pictures, speaking in so low a voice that they can hardly be heard in the strident clashes often emitted from museum walls, were painted to hang over the fireplaces of private homes, where they distilled their sweetness quietly into the domestic ear. And, as drays moved noisily outside on city streets, Kensett's rendition of healing mountains and waters and fields soothed the poetic souls of businessmen home from their countinghouses.

Kensett was probably the most influential member of the second generation of the Hudson River School. However, he was later so completely forgotten, with the whole school he led, that so knowing a cultural historian as Lewis Mumford, in his *The Brown Decades* published in 1931, attributed the early growth of American artistic interest in nature almost altogether to writers like Thoreau. He passed over the Hudson River School (getting its name wrong) in only part of a sentence:

---

*An earlier version of this essay appeared as the Introduction to John Howat's *John Frederick Kensett, 1816–1872* (New York: The American Federation of Arts, 1968).

"A definite school of landscape painters, the Catskill School, had at least a sense of locality, if only feeble power of personal absorption." He equated the landscape painters with Currier and Ives prints.

But now all the old misapprehensions are being righted as interest in mid-nineteenth-century American painting augments like a cresting wave. This handsomely assembled exhibition in a further happy indication of the new knowledge. Some viewers, unfamiliar with the Hudson River School esthetic, may need to pause and readjust their sights a little before they can truly appreciate Kensett's art. But the effort is well worth making: here is a painter of great sensitivity and taste who created, in his best works, pictures of deep and moving beauty.

MONOCHROMATIC DRAWING: A FORGOTTEN BRANCH OF AMERICAN ART

The greatest enemy of naïve American art is the spring cleaning and its ruling genius, the housewife with blood in her eye.* In order to survive for a century, a picture has to live through endless raids by commandos armed with mops under the direction of generals who are determined to see the attic tidy. Through the agency of dealers whom they have inspired, collectors sometimes arrive at the last minute like the United States Marines to save invaluable old canvases from worse than death on scrapheap or bonfire. But if the collectors are apathetic, God help the poor picture!

A whole school of painting will vanish almost without a trace if during the century or two after the pictures were made no one is interested in preserving them. An example of such disappearance is supplied by the amateur canvases of the eighteenth century. The advertisements of drawing schools which often appeared in newspapers, and the references to amateur artists found in contemporary documents, make it clear that many American colonials drew for pleasure. Yet only a few isolated examples of their production are known today. Portraits executed by professional artists during that early period remain because they were treasured by descendants as a source of dynastic pride. But when a musty old amateur picture, odd in execution, shedding paint like a chicken in molt, turned up in a corner of an attic, nobody was interested. What would today create the greatest excitement was regarded as a piece of junk and treated accordingly.

It is a universal rule of taste that the parlor piece of one generation is the attic piece of the next. The third generation, however, usually comes to the rescue. The same tide that washes mother's Horatio Walker up into the lumber room brings down grandfather's Thomas Cole. But this

---

*An earlier version of this essay appeared in *Magazine of Art* (February 1945), 62–65.

rule has its exceptions. If grandson is as myopic as his father, the school of art which he does not appreciate is likely to be lost forever. Thus it is our duty to survey the achievements of our grandparents to make sure that everything worthy is preserved.

Within the last twenty years a great interest has arisen in the work of America's less sophisticated artists, commonly misnamed "American primitives." Like a vast suction machine, this interest has drawn out of attics all over the land innumerable nineteenth-century canvases, some fresh and brilliant, some merely amusing because of their incompetence. Probably when all the returns are in a generation from now, this fad will be principally memorable because from among the thousands of pictures it has preserved there will emerge a few hundred of real merit that have been saved from taking their last ride on the ash man's tumbrel. Certainly we have cause to regret that no similar movement impelled the citizens of 1845 to rescue the less conventional work of the eighteenth century.

One important branch of the work of our amateur artists has for some reason fallen through the chinks of contemporary interest; if it is not called to the attention of collectors and their attendant dealers, all trace of it will be gone in another generation. Indeed, I have had considerable difficulty finding examples of the vanishing medium. An examination of the established sources on "American primitives"—books collections, the shops of metropolitan dealers—would hardly show that such pictures existed. I had to go into the back country and find the drawings for myself. During the days before gasoline rationing, my wife and I never passed an antique or junk shop without stopping; sometimes, particularly in the junk shops, we found such a picture as we sought. More recently, we have persuaded a group of friendly dealers near our home in Connecticut to rescue the drawings from the attics where the average dealer would have left them as being of no value.

The pictures for which we hunted were black-and-white pastels made particularly during the third quarter of the nineteenth century, by amateurs and, of course, by their instructors. For reasons which we will discuss later, this medium removed many of the purely technical difficulties of execution which in an oil painting stand between the unsophisticated artist and realization of his vision. Thus the pictures were an accurate mirror reflecting the tastes, the dreams, and the esthetic ambitions of our citizen-artists. And when, as sometimes happened, the mind reflected in the pastel was the mind of a mute inglorious Cole or Bingham, the result was well worthy of admiration, and of preservation as part of our esthetic heritage.

The medium, which came to be known as monochromatic drawing, was originally introduced to the public as part of a more elaborate technique which some brilliant publicity man dubbed "Grecian painting." From the first, it was promoted as a short-cut to impressive results. In his "The Artist, or Young Ladies' Instructor in Ornamental Painting, Drawing, etc." (New York and London, 1835), B. F. Gandee writes that Grecian painting is "perfectly easy of acquirement to anyone who can draw a little with a pencil." The art, which "is of quite a recent invention," was given its name, Gandee confides, because of the near resemblance of the result of several paintings discovered on the walls of Grecian palaces. The work of a few hours in this medium, he adds temptingly, has so high a finish and so exquisite a softness that it would be mistaken for the result of days of close application.

To prepare the ground on which the painting was to be executed, the young artist took millboard, covered it with varnish (which could be colored if desired), and then sifted through muslin onto the sticky surface finely ground marble dust secured from a stone mason. After the result had dried for a week, it was to be well brushed with a clothes brush to take off any loose dust, and then rubbed with fine sandpaper, but not to too great a smoothness. "The numerous advantages referred to are gained simply by applying colors to an unusually rough and hard surface."

Next the young lady artist places on the board about as much lamp black as will lie on a sixpence. With a piece of soft leather, she "rubs on the sky," commencing where it is darkest and working toward the light. After the forms have been thus defined, she scrapes in the highlights with the edge of the leather, or a knife. From the sky, she moves on to the middle distance and then to the foreground, where to make very sharp forms a stick of black chalk may be used instead of lamp black. The advantage of this method to the amateur, Gandee points out, is that it is unnecessary to sketch an outline. Form is defined gradually by pushing the pigment from the center toward the edges. If a mistake is made, it can easily be altered by a little rubbing, and a whole section of the picture can be washed out with soap and water without disturbing the rest. The artist can revise until she is completely satisfied; then she applies fixative and varnish.

In Grecian painting the black-and-white drawing was only one step toward the final result, yet the author realized that a finished landscape in lamp black could stand by itself as a decorative piece. Thus, before proceeding any further, Ellen, the protagonist of the volume, is encouraged to mount one of her first efforts as a fire screen for her mother.

To complete a Grecian painting, however, Ellen must work over her black-and-white drawing with transparent colors. Relying on the undercoat of lamp black for shading and the definition of forms, she needs merely to spread the colors in appropriate places, in the manner used by professional colorists of the period to tint engravings. This done, she had an impressive picture which, so Gandee assures us, only a sharp eye could distinguish from a conventionally executed oil painting.

As the years passed, the two processes involved in Grecian painting separated. Undoubtedly one reason for this was the emergence in France of charcoal drawing as an independent art form. For years charcoal had lain in color boxes of professional painters, but it was used merely to define an outline on the canvas which would later be painted over. The charcoal and chalk drawings made by the Old Masters had been largely forgotten when Decamps and Troyon began making elaborate renditions of landscapes in charcoal for their own sake. In a short time the medium became very popular; by the 1860s and 1870s the drawings of such artists as Allonge, Appian, and Lelanne were enjoying a great vogue. When mama had a reproduction of a charcoal drawing by a famous artist hanging in the parlor, there was no reason for daughter to add color to her black-and-white pastel.

The end of the development is described in "Art Recreations," by Mme L. B. Urbino and others, published in Boston in 1860. Instead of bothering herself to make a drawing in lamp black, the young lady buys from an art store a specially designed print, the back of which she treats with "Grecian varnish" to make the paper transparent. Then she puts her colors on this varnished surface, relying on the print for the shading that defines the forms. She does not even have to use her own ingenuity on the coloring, for instructions on how to tint each part can be procured with the engraving.

Altogether separate now from Grecian painting is "monochromatic drawing." The use of marble dust is still recommended (if there is no stone mason near, you can pulverize a cake of marble by "burning it"), but mass production offers a cheaper sand paper, called "monochromatic board," made gaudy sometimes by a sprinkling of flecks of mica. Charcoal or black crayon is used instead of the lamp black recommended by Gandee; yet the techniques for applying the color are almost the same. The citizen-artist still puts a little pile of black where she wants a heavy shadow, and then pushes it out toward the light. Mme Urbino and collaborators, however, had some tricks of their own to recommend: "For water, scrape some black crayon into a powder, and lay it on your board with the kid, working it horizontally, and making the lights and shades stronger as it comes nearer. Your sponge may do good in rendering the water transparent." The completed pictures were framed under glass without any addition or fixative or varnish.

The authors comment "Ruins overgrown with moss, and dilapidated buildings make pretty pictures. We have seen moonlight views in this style of painting more beautiful than anything else." Many of the monochromatic drawings now found show moonlight, but every kind of outdoor subject matter that appealed to the amateur artist is depicted in this medium. We find landscapes ranging from the most widely romantic creations of the imagination to portraits of houses and views of identifiable places; often there are figures in the foreground. Indeed, some of the landscapes are so crowded with action that they go over the line into genre. Scenes illustrating romances and plays are done with great gusto and belief, the more grandly awful the better. Portraits were attempted too, but I have never seen a successful one, probably because the medium discouraged the use of sharp lines, and it takes great technical skill to achieve a likeness in a haze. (We must distinguish between monochromatic drawings and the charcoal likenesses make by craftsmen in photographers' studios who drew over enlarged photographic prints.)

The technical skill of the artists varies greatly. Some drawings are so expert one is inclined to think them the work of professionals linked to the Hudson River School; perhaps these were done by adults who taught the medium. Also professional in execution, *The Balloon Flight* presents a problem; could the picture have been drawn as the model for a woodcut illustration in a magazine? On the extreme is the view of a Connecticut river town which is clearly the work of a child. Between lie such pictures as *The Village Green* and *The Magic Lake*. These heartfelt productions of young ladies, hanging in the parlor over the piano, were a type of flypaper for the catching of impressionable young men.

The question of how far these drawings were original, how far adaptations of commercially produced pictures, is one with the whole knotty problem of the sources of American amateur art. I have discussed aspects of the problem in the *Magazine of Art* of May 1943, and elsewhere; suffice it to say here that amateur pictures which did not lean on some printed source of inspiration are the exception rather than the rule. The more gifted citizen-artists, however, modified the subject matter of their sources according to their personal tastes, producing independent works of art.

Such monochromatic drawings as I have been able to find have all been done in charcoal or black crayon; no varnished drawings in lamp black have come to my attention. As far as I have been able to determine, the existing drawings all date from the third quarter of the nineteenth century. This was probably the high period of the fashion, although it may be that older pastels remain to be found.

The best monochromatic drawings have an elegance rarely found in other American amateur productions, perhaps because the simplicity of the medium allowed the artist to move with great sureness. That the color is limited to gradations of black and white reduced the problem of shading to most basic considerations and encouraged boldness of contrast. The technique of rubbing on the color with a chamois encouraged smoothness, the use of broad forms, and the subordination of detail; only rarely was white chalk used to put in highlights. And the soft texture of the medium lent itself well to the expression of that brooding melancholy which is one of the characteristics of the adolescent mind.

I do not mean to suggest that the best esthetic technique is the simplest; that we create great art by giving children charcoal or finger paint to play with. Art, to my mind, is as various as the people who create it. The finest flowerings of the human genius are created by highly complicated individuals who, in order to express profound emotion, make use of a highly evolved technique. Admittedly, an artist can never climb to the topmost rung of art as long as he is an ill-trained amateur. But because we admire the majestic blooms in an intensively cultivated garden, we do no have to despise the blue-eyed grass and violets by mossy stones. In order to understand amateur art we must accept its limitations and look for the compensating virtues: a naïve freshness of viewpoint that is as different from the profound booming of great art as the taste of a wild strawberry is from terrapin à la Maryland.

It is on this plane that I beg indulgence for monochromatic drawing. These pictures are to be compared, not with Titian, but with the other productions of nineteenth-century amateurs, the "American primitives" now being so avidly collected. In this company, I claim, the drawings hold up their heads very well, and it is not impossible that a few examples, culled from thousands, may be found to have strength that will enrich our national art heritage.

THE PEACEABLE KINGDOM

Edward Hicks was a nineteenth-century American who painted altogether in isolation. He knew no other artists and probably never visited a museum. His *The Peaceable Kingdom* is an intensely personal picture.* It summarizes his own experience. Yet, more than most pictures, it explains mankind's deep dilemmas.

The painting is one of roughly a hundred similar canvases which Hicks based on a prophecy in the Bible (Isaiah xi):

> The wolf also shall dwell with the lamb, and the leopard shall lie down with the kid; and the calf and the young lion and the fatling together; and a little child shall lead them. And the cow and the bear shall feed; their young ones shall lie down together; and the lion shall eat straw like an ox. And the suckling child shall play in the hole of the asp, and the weaned child shall put his hand on the cockatrices' den. They shall not hurt nor destroy in all my holy mountain; for the earth shall be full of knowledge of the Lord, as the waters cover the sea.

The leopard lies down with the kid near the right edge of the painting. Directly to the left, the wolf dwells in peace with the lamb, and above these two groups a little child is leading the young lion, the calf, and the fatling. In a minor deviation from the biblical text, the suckling child holds the asp happily in its hand while the weaned child looks after her with motherly care. A fourth child feeds both the American eagle and the dove of peace. The composition is dominated by the mature lion and the ox. Protruding from behind this magnificent pair, the cow and the bear chew on the same ear of American corn.

The additions Hicks made to the biblical scene were all of local reference. We are not on a holy mountain but in one of the most lovely places in his native Pennsylvania, the Delaware Water-Gap. Hicks

---

*An earlier version of this essay appeared as "The Peaceable Kingdom: Painting by Edwards Hicks, America, 1780–1849," in *Man Through His Arts*. I. *War and Peace*, ed. Anil de Silva, Otto van Simon, and Roger Hinks (London: E. P. Publishing Co., 1963), pp. 55–56.

painted in the middle distance a scene which applied the biblical allegory to modern history: William Penn, the founder of Pennsylvania, buying the land peaceably from the original inhabitants. Hicks himself thus characterized this event: "PENN'S TREATY with the INDIANS made in 1681 without an Oath, and never broken. The foundation of Religious and CIVIL LIBERTY in the U. S. of AMERICA."

Hicks was born in 1780, during the Revolution in which the American colonies achieved their independence from England. His parents, who had been officeholders under the British crown, were ruined by the establishment of the United States. The mother died, the father drifted away, and the three-year-old boy was taken care of by a coloured servant girl. Then some of his parents' friends raised him on their farm until he was thirteen, old enough to be apprenticed to a coach-maker.

Before the Revolution, the Hicks family had lived in a mansion and looked down on such artisans as the boy was now being trained to be. He wrote that his dead mother, "used to moving in the gayest and highest and most extravagant circles," had been "the very reverse of a perfect woman." As for the father who had deserted him, that drunkard proved how education led to misery, pride to a fall. The very vehemence with which Hicks denounced his family's former grandeur indicated that he was not altogether reconciled to the loss of it.

To escape from one inner conflict, Hicks engaged in another. He found relief in drinking, and riotous living, but always with the same sense of sin. "The strength of my passions and the weakness of my resolution" were, he feared, rushing him into "the pit of pollution." He made a sharp break; he became an adherent of that extremely pious and strict sect, the Quakers.

As a coach-maker's apprentice, Hicks had most enjoyed painting the vehicles. On his own, he had become a sign painter. Now, as a Quaker, he was forced to conclude that painting was "the inseparable companion of voluptuousness and pride. . . . It stands enrolled among the premonitory symptoms of the rapid decline of the American republic." He became a farmer, "for which I had no qualifications whatsoever." Complete ruin was averted only when he discovered that he had great gifts as an evangelist.

Traveling about the countryside to preach the Quaker doctrine of universal love and peace, he found himself hating all who disagreed with him. From many a religious meeting which he had turned into a doctrinal battle ground, he retired in tears, accusing himself of the sins of belligerence and pride. Did not the early Christians "work with their hands, avoiding idleness and fanaticism"? As a compromise that would enable him to support his family, he returned to his only manual skill, "my peculiar talent for painting." However, he was perpetually worried to be in the eyes of God "nothing but a poor old worthless insignificant painter."

At least he could prevent himself from being one of those "fine painters" who undermined society. Limiting himself to what he considered utilitarian practice, he decorated carriages, illuminated signs, and created visual sermons like *The Peaceable Kingdom*. Although he lived near the cultural center of Philadelphia, he shunned its museums which he feared would carry his art beyond "the bounds of innocence." To his dying day, he painted in the direct uncomplicated manner of the sign painter and he did not hesitate to copy any printed pictures that served his ends.

His source for *Penn's Treaty with the Indians*, a subject he not only put into *The Peaceable Kingdom* but executed for its own sake, was an engraving after a celebrated painting of the treaty by another Pennsylvania Quaker, Benjamin West. The difference between West's canvas and Hicks's adaptations shows how far the sign painter deviated from the dominant tradition of the fine arts in America. West painted the scene as it might have appeared to us had we been there. But Hicks's naïve brush was incapable of simulating reality. He was forced to simplify space into an almost flat pattern, shape into symbol, and in the course of this transformation, his powerful imagination took over.

Hicks's own experience told him it was not easy to be peaceful, yet surely it was worth the labor. In the heat of his sermons, the preacher-painter attacked with violence all religious persuasions other than his own. But when he could struggle away from his imperfections, "my soul," so he wrote, "feels sweet union with all God's children in their devotional exercise, whether it is performed in . . . an Indian wigwam or by the wild Arab of the great desert with his face turned towards Mecca."

Hicks painted no relaxed allegories in which wild animals find it easy to be tame. He shows, instead, "man's cruel selfish nature," as symbolized in the carnivores, controlled by will rather than completely routed. The wolf, the leopard, and the lion do not, it is true, hurt the domestic animals, and those helpless creatures are not afraid of them, yet the great beasts, who were once infected with the lust for meat, are afraid of themselves. They stare blindly ahead with strained eyes that reflect inner conflict. The war against savagery has moved back into its primeval seat, the individual mind. It is never altogether won. There is backsliding as well as advance. Day by day the fight goes on. It is the most heroic of all wars.

"Oh!" wrote Hicks in his diary, "that I had more faith that works by love, which is that charity that suffereth long and is kind, and oh! that I had more hope that would be an anchor to my poor soul, which seems tossed upon the tempestuous billows without sun, moon or, stars." Thus Hicks spoke for himself. To the world, he said, "Dear Friends, . . . be perfect, be of good comfort, be of one mind—live in peace—and the God of mercy and peace will be with you."

WILLIAM RIMMER

William Rimmer, who lived between 1816 and 1879, was, among important American artists, the least amenable to esthetic or historical classification. This has blocked recognition of his striking genius, since the art historical establishment—critics, professors, museum curators, etc.—are made·uneasy by works that refuse to fit into established esthetic categories. Thus Thomas F. Stebbins, curator of American art at Boston's Museum of Fine Arts, mourns the impossibility of locating Rimmer "within the context" of other mid-nineteenth-century American art.

Explanations of Rimmer's peculiarities can be found if we look outside the acceptable scope of esthetic criticism. His father considered himself the rightful king of France, and the artist as the eldest son was in succession to the crown.

During the Terror, Louis XVII and Marie Antoinette were publicly guillotined, but their heir, the Dauphin, was said to have died in prison. It was, however, rumored that he had been spirited off and hidden away by royalists who hoped eventually to put him on the throne. But, in the need for secrecy and in the revolutionary confusion, he had got lost. This situation permitted many individuals—including Audubon—who judged themselves superior to their supposed birth, to wonder whether they were not "the lost Dauphin." Usually, this speculation, as in Audubon's case, was taken more or less lightly, a spice to living. But Rimmer's father made this self-identification into the core of his and his family's being.

After Napoleon had been defeated, the elder Rimmer waited hourly for the messenger who would kneel before him—but venal politicians crowned instead his "uncle" Louis XVIII. In despair the elder Rimmer married an Irish serving-girl, set up as a cobbler, and drifted to America. When the future artist was ten, the family settled in a Boston slum. Believing that they were in daily danger from Louis XVIII's assassins, they lived in utter isolation, moving behind locked doors in a private world. The father made each of his seven children a silver flute, read them romances, and urged them to re-enact old battles. Poverty tattered the furniture, yet when the future artist stepped into the street, he seemed to descend to the sordid from what were, however disturbingly, heights.

Rimmer's art reveals obsessive identification with his father, a natural outgrowth of royal succession, where the son steps into his father's place. At the age of fourteen, William made in gypsum a small statue called *Despair* which is said to be the first nude sculpture in American art: it contrasted isolation and emotional turmoil with nakedness to the world.

The son drifted from one occupation to another. He set type, made soap, molded Indian rubber, secured his only artistic training in a lithographer's shop, studied anatomy by dissecting cadavers, practiced medicine as a self-taught doctor, tried his hand at religious painting which did not suit him, and tried portraiture but could not get on with his sitters, being, as contemporaries testified, stubborn, unmanageable, and thin skinned.

After his father, a half-insane alcoholic, had died, Rimmer set to work on a life-sized statue of a falling, mortally wounded gladiator. Enclosed in a cramped basement, he naïvely carved rather than modeled clay. In his ignorance he did not use a central armature to hold the mass together. The clay fell off on warm days—he tried to hold it in place with sticks— and on cold days, froze too solid to be workable.

Completed after some one hundred hours of labor, the *Fallen Gladiator* was a naked body covered with a net of muscles tensed with the ultimate of exhaustion and strain. It was as far as it was possible to be from the classical serenity of the then admired American sculptors who usually had studios in Italy.

Those modern critics who deign to pay much attention to Rimmer argue whether he is to be most praised as a sculptor, a draftsman, or a painter. Efforts to find sources for his work in these three directions end up as a disorderly mob scene: Rodin would be included if he had not been born two generations later. The Bible, Dante, Shakespeare, Bunyan, Michelangelo, Rubens, the German romantics, and the French academics who were also concerned with blood sports in the Roman forum. And so on. If I had to vote for one, it would be William Blake, but it is quite possible that in mid-nineteenth-century Boston, Rimmer was unfamiliar with Blake.

From work of art to work of art Rimmer seems to have followed an obsessive vision without any consciousness of whence visual influence may have come. Again and again he was inspired by the plight of his father which was also his own, as in his truly beautiful drawing, *Evening*

Fall of Day, where extreme emotionality is given strength and body as a result of the artist's anatomical studies.

Rimmer was most uneven as a painter, perhaps because it was here that he periodically made his living: there exist pictures imitating commercial illustration. He was secretive about his best work, his masterpiece having been given to a friend. It remained unknown until the twentieth century.

On being rediscovered, the picture was given the title *Flight and Pursuit*. Rimmer's own notation on a preparatory sketch, "Oh for the Horns of the Altar," was pushed aside as incomprehensible. No one thought to consult the Bible, Kings I. There we are told how David established his successor as king of Israel. The rightful heir, being the oldest son, was Adonijah, but David's young wife, Bathsheba, persuaded the dying sovereign to designate her own son, Solomon. This put the life of the true heir in danger. Adonijah fled to the temple and established sanctuary by holding onto "the horns of the altar." He would let go only if Solomon swore "he would not kill his servant."

The painting is thus revealed as an allegory of the plight of Rimmer's father—and perhaps the artist himself—made no happier by the fact that David persuaded Adonijah to let go and then he was killed. The discovery of this source goes far toward explaining the emotional impact of the picture. But Rimmer's composition goes way beyond a single, consistent explanation.

The action is set in an interior, imaginatively Moorish in architecture and decoration, so spacious as to imply a royal palace. Dominating the composition, a dark-skinned man, clad in plebeian clothes utterly out of keeping with the grandeur of the setting, daggers in his belt, running, eyes straight ahead, with almost superhuman vigor toward steps leading out beyond the edge of the picture. Through a high archway, we see as in multiple reflecting mirrors, a succession of similar halls shrinking with distance. Down the nearest of these, a second figure is running almost level with the first. We are made to feel that this is not another individual but an emanation from the foreground runner. The alter ego is somewhat transparent although tangible, shrouded from head to his running feet. His bodily position is almost a reflection, but he looks at his double toward whom he is pointing an arrow.

In the foreground, behind the principal runner, there is the advancing shadow which inspires the "pursuit" in the modern title. Rimmer shows, however, nothing but blackness thrown from outside the canvas.

Rimmer, whose training and much of his practice was in draftsmanship, achieved his effects less with color than on the scale of "black-and-white values." His composition is alive with light and shadow. The total effect is verisimilitudinous but, if we examine closely we realize that the light effects would in a real scene be impossible. The dazzling brightness, as if thrown by a searchlight, on the foreground and the panel against which the runner is displayed is mysteriously quarantined from the rest of the umbrageous setting: hardly a glint splashes over. There is no possible naturalistic justification for the shadow of elaborate architecture thrown on the panel that matches the position of the altogether bright arc. Throughout the picture, light and shade are organized arbitrarily but with such conviction that we accept the reality with a heightened sense of strangeness.

The picture conveys a deep meaning in which the viewer is emotionally entangled, but what is the meaning? We may assume that the foreground runner is the painter and also his father. But why is the sanctuary implied by the title and so passionately sought not included in the picture? And why is the menace that pursues not particularized beyond a shadow? Although the background figure seems to be his ego, the foreground runner remains unconscious of its presence. This emanation presents the only danger depicted, aiming an arrow.

Did Rimmer communicate that the menace under which he, like his father, suffered was not in the world around him but an emanation from his own unconscious mind? Or, as seems more probable, did the artist put down a vision as it came to him without any seeking for a conscious message.

Oh, for the Horns of the Altar manifests hallucinatory power similar to that of Coleridge's *Kubla Khan*.

Rimmer's masterwork was not discovered until 1926, years after it had been painted. Can we look forward to further stupendous discoveries? If *Oh, for the Horns of the Altar* were reinforced with one or two more such tremendous achievements, even those who find him too off-base for serious consideration will have to allow William Rimmer, the outcast, into the pantheon of major American artists.

THE ROOM ON THE WALL

If you have a house or a room to decorate in an authentic American manner; if you have an antique chair that needs reupholstering or a reproduction which you wish to place on the right kind of carpet; or if you have a more general interest in knowing how great-grandfather lived, go to your art museum and examine the canvases by old American painters. You will see all kinds of people—rich and middle-class, purse-proud and simple, ordinary citizens and heroes like Robert E. Lee—in the rooms they inhabited generations ago. Around them are their posses-sions, arranged just as they were in real life. Perhaps you will have the excitement of discovering the table in your living room duplicated in the vanished parlor of some long-dead worthy.

Sometimes you may be surprised by what you see in the pictures. Our ancestors did not have that hatred for color which has been imposed on their memory by the dimming effect of time and the vandalism of igno-rant restorers. They were more likely to gay up a table with nice bright paint than to scrape it down to the bare wood. Nor was a consistent attempt made to be true to what historians would later consider the style of the period. In those years, as today, a piece of furniture was likely to be used as long as it was serviceable. Thus the decor of a room was less often a shiny novelty than a slice of family history; grandmother's chair, father's highboy, and the sideboard the present owner bought after he had made a killing selling beaded necklaces to the Indians.

No other source gives us so intimate and accurate a view of the Amer-ican past as do the paintings our ancestors commissioned themselves and criticized carefully before they hung them on their walls. We do not have the formal arrangement of unusual and therefore valuable antiques which is the stock-in-trade of American wings in museums. The figures are not wax fugitives from department store windows smirking eternally over the clothes wished on them by some curator of textiles. These are real rooms inhabited by real men and women. Everything is spruced up, perhaps, as for a party, yet the elegance is elegance our ancestors themselves created. And, as always, life changed the planned and the perfect into that comfortable imperfection that is home.

Appearing after the American Revolution, such exact renditions of domestic life expressed a new national self-confidence. During Colonial times, Americans were ashamed of their humble environment; they begged the artists to make them look like English lords. But when at last the redcoats had been overwhelmed by a ragged militia, and King George had surrendered to citizen diplomats, Americans decided they were proud of being exactly the kind of people they were. No longer pretending they inhabited palaces, they demanded images of the rooms in which they lived, with every stick of furniture in its rightful place.

In 1792, the Connecticut master, Ralph Earl, painted Oliver Ellsworth, who was to precede John Marshall as Chief Justice of the Supreme Court. Because of the depression which followed the Revolution, most Americans had to put up with the ratty old furniture (now worth thousands of dollars) they had bought before the conflict, but Ellsworth was a rich lawyer. Following the latest English fashion, he had just acquired some Heppelwhite chairs, complete with shield backs and draped nail heads. Naturally he wanted them in the picture, and, since he was a loving husband, he included his wife, although her voluminous skirts almost hid one of the chairs. The couple sit in the library of their Windsor, Connecticut, home. Beneath their feet is an elegant woven rug, and in the background we see banks of leather-bound law books. Ellsworth holds in his hand a copy of the Constitution, for the ratification of which he worked so valiantly.

The artist could not resist shaping the composition with a crimson curtain that undoubtedly was not there, yet in his heart he wished to define with exactitude his sitters' environment. So great was his desire to crowd in every detail that he violated all logic by showing through the window the exterior of the very home in which the Ellsworths are sitting. The eighteenth-century mansion we see is conventional in most details, but what do we make of the roof? A modern restorer would be horrified at the suggestion that he paint such a roof red, yet the Ellsworths, not realizing what their descendants would expect of them, reveled in this gay note and even used what paint was left over on part of the handsome fence. Around the house are the thirteen trees which the patriot planted in honor of the states of the Union.

The portrait of the Rev. Ammi Ruhamah Robbins reveals how Ellsworth's simpler neighbors lived. Where the patrician lawyer had a woven carpet, the minister covered his floor with a greenish-brown cloth on which a clumsy design was painted in red and black. Robbins did not splurge on new furniture. The chair on which he sits, with its yoke back, cabriole legs in front and straight legs behind, is in the Queen Anne style. Although you might have to pay well for it in an antique shop, the table was in its own day a humble piece, the work not of a cabinet maker but of a joiner. The base was probably made of maple; the top, of pine. Since there was a horizontal support below knee height and another a few inches above the floor, Robbins was forced to do his writing in the clumsy position shown. Clearly more interested in the mind than in the body, the minister has covered this cheap table with expensive books, beautifully bound in vellum. However, he indulged in at least one fleshly pleasure, as the clay pipe, so lovingly placed in a conspicuous position, shows.

Even prominent people did not necessarily keep up with changing furniture styles. A leading New England minister, the Rev. Jedediah Morse became famous as America's first important geographer. That in the 1810s he was still using Chippendale furniture, although it was a half-century old, is revealed in a family group painted by his son Samuel F. B. Morse. The boy, who shows himself standing between his parents, is one day to invent the telegraph, but at the moment he is dying to become a painter. He has pulled from the wall a console table and, in honor of his father's interest in geography, placed upon it one of the globes that were manufactured in England during the 1780s and 1790s after Captain Cook's discoveries had excited great interest in distant places. The globe bristles with gadgets and has a compass between its feet.

The highly sophisticated paneling, with its eared moldings, dates from mid-Georgian times. A more plebian and more modern note is struck by the carpet, which shows that we have now entered the period of machine-made rugs; the Morses' was undoubtably imported from England. As for the cat near the sewing basket, she may be a lady, and thus, in deference to the sex, we shall not attempt to estimate her age.

After young Morse had studied art in Europe, he considered his American environment too mean to be worth recording. But he never really identified himself with any foreign culture; he was left with nothing to paint in which he believed. One result was increasing frustration that led to his eventual abandonment of art for invention. Another result was such pictures as *The Family of Richard C. Morse*, which shows his nephew's wife sitting in a most impossible classical room that is chopped up into transverse sections by banks of marble pillars. Certainly, the little girl will catch her death if she squats for long on the floor that is parqueted in rare marbles, tan, dull rose, and blue-gray. This exaggerated picture reveals that now that the elation of the Revolution was far behind them, Americans had become ashamed, as they had been in colonial times, that their homes were not castles or temples.

What Mrs. Morse's room actually looked like is indicated by O. T. Eddy's *Rebecca Jane Griffith,* also painted about 1835, when Greek Revival architecture was the rage. The walls of the relatively small chamber are topped with tremendously heavy moldings, while the doorway is flanked by fluted columns in which wood substitutes for marble. The tendency of the later nineteenth century to mix styles is already manifest in the capitols, where some Egyptian ideas have got entangled with the Greek. The furniture is in transition between Empire and Victorian, as shown by the scrolls which, although neo-classical in conception, are coarse and heavy. The charming young mistress of all this elegance never married, which seems to show lack of enterprise among the swains of Montgomery County, Maryland.

Observing a dinner party, given and painted by the artist Henry Sargent in Boston during the early 1840s, we see from the postures of the guests that the furniture is Sheraton. When modern decorators buy a Sheraton dining-room table, they are likely to place around it chairs in another style, lest the guests loll as did Sargent's a century ago; higher backs are needed to hold diners upright. The sideboard was certainly made in America, since it is several inches taller than English ones. Today, we would not hang over it, as Sargent did, two full-length portraits lest that part of the room be over-weighted. But no one could object to the draping of the red curtain which follows an illustration in one of Sheraton's books.

In the foreground we see a wine cooler, an elegantly disguised metal-lined tub. So its altitude can be adjusted to give just the right amount of light, the chandelier hangs on pullies. The figured rug that stretches from wall to wall is protected in the neighborhood of the table from the rubbing of chair legs and the spilling of guests by a plain blue carpet. The footstool which looks like a booby trap, put there to trip up servants, was probably added by the artist to fill a hole in his composition; and the huge archway opening the room almost from wall to wall seems exaggerated from reality to fill an esthetic need.

By 1865, the clutter so dear to Victorian hearts was in full sway. When Alexander Lawrie painted *Lady Writing in Her Parlor* he cleaned out the foreground, lest he seem to be painting a forest, but showed with great accuracy the objects near the far wall. We see typical chairs, vaguely Gothic in design, with every piece of wood shaped by the lathe into an anthology of bulbs and bumps. The mirror in the corner, uplifted on legs, was the latest squeak, but the table on which the statues stand is Empire. By the window is that explosion of plants that was so friendly to the young in those theoretically proper days. Indeed, no modern parlor offers such effective cover behind which to steal a kiss.

The tremendously high ceiling forces the window to be designed in two parts, and inspires the awesome valance of fretted and stenciled cloth that went by the fancy name of a lambrequin. Despite the vast reaches above, the objects of art are kept low and crowded violently together, busts on brackets, ornamental plates, and paintings of various sizes forming a frieze, two or three layers deep, that stretches around the room. Although this method of showing art objects produces an extremely rich effect, you would be laughed at if you attempted it today. Indeed, the whole decor seems much more old-fashioned than the much older styles we have been examining. However, the lady writing eternally at her desk need not despair. Unless history refuses to repeat itself, the time is not far off when the decorative scheme will be antique enough to return to fashion. Thus, if you possess a much-spindled Gothic chair, put it in your attic if you must, but do not chop it up for firewood. Your daughter will be delighted to bring it down again into the living room, and will even smirk a little at the old-fashioned taste that made you banish it.

The prosperity of the victors in the Civil War is examplified by Eastman Johnson's immortalization of the Hatch mansion at Park Avenue and Thirty-Seventh Street in New York City. Mr. Hatch, a stockbroker with the delightfully double-barreled first name of Alfrederick, sits negligently in his library before his desk, while his wife strikes a pose at the mantlepiece. His father reads, her mother sews, and eleven children wander around. The baby was born after the picture was completed, but Hatch quickly paid the artist an extra thousand dollars to add her to the scene.

A contemporary art critic wrote, "The highest esthetic luxury in which a Wall Street man indulges in his period of good fortune is works of art. There are auctioneers and picture dealers who have grown rich off the New York Stock Exchange alone, and there are few, even among the small fry of the Street, who have not in their time made some sort of collection." As president of the Exchange, Hatch had found it incumbent upon him to buy 150 pictures and sculptures, which the critic characterized as a "Wall Street collection," for it contained some "serious and thoughtful pictures" bought when Hatch's "mind was at ease," as well as "many light and trifling ones, bought to relieve the depression of an anxious hour, just as a man goes to see a rough and tumble comedy to forget the troubles of the day."

Although Hatch's collection plays no prominent part in Eastman Johnson's painting, there are plenty of objects and colors. Indeed, every surface has been complicated with paint, carving, fancy cloth, or cast plaster. Even the upper parts of the high walls have been shaped with blue lines to simulate panels. The center table is carved to within an inch of its life, and further variegated with different tones of wood. The only quiet note is struck by the little doll's chair, which seems to be an heirloom stemming from the eighteenth century.

Hatch made his fortune by floating Union loans during the Civil War, which gives particular significance to the contrast between his library and the office which the Southern hero Robert E. Lee occupied in his final role as president of Washington College in Virginia. Lee's room boasts no new furniture. An Empire sideboard has been converted to office use by the addition of a later superstructure that may once have held plate but now holds papers. The cabinet and the smaller chair are also old Empire pieces, while the armchair in which the statesman sits, although the most modern piece in the room, dates from before the Civil War. When compared to Hatch's library, Lee's office is unbelievably bare. Southerners may comfort themselves with the thought that Hatch went bankrupt while Lee lives on in history as a great American.

Our show of painted interiors comes to an end with a rendition of his father's study by a major artist, Thomas Eakins. This picture communicates a powerful sense of time and place, of the essence of an environment, yet the objects shown are difficult to identify. Everything in the rear is half-lost in shadow. We cannot be sure whether or not the walls are paneled to the ceiling, the mantlepiece is a vague blur, and the quite amazing urn which stands upon it is no more than indicated. Even the tables in the foreground, although they play a major part in Eakins's composition, lack specificness of detail. The round one probably has a marble top, but we cannot be sure. Is the chess board inlaid in the other table or placed upon it?

New tides of esthetic taste were banishing from the work of sophisticated painters exact and literal reproductions of rooms and houses. Where once artists drew carefully what they saw, now they were less concerned with the shape of objects than with the emotional reaction objects induce in the mind of the viewer. Impressionism was on the march in Paris, and, although Eakins was by no means an impressionist in the French sense, his art was inspired by the same world currents of thought and visions.

After the 1870s, American habitat groups became a swirl of pigments which indicated light and color but subordinated detail. The pictures make us feel what it was like to live in those days, but do not record individual chairs and curtains. Art critics regard this as a step forward, yet the historian may well regret the passing of a type of art which, during the first century of America's life as an independent nation, gave us so literal and loving a view of our ancestors and the world they lived in. The pictures were sometimes beautiful and always documents of the greatest importance.

THOMAS SULLY

Ever since our culture took on a national character in the mid-eighteenth century, the vast majority of American portrait painters have been primarily concerned with recording individual personality.* The urge to put on canvas what Stuart called "the animal before you" is manifest in the crabbed patternmaking of most primitives, in emphatic likenesses by Copley, suave likenesses by Stuart, Eakins's monumental figure paintings, Speicher's strongly lighted studio pictures. The list could be extended indefinitely, since emphasis on personality rather than on manners or class reflects the individualism basic to democratic thought.

Among the few important American portraitists who have submerged character in an effort to achieve a generalized and ideal image, be it of beauty or wealth or virtue or social class, Thomas Sully was one of the most remarkable, for he flourished in a period when opposite artistic tendencies were at their very strongest. Never before or since have the great majority of American likenesses been as downright as they were in his environment.

That Sully was born in a different environment, in England, and spent his first nine years there, is significant, but probably not so much as the fact that his mother and father were actors. Make-believe was a basic part of his nature from the very start: lights, costumes, grease paint that, when the curtain rose, changed ordinary men and women into beings from a strange and wonderful clime.

Sully's parents were worried by the stars in their son's eyes. As they struggled along in the theatrical company at Charleston, South Carolina, which they had joined during 1792, they visualized for their son a safe business life: they apprenticed him to an insurance broker. The only figures he was interested in, however, were human figures and, after he had spoiled his quota of ledgers with drawings, he was allowed to become a portrait painter. His meager training made his first canvases hard

---

*An earlier version of this essay appeared in the *Catalogue of the 150th Anniversary of the Pennsylvania Academy* (Philadelphia: Pennsylvania Academy of Fine Arts, 1955), pp. 27–31.

and dry: yet there was a striving for dash and grace which every month brought nearer to realization. In 1807, when Sully was twenty-four and had been a professional for six years, the real test of his artistic preferences and their strength came. He went to Boston to sit at the feet of Gilbert Stuart.

Stuart's influence was establishing the dominant portrait style of Sully's generation. Stuart taught both in person and by the example of his work that a portrait should consist of a face painted accurately against a plain background designed to bring out its colors: the body and costume should be kept as inconspicuous as possible so that they would not distract attention from the features. In Stuart's studio, Sully was pushed into no such extremes of bare, literal rendering as were many disciples: he was more interested in the richness of the master's color, which most of the other disciples missed.

During 1809 he went to London, and there he found exactly what he wanted in the elegant forms and flashy conceptions of Sir Thomas Lawrence. Bringing home with him much of the English society painter's virtuosity, he applied it to American faces and figures for the rest of his long career. He never lacked business or admiration; he was the cheeriest, most flattering, most decorative portraitist in the land; yet for years his influence on his colleagues was almost negligible.

Other American artists who reached London were unanimous in considering Lawrence vastly inferior to Stuart. They joined with their contemporaries who did not get abroad to produce a flood of unpoetic, realistic likenesses. Lacking Stuart's maturity of style and depth of psychological insight, they avoided ostentation and flattery by veering too far in the other direction, producing the ugliest group of images ever created in the United States by leading portraitists. That their canvases were hung in the best drawing rooms shows that American life was still dominated by men (who came off better in the pictures than the ladies) and American thought by the conception of rugged, democratic simplicity. Only when the social climate changed, toward the mid-nineteenth-century, did Sully have artistic followers.

Almost alone among the sophisticated artists of his own generation, Sully was at his best in depicting women. How lucky were the ladies who were painted by him rather than by one of his colleagues! Instead of being shown as horse-faced, bull-necked, and arrayed in incongruous finery, they became glamorous visions of feminine delicacy. Their refinement was extreme, although not altogether convincing even to Sully's contemporaries.

In 1823, the critic John Neal wrote, "He throws, like a poet or a dramatist or an actor, something of himself into all the workmanship of his hands. His women, therefore, are full of fire, and instinct with spirit where it is possible for him to find any justification for it. . . . His characteristics are elegance and taste. He is not remarkable for strength or fidelity or workmanship." Neal stated that he would go to Sully for "the portrait of a youthful, passionate enthusiast, male or female; but if I wanted a likeness of a sober-minded man or woman, I would go to Mr. [Rembrandt] Peale; and to Stuart for whatever was awful [awe-inspiring], distinct, and *real.*"

Charles Robert Leslie, who was given his first instruction by Sully, later told his master, "Your pictures look as if they would blow away." They seem, indeed, only lightly linked to that reality which most American portraitists have sought. They are such images as the actor's son saw when the lamps were dimmed in the hall and sequins were turned into diamonds on limbs of finer, lighter stuff than flesh and bone. Since his imagination was less strong than facile, less deep than high-spirited, his comedy of manners was dedicated to prettiness and gentility; yet it is of the true theatre, and we are glad that the curtain will never fall on Sully's painted stage.

JAMES ABBOTT MCNEIL WHISTLER

Since no man is elected to the Hall of Fame while yet alive, the painter James Abbott McNeill Whistler could never express his reactions at being enshrined in a becolumned institution as one of a group of Americans that includes statesmen and inventors and captains of industry. However, we can be certain that, had he been able to do so, Whistler would have denounced the whole proceeding. For he made jokes about formal institutions, often denied that he was an American, and always insisted statesmen and inventors and captains of industry were completely unworthy to be in the same room with an artist.

The great French painter Degas once said to Whistler, "My friend, you behave as if you had no talent." He himself drew as his signature a butterfly with the sting of a wasp in its tail. This was an accurate symbol of the personality he showed to the world, but we would not be discussing him today were there not much more to him than that. He was among the most original and influential of all English-speaking artists.

However, Whistler never put down roots in any single place or nation. He was born in Massachusetts on July 10, 1834, son to a civil engineer who moved from task to task. While still in short trousers, the boy lived in three American communities, in England, and in Russia where his father was called by the czar to build a railroad. He was enjoying the luxuries of the world's most lavish imperial court when the father died and he was shifted to a frozen New England farmhouse to be kept by his mother perpetually engaged in chores. He was sent to West Point, but dismissed for failure in chemistry. "Had silicon been a gas," he was to explain, "I would have been a major general." He worked in a locomotive works and then in the Coastal Survey. All this before he was twenty-one!

At twenty-one, Whistler left America forever. He sailed to a physical France, but actually he struggled on sinewy butterfly wings toward the only region where he ever felt at home: the world of art. For the rest of his life, his mind tried to inhabit that visionary land while his feet walked more tangible bottoms: the alleys and damp studios of Paris's artistic

Bohemia; the embankments of London's industrial Thames; the parlors of stuffy dowagers and boudoirs of amorous models. He had companions: Jo who appears half-human and half-apparition holding up her heavy red hair in many of his pictures; fellow painters with whom he caroused and argued; patrons; critics he denounced; friends; enemies; and those bourgeois—Philistines he called them—who turned white faces to stare as the now famous painter strutted by, an esthetic dandy, with his mustachios and his cane and his little, pointed shoes. All these things he experienced half-reluctantly, refusing to admit that worldly matters had for an artist any importance. When he painted the individual who had most influenced his life, he called the picture *Arrangement in Gray and Black*, and wrote that it could be of no possible interest to anyone but himself that the portrait was of his mother.

Of all the figures Whistler depicted, his mother seems to belong most completely to a tangible world. That most of his figures fail to stand solidly on the ground, we do not mind for they move solidly in the imagination. Whistler's artistic forte was a subtle, withdrawn, decorative charm. As an etcher—and he was one of the world's best—he used delicate lines to create cities that seem to rise without weight. Avoiding, in painting open-air scenes, the brightening sun that so fascinated his French friends, the Impressionists, he became a majestic depictor of half-light, the time when, as he wrote concerning London's waterfront, "the poor buildings lost themselves in the dim sky, and the tall chimneys become campanili, and the warehouses are palaces in the night, and the whole city hangs in the heavens, and fairyland lies before us."

It was in London that Whistler spent his most productive years. However, the dictator of English taste, John Ruskin, was outraged by his passion for suggestion rather than statement, by his "arrangements" and "nocturnes" in which dim space often called more strongly to the imagination than defined form. Ruskin believed that the more exact detail with which a picture was crowded, the better that picture was. He wrote concerning a shadowy night scene that Whistler called *Black and Gold—A Falling Rocket*, "I have seen and heard of much cockney impudence before now, but never expected to hear a coxcomb ask two hundred guineas for flinging a pot of paint in the public's face."

Whistler sued Ruskin for libel. Then there was a great movement to the witness chair of conservative English artists who stated that Whistler would do much better to depict everything the way they themselves did. And in his own testimony, he enraged the court: He insisted that lawyers, judges, and jurors could not expect to understand art. And he laughed at the conventional English belief that an artist's primary task was to imitate nature.

"Nature," Whistler liked to say, "is usually wrong," rarely exhibiting "a perfection of harmony worthy of a picture. . . . Nature contains the elements, in color and form, of all pictures, as the keyboard contains the notes of all music. But the artist is born to pick and choose. . . . To say to the painter that nature is to be taken as she is, is to say to the player that he may sit on the piano."

Such sallies convinced the court that, although Whistler had in fact been libeled, his reputation had no value. He was awarded the insulting damages of one farthing. And the costs of the suit drove him into bankruptcy. He became more bitter, more determined to fight the world.

Whistler insisted that artists have no nationality and in his case this was undoubtedly true. American-born, he lived in England more than any other land. The English consider him a member of their school. However, English art had no more effect on his style than American. He was more receptive to influences from France, where he sometimes resided, and from Spain and Japan, which he never saw.

Whistler's own experiences made him a propounder of the esthetic theory known as "art for art's sake." Artists, it is postulated, create independently of physical environment. Living in and for art, they degrade themselves if the pictures they produce tell a story or point a moral or have any significance beyond the purely esthetic. Furthermore, any concession to popular taste is prostitution: Only artists can appreciate a true work of art. These theories did much to prepare the way for modern abstractionists.

However, Whistler's own actions reveal that he himself by no means subscribed wholeheartedly to the doctrines of "art for art's sake." Always he painted the world around him, even if he refined it to a personal vision. And, instead of turning his back on the unesthetic people he damned as Philistines, he was perpetually shaking his fist under their noses, he was perpetually posturing for their admiration.

In his heart, he wanted to be accepted by the groups he chided. Had he been alive when his sculptured likeness was placed in America's Hall of Fame, however loud his public sneers, secretly he would have been delighted.

FROM THE SOCIETY OF AMERICAN ARTISTS TO THE ASH CAN SCHOOL

Throughout the history of our nation, American painting has been confused and impeded by physical and cultural isolation. First-class old master canvases have always been rare in this land, available only in a few cities. Although examples of the European art then contemporary have been imported in every generation, the men who created them and the studios in which they were created have remained across three thousand miles of ocean. Foreign traditions have never been assimilated in the United States, and yet no intelligent man can deny that these traditions have, down the ages, created a greater art than our own.

From the beginning, this situation has placed our painters in a dilemma. The America that was their birthright was an exciting land, and, in any case, it was irrevocably built into their personalities, by environment even if not by heredity. On the other hand, the masterpieces which seemed in every lifetime to be signposts pointing the way to immortality were created in distant lands under different conditions to express another way of life. Blending European skill with American experience has always been a most puzzling labor. Most artists have found it easier either to forget the great traditions or to forget the United States. As time has passed, these two solutions have been accepted alternately, in a sort of rough pendulum swing.

Although American painting dates back to at least 1660, not till 1760 did an important American painter set foot in Europe. The art of the Colonial period was, of necessity, largely a native growth. However, the same increase in power and prosperity that inspired the American Revolution propelled our painters abroad. For two generations, American artists played a role on the world stage. The first of these generations adhered to native roots and prospered; the second attempted to become completely Europeanized and failed so dismally that the pendulum suddenly leapt to the other extreme. In the 1830s, the members of the Hudson River and related schools became passionately dedicated to depicting American life and landscape; they based their painting techniques on the crude sources that were easily available to them in the United States. Again there were two generations. At the outbreak of the Civil War, the second was in the ascendant. American exhibitions were dominated by huge canvases—which showed the natural wonders of the continent, and which brought greater prices than were paid for imported European art.

When peace returned, the majority of the young painters arising throughout the land, disillusioned by warfare, looked at these Hudson River School pictures with new eyes and saw only their faults. They noticed a lack of subtlety without noticing strength; they noticed a directness of technique which often seemed to contrast unfortunately with such European canvases as they had seen. Paying little attention to such sophisticated workmen among their elders as George Innes, completely ignorant about the native painters of previous epochs, they told each other that there had never been an American art. The opportunity to create an American art they believed to be their own, and they thought they knew how to do it—import everything from Europe. One by one, the young men sailed abroad.

The first Mecca that attracted them was Munich, in the 1870s a fashionable art center although the work done there was not to stand the test of time. Among the many students at the Bavarian city, two men from the Middle West were to attract particular attention. William Merritt Chase of Indiana and Frank Duveneck of Ohio became expert at painting professional models posed in clothes hired from a theatrical costumer, and in giving the resulting pictures an all-over yellowish tinge which approximated the effect of age on Old Masters. Since flashing brushwork was the trademark of the Munich School, they dashed their paint-loaded brushes against canvas as if fencing with an invisible opponent. That nothing they were doing in any way connoted their native land made it all seem the more exciting, the more valuable for reforming American art.

Duveneck had stayed for a time in Munich, where he instructed his young compatriots who continued to flock there. Chase had joined the flood of students who were returning home, each clutching a favorite formula. They not only had worked in Munich, but had also shopped around among European traditions, like bargain hunters in a department store, picking up something here and something there until their styles were as polyglot as they were lightly felt. Eager to share their discoveries, they organized schools in New York, the Art Students League, and, when the older painters who controlled the National Academy slighted their pictures, they formed, in 1877, an academy of their own, the Society of American Artists. Their ranks swelled yearly, as more young men sailed in from abroad. Since Paris was becoming increasingly ascendant in European art, French influence gradually replaced Munich as dominant in the Society of American Artists.

The painters of the new movement generally avoided depicting American life except in its most refined and idealized aspects. Subscribing to the doctrine of "art for art's sake," they insisted that subject matter was of very secondary importance as compared to technique, and indeed it was in the realm of technique that their contribution to American culture lay. However, the leaders of the Society of Artists, in their reaction against what they considered the crudeness of their environment, refused to see and feel. They created superficial pictures.

Today we regard as our greatest artists of the late nineteenth century those men who never tried by an act of will to cut themselves off from their American roots. Building through personal experimentation on his early training as a magazine illustrator, Winslow Homer became one of the world's greatest watercolorists, and a majectic painter in oil of the ocean as it battered the coast of his beloved Maine. Albert Pinkham Ryder, a gentle, gigantic bearded hermit, invented for himself the weird technique with which he gave substance to the visions that floated naturally through his mind as he prowled New York City streets. And Thomas Eakins exemplified the most fruitful way for an American to use European study. In France, Eakins selected techniques that were peculiarly suited to his temperament, and, after his return to Philadelphia, he matured slowly an individual art based on his convictions concerning the Pennsylvania world he knew so well.

These great creators stayed apart from the fashionable artistic life of their time: The Society of American Artists continued to engender the greatest buzzing in critical and social circles. Little by little, its leaders were elected to the National Academy, and in 1906, they merged the two organizations. But already the pendulum of taste had started to move in the opposite direction.

After studying in the leading art schools of the United States and Europe, Robert Henri (pronounced Henríe) reached the conclusion that even the greatest technical proficiency was sterile unless it was mated with life. In Philadelphia, he accepted as students a group of newspaper illustrators—John Sloan, George Luke, William Glackens—and he took the revolutionary step of advising them that the street scenes they drew for their commercial employers were suitable subject-matter for serious art. The resulting canvases of gas-lit bars, shopgirls hurrying home, and ragged urchins dancing in the gutter shocked the exponents of art for art's sake who now controlled the National Academy. Again secession became a necessity.

In 1907, the painters of city scenes joined with other advanced artists to form "The Eight" and hold their own exhibition. Although they were mocked as "The Ash Can School," their pictures were in keeping with a time when writers were increasingly concerned with realism, economists with the problems of urban life. Their reform showed signs of sweeping everything before it when the greatest artistic revolution in 600 years roared into a much louder explosion.

Since the end of the Middle Ages, the ideals of Renaissance art had dominated Western culture. But at the beginning of the twentieth century, men of many nations, including a few Americans, developed in Paris what has been called modernism: an art with very different ideals. The wave of confusion and achievement thus set up moved slowly across the ocean to reach the United States in 1914, in the famous Armory Show. Even leaders of "The Ash Can School" were caught up in the wave that washed American painting in new and strange directions.

THE HOMER SHOW: "FEW PAINTERS HAVE SO POWERFULLY EXPRESSED THE VASTNESS OF THE WORLD"

Published in 1944, Lloyd Goodrich's book on Winslow Homer was a precurser and long-range incitor of that deep concern with the tradition of American painting that had, during the last decade, become a phenomenon of American taste.★ Goodrich's multiple activities have included further publications on Homer and now, 30 years after his first book on the painter, he has staged a major Homer exhibition for the Whitney Museum.

Goodrich told me that the exhibition was not as comprehensive as that put on in 1958–1959 by the National Gallery and the Metropolitan Museum (200 pictures to 224). However, he could think of no other exhibition larger than the present one. And, he added, it was unlikely that there would be another show in the foreseeable future as big and representative, since institutions and private individuals are becoming less and less willing to lend works of art.

Although Goodrich was unable to secure everything he wanted, it took a hard heart to refuse such an expert. He is happy with what he has brought together. And he has every right to be proud. It is an impressive show.

The show is plenty big enough to challenge the capacity of a full floor at the Whitney. The pictures are, indeed, more crowded on the walls than modern ideas of museum installation encourage. But surely exuberance is a lesser fault than caution, and in Homer's own day, when so many canvases found their places in private living rooms, pictures were hung much closer together. The result can have a great richness.

Indeed, my first reaction when I entered the galleries was to feel roll over me a great wave of color. One is inclined to forget how quickly, after he moved from black-and-white illustration to the use of pigments,

---

★An earlier version of this essay appeared in *Art News* (May 1973), 65–67.

Homer revealed his potentialities as a major colorist. His *Pitching Horse-shoes*, painted when he had been working with oils for hardly more than a year, is a sensuously moving depiction of bright sunlight as it illumines soldiers playing in a Civil War encampment. Homer had been lured into a high key by the picturesque costumes of the Zouaves, northern troops who went to battle tricked out, as at a fancy dress ball, in imitation of Algerian soldiers in the French army.

Homer's color sense grew steadily throughout the rest of his career, reaching its apogee when he was in his 60s and early 70s. This growth was not what one might expect to come with great maturity—it is not a development toward heavier resonances reflecting the tragic complications of the human spirit; it is, rather, an ever more eloquent lyricism.

Goodrich has, he told me, selected the pictures to emphasize the painterly quality in Homer's work, which was too often overlooked through attention to subject matter. Homer, he pointed out, was not only a great colorist but a designer concerned with the conscious structuring which we today particularly value. The exhibition is aimed at bringing forward those aspects of Homer's work "most alive today."

This concern encouraged emphasis on the pictures painted at Tyne-mouth, England, when, after suffering from "painter's block" Homer labored on the shores of the North Sea to evolve new directions. The resulting works, in which subject matter was often primarily a vehicle for form, were the most esthetically contrived Homer ever produced. I myself find them among the least successful. They seem to me to lack inner conviction, to be the only art Homer ever painted that was derivative and could have been created by another man. Homer's own later reaction to his Tynemouth work seems to have been ambivalent. He continued to consider *Voice from the Cliffs* one of his best canvases. However, after his return to the United States he completely submerged what he could use of his formal experiments into his naturalistic style.

I have my own *idée fixe* concerning the aspect of Homer's work that is most sadly overlooked. We think of him as a powerful, burly glorifier of physical stress, of nature at various extremes, of masculine adventure. In considering his early work, we think of homely farm scenes, plank fences, urchins lolling in ragged clothes. But there was also in the early Homer a lyrical delicacy and elegance that, as he pursued other paths, we would least expect: for instance, in that poetic, color-drenched re-creation of an ocean only gently troubled, *Cannon Rock*. This side of Homer's art is not omitted from the present exhibition—for instance *Long Branch* and *Grace Hoops*—but it seems to be somewhat muted.

Goodrich is too experienced and wise a hand to exclude, whatever he may emphasize, any aspect of Homer's achievement. The viewer is impressed both with the consistency (despite some exceptions) of Homer's output and its great variety. As was the situation with his color, while his art deepened, his fundamental attitudes and technical resources did not really change.

He never painted city scenes (although as a youth he sometimes drew them). Only a few times did he depict an interior, and then, as in *The Country School*, he was most successful when large windows let in so much light that the room could be illuminated as if it were out of doors. His visit to the front during the Civil War did produce a few battle scenes, but he preferred to show soldiers relaxing and playing, which links the war pictures to his rural scenes of boys sporting. Until the last years of his life, his landscapes and seascapes were always inhabited, even if sometimes by trout instead of humans, the figures strongly presented in the foregrounds.

Toward women, whether they were picnicking belles or endangered fishergirls, he always expressed a delicate sympathy that in the work of a lesser artist might have been sentimental. Although he dwelt more explicitly, as he grew older, on the fierceness of nature, there was from the very start in many of his oils a feeling that menace was part of the mystery and beauty of the world. From the first to last, his oil technique was simple, his brush always lacking what Henry James called, in criticizing his early oils, "secrets and mysteries and coquetries." Yet, all limitations admitted, we feel, as we wander through this exhibition, a greatly various panorama of the human experience and the world.

An insight which I found surprising came to me because, when I first visited the galleries at the Whitney, all of the pictures had not yet been hung: many still leaned against the walls, resting on the floor, occupying the same environment with various ordinary implements and with my own feet as I walked around. Thereby encouraged to view the pictures as purely physical objects, I realized with a shock how small they were.

In the entire exhibition there are only two pictures which measure in their longest dimension more than four feet and a trifle. *Pitching Horseshoes* reaches five feet, five and a half inches; the very biggest, *The Fox Hunt*, five feet, eight inches, Indeed, most of the paintings are considerably smaller than four feet. The powerful *Dad's Coming*, which contains three figures, a foreground rowboat, beach and ocean, each with details, measures nine by $13^{3}/_{4}$ inches.

The realization of how small Homer's paintings are brought another thought equally startling: during his entire career, Winslow Homer almost never depicted anything—a bush or a rock or a bowl or an arm or a portrait head—at life size. (The only important exceptions seem to be the face, hat, and beard of the lookout in *All's Well* and perhaps the fox in *The Fox Hunt*.) The faces of the protagonists in the vast majority of Homer's paintings, even in those most dependent on human participation, could easily be covered by a fifty-cent piece. Homer usually worked on the scale of a miniaturist.

Winslow Homer a miniaturist? The ridiculousness of this conception is a measure of the strength of the human imagination and the magic of Homer's art. When, being elevated on walls, the canvases are so separated from their surroundings that they can dictate their own scale, the physically tiny becomes visually and emotionally huge. There are few major painters (other than manuscript illuminators) in the history of Western art who have worked, so almost without exception, in small scale as did Winslow Homer. And there have been few painters who have so powerfully expressed the vastness of the world.

Who says that the age of miracles is long dead? Surely it is a miracle to distill with no loss the macrocosm into the microcosm.

How such effects were achieved is more a mystery in relation to Homer than would be the case for a European artist of equivalent stature. Homer subscribed to the Hudson River School tradition that the object of technique was to hide technique. The less a painting looked like a work of art, the more it looked like unedited nature, the more the artist congratulated himself. This esthetic is responsible for the universal first reaction to Homer's work: the sense of the overwhelming importance of his subject matter. But a long look will reveal that the result goes far beyond what the subject seems to allow.

It is Goodrich's point that Homer enhanced his effects by expert use of the vocabulary of art—color, form, composition—and this is indeed the case (the more so, the more effective the picture). Yet it seems to me that Homer's approach to creation determined much: As far as we know, Homer never considered a painting primarily as an esthetic problem. Rather, he selected from among the millions of visual images that passed before his eyes those that triggered some emotion which, consciously or unconsciously, he yearned to express. He then painted the subject as it appeared to him, viewed in terms of the emotions it had inspired. The mysterious chemistry of art fused the two together. Since Homer saw everything in its largest implications, largeness of effect, expressed in his astonishing sense of monumentiality, was inherent to his work.

Winslow Homer was among the greatest painters of the nineteenth century, and is surely comparable with any one of the great French Impressionists. Lloyd Goodrich remains, as he has been for a generation, the most knowledgeable and perceptive authority on Winslow Homer. To view the rich exhibition which Goodrich has brought together is a privilege which no one should forgo.

WILLIAM SAWITZKY (1879–1947)

The death of William Sawitzky on February 2, 1947, was a great blow to scholarship in early American art.★ When he entered the field shortly before the First World War, it was still a playground for dilettantism, too many of the workers being concerned with pretty theories or ancestor worship. Wolves of error stalked the woods, falling unhindered on the little settlements of amateur scholars, and slaughtering their sheep-like publications. With incisive insight, Sawitzky realized that the most valuable contribution he could make would be to get back to first sources, to documents, to the attribution of individual pictures. Too much of what he called "aesthetic twaddle" was being written, too many airy theories were being built on misattributions or downright fakes. He would look at the pictures with a cold, scientific eye, laying firm the foundations on which his successors could build.

There was heroism in this resolve. Academic institutions ignored American art; the organized structure that supports basic scholarship was non-existent; he was forced to push ahead on his own, with little possibility of financial reward, through a most tangled wilderness of error. He may even have had to fight personal temptations too, for there was much of the artist about him; he could have written appreciation and theory, had the time been ripe. His monographs, indeed, are composed with a facility of style rarely found in such publications. His dedication overcame all obstacles; he used his esthetic insight to solve the seemingly tiny problems which are the basis of all knowledge; with little encouragement, he struggled on for years. His great abilities, his fine seriousness, his profound integrity won out in the end. He became an inspiration to the younger scholars in the field; men who disagreed on almost everything else could usually find common ground in their admiration of Mr. Sawitzky. And in 1940 he was appointed Advisory Curator of American Art at the New-York Historical Society under a special grant from the

★An earlier version of this essay appeared in *College Art Journal* (Summer 1947), 301–302.

Carnegie Corporation of New York. As a lecturer at the Institute of Fine Arts, New York University, he gave during 1940 and 1941 two brilliant courses.

The first of these was quite a phenomenon. Graduate students found themselves a somewhat embarrassed minority, for at Sawitzsky's feet sat most of the mature scholars in the field. Curators, dealers, editors, authors of already published books and monographs took notes as if their lives depended on it. For the first time in history, a lucid and accurate description was being given of the beginnings of American art; no wonder we all leaned forward so as not to miss a word.

Already the great scholar was in bad health. Walking to the platform, he had to stop every few steps to regain his breath. Yet this stricken figure was not pitiful; from him flowed tremendous strength. The long face, with its high forehead and vigorously cut features, bore an expression both stern and affable. Here was a man not to be trifled with, not to be underestimated, to be feared a little and yet loved.

In one particular at least, Sawitzky reverses the usual practice of mankind. People are inclined to compliment colleagues to their faces and deprecate them to their backs. Sawitzky, of course, would damn a thoroughly bad piece of work at all times and anywhere, but if a publication had virtues, he was inclined to dwell on them when the author was absent. It was to the author himself that he pointed out errors, sometimes very gently, sometimes less so. Fired with a vision of perfection, he occasionally, when he allowed his mind to run on error, attacked it with all the energy of an Old Testament prophet cursing Babylon.

Sawitzky's range of appreciation was wide. Younger workers could rely on warm words of encouragement, if they deserved them. Some evening the phone would ring, and there would be the veteran scholar, calling long distance. "I understand how much work went into the publication," he would say. And then, remembering perhaps his own struggles, he would add, "I want you to know that there is at least one person in the world who appreciates what you have done." Such praise was to be cherished, and often thought of in moments of discouragement. But there was always another, terrifying possibility. Many a young worker had in his mind's eye seen that stern face looking over his shoulder, and had hurried back to a further investigation of sources lest he be taken to the intellectual woodshed for a well-deserved whipping.

Sawitzky was a powerful personal influence on his colleagues. This must be emphasized today, for the record will die with those who knew him. Important as his publications are, they are only part of his contribution. William Sawitzky was a human embodiment of serious purpose, of accurate research, above all of uncompromising integrity.

Facts and bibliography have been given in so many obituaries that I shall only summarize them here. Born in Latvia in 1879, Sawitzky became an ornithologist. In 1911, he came to America as a newspaper correspondent, but two years later an unconquerable interest in art induced him to become librarian of Knoedler & Co. Soon he was an independent scholar, picking up support where he could get it, traveling all over the Atlantic states as he examined the first monuments of American art. In 1927, he secured a charming, faithful, and intelligent collaborator through his marriage to Susan Clay, of Lexington, Kentucky. He edited, for the Frick Art Reference Library, Lawrence Park's monumental work on Gilbert Stuart, and he was always generous in giving that important institution information and advice. He catalogued the paintings in the Historical Society of Pennsylvania, published a monograph on Matthew Pratt, and articles on Stuart, Ralph Earl, Benjamin West, and William Williams. At the time of his death, he had almost completed a monograph on Earl, and another on three New York artists Lawrence Kilburn, Abraham Delanoy, Jr., and an unidentified workman. We may look forward to an increasingly rich harvest of his scholarship, since more of his researches are to be put into final form for publication by the New-York Historical Society.

MASTERPIECES—LOST FOREVER?

The conclusions finally drawn from the current controversy concerning the Metropolitan's "deaccessioning" paintings from its collection will influence future museum policy in America.* It is thus unfortunate that little emphasis has been placed on the most serious menace of such "deaccessioning" to the cultural heritage of the human race.

The worst catastrophe does not immediately hang over objects sold by a museum for an impressive sum. Although faith to donors may be violated; although the museum may not secure maximum prices; although its collection may be impoverished to the detriment of the community, the chances are that the objects, being regarded as valuable, will (at least until there is a major change in taste) be preserved. But if museum objects are dumped at a time when they are considered of minimal value, they may, since at that moment nobody cares, be lost forever to the world of art.

The only certainty concerning artistic taste is that it changes: today's position will be abandoned tomorrow. Since this situation is so irrefutably demonstrated by history, it is amazing to find supposedly sophisticated individuals who believe that taste has at last been solidified in their eyes and their erudition. They claim that, having conducted research according to their own lights, they have soared above their own times into universal infallibility. They see no reason why they should hesitate to restructure for the entire future of mankind the collections temporarily entrusted to them.

Defending his museum's policy in a letter to *The New York Times* last fall, Douglas Dillon, the president of the Metropolitan, stated that the precautions taken before an object is sold are scaled to the presumed sales price. Considerable care is taken if the assessment is over $25,000; some care if the work is "valued by the curator at $10,000 or over." Nothing is said of any checks on the dumping of objects judged to be worth less than $10,000.

---

*This essay originally appeared as an Op-ed page article in *The New York Times*.

The assumption behind this policy is that esthetic values and sales values are identical. That theory presents, of course, a method of automatically creating, in the very act of acquiring it, a masterpiece; pay more than a million dollars for it. However, it is of much deeper concern to civilization that the policy demonstrates indifference to objects not currently prized in the marketplace.

As a common rule, people despise the art admired by their fathers and rediscover the art of their grandfathers. According to the Metropolitan system, curators may follow an inner glow of self-satisfaction in clearing out the "trash" acquired by their predecessors. The fact that their successors may, with an equal glow, clear out the "trash" they acquired, contributes a note of comedy. But the tragedy is deeper. As Edgar Preston Richardson, former director of the Detroit Art Institute, has pointed out, a museum cannot meet its responsibilities if it functions like a revolving door.

Swings of taste much more extensive than those caused by the generation gap must also be recognized. Had the Catholic Church in Spain deaccessioned during any one year out of two and a half centuries, we would never have heard of a painter whose work sank beneath civilized interest shortly after his death in 1614 and did not truly emerge until the twentieth century: El Greco. Since American mid-nineteenth-century painting has only recently escaped a long eclipse, I myself have seen major exemplars of our national heritage dumped by major museums, including the Metropolitan, which could not now buy them back at ten or even a hundred times the pittances they then received.

The adventures of the Metropolitan's little Greek horse which was declared a fake and then reinstated demonstrate that reassessment of genuineness does not justify deaccessioning. Pruning examples of an artist's work to keep "the best" requires definitions that time will change. Since shifts of taste can be extremely violent, even pictures sold for a large sum are not in the long run safe from destruction.

We must insist that, when a work of art is considered worthy of a public collection, that collection has entered upon a compact with the human race to preserve the work indefinitely. The only viable exception would be in relation to a work of art that proved to have been stolen.

A major institution like the Metropolitan can enrich the whole nation by lending to other institutions. But it should not abdicate its responsibility to see that the works are cared for according to its own high standards.

Works currently too out of fashion to be of immediate interest can be placed in dead storage in a museum-controlled warehouse. Every ten years or so, the then-current officials could undertake a safari, bringing out what has returned to interest and putting in what they do not care for. Much would undoubtedly remain in dead storage but much would not, and there is always the possibility that the explorers would extract a latter-day El Greco.

BIOGRAPHY

Biography as a Juggler's Art

Biography is a complicated art that combines things seemingly irrecon-
cilable.* Concerned with the depiction of personality, the biographer
must be an imaginative writer; concerned with the resurrection of actual
men and events, he must be a meticulous scholar. On the one hand, he
leans toward the technique of the novelist; on the other, toward the
technique of the documentary historian. Somewhere between these two
poles lies his own technique. Finding the golden mean which is most
suited to his art is the fundamental problem which faces every writer of
lives.

The easy way out is to go to one extreme or the other. Many a
biographer, deeply conscious of his duty as a scholar, has forgotten that
he is dealing with people who once lived and thought. We may learn
from his pages where a man was at a certain date and the actual physical
facts of what the man was doing. Those letters and papers which the
biographer considers relevant he paraphrases or quotes. And, having
done this, he claims to have gone as far as a biographer may go; these
are the facts, anything else is fiction. Even if his books are not vivid,
they are, he insists, completely impersonal and non-partisan, entirely
accurate.

We may agree at once that such books are not vivid, but are they
impersonally accurate? That is open to question. Although the author
has quoted the documents he has used with rigid fidelity, keeping in
every misspelling and every omitted comma, the fact remains that he has
made a selection among the many papers at his disposal. If he has written
the life of a great character in history, we may be sure he has been able
to quote only one document in five hundred, or a thousand. Of course,
he has dwelt on the papers he considers most significant, but his judgment has depended on his own personal interpretation of his subject's
career. Thus, if he considers his subject an honest man, he will regard

---

*An earlier version of this essay appeared in *Saturday Review of Literature*, October 9,
1943, pp. 3–4, 19.

suggestions of questionable practices in contemporary memoirs as undoubtedly inspired by jealousy and malice; it would distort the picture,
he feels to make much use of such irrelevant things. If, however, the
biographer is convinced that his hero was an evil influence, these same
evidences of wrongdoing will be given great weight. Admittedly this is
an extreme example: the point is that no author can escape evaluating
documents according to what remains, despite the most thorough scholarship, his own personal judgment.

Indeed, it may be contended that biographies made up entirely of
facts, dates, and quoted source material are in one way more misleading
than those in which the author permits himself some leeway. When a
writer draws his conclusions on paper instead of solely in his mind, we
may recognize his point of view and take it into consideration as we
read. But when an author keeps himself always in the background, we
may only discover his prejudices by making a new study of the source
material.

A purely factual biographer is forced by his method to present reality in
an unnatural manner. Experience has trained every individual to evaluate
the people he meets as living, active entities; he is not used to judging
men from quoted documents. When we re-examine a packet of letters
from an old friend we realize that much of the meaning lies not in the
words written but between the lines. Probably factual biographers would
admit this, but they would add that there is nothing to keep a reader
from looking between the lines of the documents they have quoted.
True, a reader can try; but he is in a much worse position to make an
interpretation than is the biographer, who has studied five hundred or a
thousand papers to the reader's one, and who has a much better background of knowledge of the period in which the subject lived.

Although a purely factual biography can present neither an entirely
non-partisan interpretation nor a vivid picture of a living man, we must
remember that the labor that goes into such a book is often extremely
valuable in blazing new trails of knowledge. The expert documentarian
is in his own way a worker of great ability, a Sherlock Holmes of the
library shelf. Following clues as subtle as those employed by any detective of fiction, he undertakes an exciting search for the missing fact, the
paper that has vanished. Back and forth across the world his magnifying
glass moves; now he is rummaging in the attic of some descendant of his
hero, now blowing the dust from documents in an historical society
cellar. And often when he returns to the light of day at last, he is carrying

carefully distilled on a packet of cards new data which may well revolutionize our understanding of his subject. Such a man has made an important contribution whatever the form of the biography he writes in the end. Indeed, the book is often a secondary matter, like the article in which a scientist reports his experiments. Whether the selection he publishes from the material he has found is broad or narrow makes little difference as long as he appends a full bibliography; other writers may now follow in his footsteps, and, whatever their achievement, it will be largely dependent on his labors. Purely documentary works are source books for biographies, not biographies in themselves.

At the opposite extreme are the several schools of biographers whose only interest is in creating brilliant pictures of human beings. Not aiming at sound scholarship, they use a technique which is much closer to romance than history. Some of the most successful go so far as to make accuracy secondary to the telling of a dramatic story. Not only do they improvise conversations, not only do they juggle chronology and make up events to fill gaps in their knowledge, but, should the development of their subjects' careers not accord with their ideas of suspense and climax, they do not hesitate to change fact in a way that they believe furthers fiction. Their books are not biographies at all, but novels.

Other biographers have a respect for accuracy, but fail to undertake the labor of examining the innumerable and scattered documents which are the source material in their field. They study the obvious printed sources, making great use of previously published lives, and from the material thus culled create a new interpretation. Many of the books thus prepared have definite virtues. A fresh point of view, brilliant writing, the vivid presentation of characters who walk and breathe, an easy readability that carries the eye from page to page; these are on the credit side of the best of such works. On the debit side is a fundamental flaw in method.

As we have seen, even the most scholarly study represents in the way the material was selected a specific point of view. The romantic biographer uses several such interpretations to build up a separate interpretation, which may indeed represent an opposite approach from that which determined his source-books. Let us say that he is writing about a worthy who died at the height of the Victorian era. The original biographers of such a man, themselves Victorians, would report his life according to their ideals. But our modern biographer has discarded Victorianism, so he makes fun of his subject's smugness. Yet that subject may not have been smug at all; the biographer may be dealing not with the character under discussion at all, but with the character's previous biographers. He has no way of knowing unless he himself goes back to the original sources. This again is an extreme case, but the fact remains that the biographer who relies on rewriting previous lives can create nothing but an interpretation of interpretations.

However brilliant and comprehensive were the scholars who went before him, a writer who examines the original material in his field is likely to stumble on evidence that was unimportant from the point of view of his predecessors but which will open up to him new vistas of understanding. The more original and interpretative his approach, the more valuable he will find these personal discoveries.

Facts, dates, and documents then, all the seemingly uninspiring paraphernalia of the archivist, should be a biographer's inspiration. Both the usefulness and the authority of his book will be greatly increased if he employs notes to give the source of each of his statements. Although some publishers object to references on the ground that they may scare away readers, this attitude is extremely shortsighted, even from a strictly commercial point of view. The notes can easily be gathered in the back of the volume, designated by page and paragraph in such a manner that no numbers need appear in the text. Hardly noticed by the uninterested, these references will help the sale of the book in many ways. Serious works are often given to serious scholars for review, and the first thing a scholar does is to attempt an evaluation of source material. Furthermore, it is the experts who have a long-time interest in a field. Promotion aimed at the casual reader can keep a book in the public eye for six months or a year; after that the scholars have their innings. They push undocumented books into limbo, and keep the others alive indefinitely.

Once a biographer has mastered his original sources, his work has only begun. Now he must make a synthesis of his material similar to what a novelist makes from the observed facts of life. Before him lies the tangled record of a personality acting within a fixed period of years. He must weigh evidence and draw conclusions; he must interpret and explain. While recognizing that he cannot so far escape the limitations of the human mind as to write pure truth uninfluenced by his own personality and environment, he must nonetheless strive to do so. The broader his viewpoint, the closer he comes to a universal approach, the more valuable his book will be. There can be no possible excuse for his ever changing a fact, misquoting a document, or glossing over an event that the most non-partisan attitude of which he is capable tells him is significant. Complete intellectual honesty is perhaps the most important single attribute of the biographer.

Impartiality, however, need not imply lack of color; the best biographies carry an overtone of excitement. There has long been a tendency among some intellectuals to regard the storyteller's art as a cheap trick which appeals only to common minds. A short story, we are told, is damaged by plot; a play is not art but "box office" unless it is heavy and slow. Similarly a biography is regarded as a serious contribution in exact proportion to its dullness. This attitude represents a pointless limiting of the artist's opportunity by taking away one of his best tools.

Drama is natural to biography because it is natural to the human mind. Since most men who have shaped events have found their careers exciting, to drain off the excitement makes the picture untrue. Indeed, if a writer feels it necessary to alter events to create suspense and climax, it usually means he has failed to grasp the inherent possibilities of his subject. Facts are stranger than fiction; the imagination of nature is more audacious than that of man. What novelist could conceive of a career like Joan of Arc's, or Lincoln's?

Since all men live in time, chronology is the only natural thread on which the events of a man's life may be strung. This does not mean that the biographer must follow his subject methodically from birth to death. Like a novelist, he may anticipate major happenings and then work back through the years to the explanations, yet the basic rhythm of time which is the rhythm of life must never be obscured. Sometimes it is necessary for clarity to group like events together even if they happened in different years, but this is a dangerous expedient which should be resorted to as little as possible. No biographies are to my mind less vivid than those made up of essay chapters, each dealing with one aspect of the hero's career and headed "The Statesman," "The Poet," "The Husband and Father."

A basic problem facing every biographer is how to sketch in the historical background without violating the time element and impeding the narrative flow. On the one hand, the writer has a personality and a career to present; on the other, he is saddled with the cultural, economic, and political events of a period. Many biographers have been defeated by this seeming dualism. Some try to create pure character sketches, to separate a man's personality from his reaction to and his effect on his environment. Others have written erudite histories in which for chapter after chapter the hero is obscured from view by clouds of general data. Neither expedient, of course, can turn out a well-rounded book.

Whenever an artist becomes confused, perhaps the best plan is to return to the study of life. How, let us ask ourselves, does a man's environment actually impinge on his personality? Certainly not in a series of bursts which, like the explanatory chapters in a formal book, hit him from time to time with a great bulk of facts. A man's environment is an integral part of his life, a gradual revelation never separated from the subjective aspects of his personality.

Like the novelist, the biographer should keep his hero forever in the foreground; he should see the world over his hero's shoulder. Historical events appear in the book at the time when they became of significance to the person under discussion, and this automatically keys them into the story. A biographer may, of course, include facts and analyses that were beyond his subject's experience, as long as he makes it plain that he is doing so, and always keeps clearly before his readers the reference of these matters to the career and personality with which he is dealing. A type of sleight-of-hand is required.

Indeed, a biographer must be a juggler, expert at keeping many bright balls circling in the air. Fact and imagination, sober scholarship and dramatic writing, character study and sound history, a sympathetic understanding of his hero and yet a judicial lack of special pleading—these are a few of the balls that must forever fly around his head without colliding or dropping to the floor. But fortunately it is only in the rare moments when he masquerades as a critic that a practicing biographer recognizes this analogy and realizes the enormous difficulties of his craft. When he is back in the greasy overalls of labor, he is again a simple craftsman, struggling with specific problems which he must handle as best he may. And if he sometimes wonders how his finished book will turn out, he can only hope it will be better than might be expected.

ALLAN NEVINS

Allan Nevins's name and fame are, of course, written large across historical literature. He published more than twenty-five books and fathered
the Oral History Project at Columbia which opened a new world of
historical documentation.

Nevins could not have achieved so much had he not possessed the
explosive and purposeful energy which had, in its extremes, its comic
side. He would run up a flight of stairs even if at the top he had to
stand and wait for his more slowly companions. I remember a television
rehearsal from which, unable to sit still while the director argued with
his lighting experts, the great historian, to everyone's consternation,
vanished. A believable anecdote has it that he could not resist getting to
Grand Central Station an hour before the train left, and then, unwilling
to waste the hour, disappeared into a pay toilet from which the clacking
of a typewriter soon emerged.

His expansive kindness, based on the courtesy which can only come
from profound human understanding, is remembered with gratitude not
only by his historical peers but by all younger historians who crossed his
path. The instant I myself met him—it was unconventionally through
the television adventure "Omnibus" in which we were both involved—he extended to me such warm appreciation and generosity as
most professors reserve only for their favorite pupils. At the dinner table
his face glowed with benevolence. There was no subject of discussion
in which he was not interested, and his own contributions were always
modest. His humility, which was completely genuine, probably grew
from the same source as his determination not to waste a minute: capable
of all things, he was conscious of how much more there was in the
world than he, however fast he ran, could encompass.

CARL VAN DOREN

The year was 1936, when the author of *Benjamin Franklin* was fifty-one.★ The place, the American History Room of the New York Public Library. Then in my middle twenties, I was at work at one of the tables on what was to be my first published book when there appeared in the movement of persons up and down the central aisle a remarkable figure. He was tall—over six feet—athletic in build, and carried such an air of distinction that I stared. I watched him approach the central desk, say a few words to a most respectful librarian, turn, and walk out of the room.

To my amazement—I had never done anything like this before!—I found myself on my feet. I went up to the desk and asked, who was that resplendent figure? The answer was Van Doren, Carl Van Doren.

Carl, as I came to call him, had as much charisma as any man I have ever seen. Charisma can be a dangerous thing. At the age of thirty-one, Van Doren had become headmaster of a famous girls' school: the Brearley in New York City. How the girls must have worshiped him! He could be, as I was to discover, very overbearing in conversation, but surely his *Benjamin Franklin* is one of the most modest of major biographies.

His daughter, Barbara Klaw, tells me that her father, who worked actively on this book for five years, had been preparing it in his mind for some twenty more. So much so that his family teased him for acting like Benjamin Franklin. A sense of identification on the part of the author is by no means necessarily an advantage to a biography. Only too often the author kidnaps his subject, making the dead man wear his own face. Van Doren went the opposite way, learning to see and feel like his protagonist.

This transformation did not, despite family teasing, extend beyond Van Doren's relationship with Franklin, as is made eminently clear by a reading of the author's other works. In general, he presents another

★This essay is excerpted from the Foreword to the reprint of Carl Van Doren's *Benjamin Franklin* (Book of the Month Club).

personality: edgy, ascerbic, more reflective of the queasy twentieth century than of Franklin's optimistic eighteenth. Van Doren may indeed have resented the sway sometimes exerted over him by the benign philosopher. In his own autobiographical writings, he confides that he considered his best book was his life of Jonathan Swift, who, as he put it, "aimed at mankind the most venomous arrow that scorn ever loosed." Swift's "story," he stated in explaining his preference, "took the form of a driving tragedy" while "Franklin's was a wide-flowing historical comedy."

Whatever may have been Van Doren's reactions in retrospect, his ability temporarily to make himself over into Franklin was of tremendous advantage to his book. Great biographies can, of course, be duets, the protagonist and the author playing different instruments that sound separately and together to form an artistic whole. But Van Doren's approach was particularly valuable in solving unusual problems presented to him by his subject.

Franklin was himself an extremely able writer, surely America's first great author, and yet he was not a literary man in any ordinary sense. Van Doren, who won his spurs as a literary critic, was altogether capable of presenting Franklin as a creator of prose, but that would have warped his subject out of all recognition. Franklin's writings were always part of his active participation in other aspects of his career: they were at the same time esthetic achievements and historical documentation. This fact has made many of Franklin's best writings have only limited circulation: Van Doren could not assume that the reader would already be familiar with their esthetic qualities, as he could assume if he were writing about Swift or Dickens. To make things worse, Franklin's only work that is generally read was in competition with Van Doren's biography, since it was an autobiography. Van Doren's solution to all these difficulties was the daring one of welcoming Franklin as a writer into his own volume. He inserted in his text unabridged quotations running sometimes without break to thousands of words.

The art of biography being as various as the art of fiction, quotation is used by different writers very differently. Some believe that to give any prominence to voices other than their own will destroy the texture they wish to achieve. In his many-volume life of George Washington, Douglas Southall Freeman communicated the contents of thousands of documents, but almost without exception in his own paraphrase. Other biographers throw into their texts, between quotation marks, piquant phrases, as one might liven a stew with a scattering of salt. I myself use

quotations as a novelist normally uses dialogue to vary the text and allow
the characters to reveal their thoughts and personalities through their
own expressions. Van Doren's quotations serve, without losing other
functions, as building blocks, alternating with his own prose to hold up
the very structure of the volume.

Without any indication of a break beyond the appearance of a quotation mark, Van Doren will step back from his manuscript and let Franklin take over. Many pages may pass by before the closing quotation
mark, when Van Doren re-occupies the stage. In most biographies, this
method would shatter artistic unity. For Van Doren the technique works
because, even if the interchanging voices are pitched somewhat differently, they do not create discord with conflicting points of view.

The most conspicuous way in which Van Doren's sections differ from
Franklin's lies in the nice distinction he makes between his role as ob-
server and summarizer and his protagonist's role as the actual actor.
Franklin's autobiographical writings communicate sights and sounds and
often create dramatic scenes, in which the events of one moment progress into those of another. But Van Doren does not attempt to make
the reader see or hear; nor does he take advantage of even the fullest
documentation to lead the reader into an event, to create a scene. He
limits himself to clear and eloquent exposition.

Benjamin Franklin is in the strictest sense a biography, a matter worth
commenting on as the dividing line between biography and history is at
best difficult to draw and has been much obscured by the academic
practice of dealing with an historical figure not as a human being but as
a magnet to draw together a certain constellation of exterior fact. Van
Doren keeps his protagonist always in the forefront. The author's gift of
succinct explanation enables him, if he feels that is necessary, to sketch
in rapidly and with effect historical background, but he discovers such a
necessity rarely. He prefers to let the conclusion grow from Franklin's
experiences, only using his own insight to sharpen with a summary what
has already been demonstrated by events.

Although this is a long volume, it is remarkable for brevity, considering how extensively the author quotes from Franklin's writings, and
that his protagonist became active early and lived to be eighty-four,
functioning importantly until the end.

One way Van Doren saved space was by handling with the maximum
brevity the hundreds of people with whom Franklin associated, including the most intimate. The character and appearance of Franklin's wife
is summarized in a few sentences. People he met in the world are almost

always identified only by their place in that world and shown exclusively in their connection with Franklin. Thus baldly stated, this might appear a blemish, yet it is the gift of an artist to turn necessary restrictions into advantages. The spotlight being shone so exclusively on Franklin, his character stands out with particular vividness.

The true Franklin as here revealed is, as is commonly the case with historical characters who have entered the realm of mythology, very different from the man envisioned by popular legend. One cause is that Franklin is commonly characterized as a "philosopher"—Van Doren uses the word endlessly in the eighteenth-century sense—and the word has changed its meaning. Today we think of a philosopher as a withdrawn intellectual surrounded in his hermit's study with tomes that summarize past wisdom, building mental "systems" that aim at rationalizations of the universe or are at least brilliant quibbles. No man was ever less withdrawn from the world than Franklin. He was given to quibbles, but, far from being mental, they were satires aimed at influencing immediate events. Van Doren gives no evidence that Franklin was concerned with building into his creative life the wisdom of the past. Toward times gone by he could indeed show an irreverence as outrageous as Mark Twain's: "I confess that if I could find in any Italian travels a recipe for making Parmisan cheese it would give me more satisfaction that a transcript of any old stone whatsoever."

The eighteenth-century conception of a philosopher survives in the idiomatic phrase, "He is my guide, philosopher, and friend." A philosopher was a man who accepted rationally and dealt intelligently with the actualities around him. George Washington wrote that he would like to see the great armies of Europe drill, but, as that was not possible, he would be "a philosopher" and not repine. The steamboat inventor, James Rumsey, stated in 1789 that he had no doubt his latest contraption would succeed as he had "all the philosophers on my side."

Franklin, whose formal education was almost non-existent, was an exemplar of Yankee ingenuity carried to its highest power. From their first arrival on this continent, Americans had been faced with problems toward the solution of which neither established traditions nor techniques offered much help. They were inclined to examine a situation from every angle and then conclude, off the cuff, what to do about it. Franklin read in learned journals of a new force that had been discovered, electricity. He decided to play with it, as many philosophers at that time did, and both his curiosity and his ingenuity became involved. By fixing things this way and that way and speculating on the results he invented new apparatus and concocted practical explanations. His relationship to a man evolving in the wilderness a new way to fence in his cows is revealed by the fact that he made no rush to gain publication and credit for his discoveries. He reported them in letters to his learned friends, as the fence builder might advise neighbors struggling with the same problems. Some of the capers with which he titivated his mind he did not bother to write down. We know of his famous experiment with a kite, a key, and a thunderstorm from an account written by one of his friends to whom, after the passage of fifteen years, he had reminisced about the experiment orally.

The other main misconception about Franklin, which goes hand in hand with the misunderstanding about the word philosopher, is the belief that because Franklin spent so many of his middle years as an American representative in Europe, and because he had so many European friends, he became fundamentally Europeanized. He did learn great sophistication in relation to European manners, how to best achieve his ends with an aristocratic statesman or an aristocratic belle, but he was famous in France not for the exquisiteness of the lace at his wrists but for the American fur hat he conspicuously wore at occasions where no one else would dare appear in such an outlandish thing.

The American Revolutionary generation was far from modest in relation to Europe. They believed that in fighting the Crown they were defending the English liberties which Englishmen had become too degenerate to fight for. They believed that they were evolving and establishing conceptions of liberty that would reform the whole world. That was the time when the Pennsylvanian Benjamin West, and the American painters around him in London, extended traditional artistic conceptions in a series of esthetic inventions that were highly influential in European art for another half-century. West was elected by English artists, with the approval of George III, president of the Royal Academy.

Franklin's success abroad was based less on his conforming than on his not conforming. He became among the French, who had decided to humble Britain by supporting the revolting colonies, the enchanting symbol of the cause they could not help being dubious about.

Van Doren writes that Franklin "would have preferred to keep America independent of the rest of Europe as well as England. But for the sake of the Revolution, he went to France for European aid in getting free of Europe. . . . A cosmopolitan who had most of his dearest friends in England and France and was himself more renowned in Europe than America, he moved boldly to separate the new republic from the parent continent." He warned his European friends, although regret-fully, not to emigrate to America where they would be hopelessly out of place, but to which he returned eagerly as soon as his duties in France were over, although he feared that, because of his illnesses and age—he was then seventy-nine—he might die on the voyage.

Back home, serving as President of Pennsylvania and playing an im-portant role in the Constitutional Convention, Franklin longed for France, as for a beautiful mistress from whom he had separated because her way of life could not also be his. Van Doren quotes, " 'It is true, as you observe,' he told Madame Lavoisier, 'that I enjoy here everything that a reasonable mind can desire.' Yet all these things 'do not make me forget Paris and the nine years' happiness I had there, in the sweet society of a people whose conversation is instructive, whose manners are highly pleasing, and who, above all nations in the world, have the greatest perfection in the art of making themselves beloved by strangers. And now, even in my sleep, I find that the scenes of all my pleasant dreams are laid in that city and its neighborhood.' "

This passage of lyrical prose was written when Franklin was eighty-two. He lived to be eighty-four. What a wonderful old man: Van Doren moves with his protagonist to the very end with an eloquence that is sympathetic, understanding, informative, moving, and very real. *Benja-min Franklin* is a great biography.

George Washington in Print and on Television

Since I have been assigned to talk about my biographies of Washington in relation to the television play that is based upon them, I must first define the volumes themselves.[*] I started out with the idea of writing a one-volume biography, but finding the subject so rich and so complicated, I ended up with four volumes that were published between 1965 and 1972. Then I decided that by hitting the high spots and relying on the four volumes to supply documentation and greater depth, I could do one volume after all, which I called *The Indispensable Man*. The television script, however, as has been pointed out in almost every public statement that has been made about it, is based on the larger set, particularly the first two volumes. We all hope for another show, based on the last two.

Before I began my labors on Washington, I had published eleven books on American history and biography, and Washington made a small or a large appearance in many of these. It was as though I had met him again and again, each time in a different social milieu. I became fascinated by the fact that the man I encountered was never the man described in the books I read. I decided that when I was old enough I would write a biography of Washington. Then, the distinguished publishers Little, Brown quite independently asked me to write such a life, and I decided I was old enough.

When I told people that I was working on Washington, I was almost invariably asked how, after two centuries, there could possibly be anything new to say. Had I uncovered a mass of new source material? As it turned out, I was to discover a good many new documents, some important, but that was not the point. The emphasis placed on new documentation is an aspect of conventional scholarship that too often results

---

[*]An earlier version of this essay appeared in *Biography and Books*, ed. John Y. Cole (Washington, D.C.: Library of Congress, 1986), pp. 47–52.

in distortion. The discovery tends to be emphasized by the discoverer out of all proportion to its role in the entire record.

My intention was to read every known document—whenever it was found and however seemingly trivial—that Washington had written, and also all other papers that Washington's acts or correspondence indicated would prove significant to his career. Of course, although this is often overlooked by documentary historians in their search of what they consider hard facts, hardly anything a man writes fails to reveal aspects of his character. It was my hope, as it has been for all of my books, to join in a coherent narrative both personality and the events that shaped or were shaped by that personality.

At the start, I resolved to clear from my mind, by an act of will, everything I had previously heard about Washington: I did not know whether he was a genius or a pompous dullard, whether he was a noble or an evil man. Thus, by a stroke of will, I banished all the myths and misunderstanding, special pleadings, social theories (usually contemporary to the times of their origins), all the venal and crackbrained anecdotes that have accreted around Washington down the generations. The losses of valuable insights that might result from my working plan could be considerably ameliorated by recourse to Douglas Southall Freeman's monumental seven-volume life of Washington. Since that work was built by a brilliant scholar on material gathered by a large foundation-supported team, I could use Freeman's source references as divining rods to point at the best among the many, many thousands of secondary sources. And my method of starting, as it were, anew did give me the tremendous advantage, which is reflected in the television script, of viewing Washington with fresh, unencumbered eyes.

The devil did dangle a lucrative possibility before me. Particularly when I was writing on Washington and the American Revolution at the time of the Vietnam war, there was great pressure on me to dwell on parallels. Had I been willing to do so, I could have appeared on the best talk shows—I was invited—and could have relied on at least doubling the sale of my book. But had I given in to pressures to make my work, as it was put, "contemporary," the biography would be out of date now, and the current show would never have existed. The script and the subsequent acting have preserved the tone I maintained of adhering to eighteenth-century realities without any distortions or detours undertaken to reflect contemporary issues.

I pursued my research and my writing unblinkingly, without suppressing anything. Fortunately, there was in the Washington record nothing grievous to suppress. I moved so far from the accepted marble image, however, that I foresaw attacks from conservative patriots. As it turns out, the conservatives fell in behind me because they were glad to have the father of our country presented as a man whom other human beings could love and admire. The attacks came from the left, from radicals who wished to tear down American institutions and thus resented having Washington depicted as anything but a bugaboo.

Actually, although the presentation of Washington in my books and in the television script seems today to be a novelty, it is far from being that. Understandably, considering my method which carried me back altogether into the eighteenth century, I ended up with the evaluation of Washington, both as a person and as a public figure, which was that of his contemporaries, agreed to, after his death, even by those who had been violently opposed to him. Starting from an impartial position, I concluded that Washington was both lovable and one of the greatest leaders in the history of the world.

As my volumes were published, one after another, they were subjected to a certain amount of sniping, but they were, considering their departure from contemporary convention, made surprisingly welcome. Even the Washington-haters did not mount a coherent opposition. I received a Pulitzer Prize and a National Book Award. Sales, although not tremendous, were respectable and continuous. I was, of course, gratified, but wished that what I believed was the truth about Washington could travel beyond readers of serious books. Then I heard from my lawyer that a producer named David Gerber wished to buy television rights.

The most common question I am now asked is how far I have had the power to control the television presentation. The question is fundamentally a naïve one, since contract provisions of that nature cannot in practice, except in extreme cases, be enforced. I, myself, have no legal right whatsoever to dictate to anyone concerned with the production. Yet I have been consulted to a degree which, considering the experiences of many of my friends, is remarkable. The basis for cooperation has been a meeting of minds among people who have, each in his own sphere, the same objectives, who have come to like and, most importantly, respect one another.

I was not consulted at first, which may well have been an advantage, as I would probably have objected to the great emphasis that was being placed on Washington's life before the Revolution. But when I saw the script for the first two hours I realized how well these early years, when he was not pressed by great events, were being used to depict Washington's character.

I took it upon myself to send the scriptwriter, Richard Fielder, a long series of suggestions, both large and small, even presuming to give advice not only on factual matters but as a fellow writer. Instead of being annoyed, Fielder felt I was being helpful. We had considerable back-and-forth both by mail and by telephone, and eventually he came to New York and we went over the final script together, line by line. We ended up with the fewest possible number of disagreements.

It is proverbial that historical consultants and television writers get into confrontations that are damaging to the result, however they are resolved. One reason that Fielder and I got on so well was, I am sure, because we are both members of what the English historian J. H. Plumb calls "the republic of letters." He respected me in my line, and I respected him in his. I had, indeed, in my younger days written some television dramas that were aired by CBS—as part of the "Omnibus" show, supported by the Ford Foundation—and I was conscious of how the playwright's art differed from the book writer's. The playwright has actors as additional tools and can make use of silence, something that is closed to a book writer. It is very difficult, however, for the playwright to express general ideas without elaborate and time-consuming dramatization or soliloquies that bring action to a halt. Fielder and his colleagues opposed having an introducer like Alistair Cook—I confess I fancied myself in that role—or any voice-over. They argued that either would keep his play from standing on its own as a work of art.

Basic to my agreement with Dick Fielder and many others was a shared sense of dedication to what we all feel is a noble cause. As the project grew with production, this conviction went beyond Fielder to the producer, David Gerber, the director, Buzz Kulik, whom I have come to regard as my good friend, Barry Bostwick, who plays Washington, and the other actors, who have not only listened to my advice but asked for it, the executives at General Motors and their advertising agency, N. W. Ayer, and the personnel involved at CBS. We all felt that we were in a position to make a real contribution to American life.

Behind the almost evangelical air that sometimes seemed to prevail as the screening went on is a conviction that the fundamental values of the Founding Fathers are invaluable today in the United States—and, indeed, the world—and are under serious attack. We are engaging in no propaganda or arguments but are aiming to present the truth in one specific but vital area. We are trying to give back to America the Father of Our Country as the person he actually was.

The television show we have in preparation is not a history lesson, although it may well propel thousands of Americans to such lessons. It is an effort to delineate truthfully the character of a man who occupies a place in every American psyche, who is more than any other the human embodiment of the American flag. Away with the fallacious cherry tree, with wooden false teeth that never existed! We hope to reveal, in his youth and middle age, a man who was known in his own generation as "amiable," possessed of charm and magnetism and great physical prowess. A man who taught himself to be the person his highest ideals made him wish to be, who learned from experience to be a triumphant general and had within himself the possibility to become, as president, a leader for all the world to follow toward freedom, the democratic process, and the self-determination of peoples. A man who, although assaulted like all of us with the temptations of flesh and ego, achieved, through will power and magnanimity, a greatness that when fully revealed will shine as a guiding light down the years.

MARTHA WASHINGTON

Martha Washington was neither beautiful nor brilliant.* She lacked artistic skill, except perhaps in fine needlework. The letters she wrote were an incoherent jumble of affection and gossip. When her husband was Commander in Chief or President, she showed no interest in strategy or government. Yet, if superlative ability in one direction is considered genius (as is the case with poets and painters), Martha Washington was a genius. No person could have had a greater gift for human relations.

It was this gift that raised her into the Virginia aristocracy. As Martha Dandridge, she belonged to a family that was moderately prosperous but obscure. This changed when she met John Custis, one of the richest and most correct men in Virginia, who was half-insane. Custis continually blocked the efforts of his son, Daniel Parke Custis, to make a suitable marriage. Daniel was growing into lonely middle age when he met Martha. Diminutive, plump, with well-cut features in a gentle face, the eighteen-year-old girl did the impossible. She charmed the wicked father into allowing his son, then thirty-seven, to marry her. When her husband died eight years later, leaving her with two children, she was the richest young widow in Virginia.

Enter a huge man more than a foot taller than Martha and a few months younger. Aged twenty-six, George Washington was a French and Indian War hero. Earlier, as commander of Virginia's forces, he had year after year defended the frontier from Indian raids. But his personal life was a disaster. He had long been in love with the wife of his neighbor and close friend. Though there is no way of knowing whether or not it was actually consummated, his passion for Sally Fairfax brought him more frustration than satisfaction. It also brought him a deep sense of guilt. His marriage to Martha, undoubtedly an effort to escape, was sweetened by the fact that her property raised him to the top level of Virginia planters.

There is evidence that the marriage at first went badly. But who could

---

*An earlier version of this essay appeared in *TV Guide*, October 18, 1975, pp. 24–25.

long resist Martha? She overcame the serious handicap that the union
was childless, persuading Washington that marriage was "the most interesting event of one's life, the foundation of happiness or misery." Its
contribution to his happiness was not excitement—he had plenty of that
in his public career—but "domestic felicity." Martha became the only
human being to whom he revealed the diffident inner core of his being.

Martha's natural turf was Mount Vernon, where she could enjoy Virginia plantation life. She dangled from her belt the practical symbol of
domestic control: a sunburst of keys. Outdoor work was left to the husband. The smokehouse, the kitchen, and the mansion house were Martha's domain. She was particularly expert at curing. "You know,"
Washington wrote when he sent Lafayette a barrel of hams, "Virginia
ladies value themselves on the goodness of their bacon."

But that was not where Martha's real interest and genius lay. Both she
and her husband felt melancholy unless Mount Vernon was crowded
with guests. Martha exulted and excelled in being a hostess. "She possesses," wrote a French visitor, "that amenity and manifests that attention to strangers which render hospitality so charming."

To be pulled out of the plantation atmosphere was for Martha a sorrow, but her husband was drawn into the great world and needed her so
desperately that she had to follow. In explaining her annual rides during
the Revolution to wherever the army was in winter quarters, she wrote,
"The poor General was so unhappy that it distressed me exceedingly."
When his wife was beside him, Washington was able to forget all the
horrors and rigors of a war which it often seemed would never end
unless by the complete defeat of his inadequate army. In this way Martha
helped her husband to win the independence of the United States.

After the war, Martha was convinced that she and her "old man," as
she called him, would stay at Mount Vernon for the rest of their lives.
The Constitutional Convention cut into her happiness like a burning
knife. Then came the Presidency. Martha was too upset to accompany
Washington to his inauguration. And when she did reach the capital at
New York City, she remained resentful, all the more because her official
position hampered her movements: "There are certain bounds set for
me which I must not depart from. And, as I cannot do as I like, I am
obstinate and stay at home a good deal." At Mount Vernon, Martha
made her own decisions about whom to visit and whom to entertain. In
New York, Washington's wishes and Presidential protocol had to be
considered.

But what genius can resist the ultimate opportunity to practice transcendent skills? Her husband's ambition was to be everyman's President, leading an almost unanimous nation. But a struggle arose between the Jeffersonians and the Hamiltonians that could not be resolved and Washington came under violent attack. Martha, however, achieved her husband's ideal by remaining everyone's First Lady. She listened appreciatively and rattled away with friendly good humor that made her companions, wherever they were, feel completely at home. The diminutive lady helped her beleaguered husband to lead the Nation, as she walked the most conspicuous of stages, by making every person she met her friend.

HISTORY

How a Madman Helped
Save the Colonies

August 22, 1777.* The militia had marched and been defeated. Behind the stockades of the New York frontier, many widows wept, not for their dead husbands only but for their still living children. The invader, Lieutenant Colonel Barry St. Leger of His Majesty's Thirty-Fourth Foot, did not lead a civilized army; his troops were largely cruel Iroquois. In star-shaped Fort Stanwix on the banks of the Mohawk a few militiamen remained in arms, but a tunnel dug under the direction of British engineers approached the mud walls to the sound of scalping knives being sharpened. Casting around for a source of hope, the settlers found no comfort in the fact that Hon Yost Schuyler, a half-insane Tory in feathers, was raving by the hostile council fires.

Three weeks before, the fort's 750 defenders had watched 800 Tories and British regulars and roughly a thousand Indians surround the wilderness clearing in which Stanwix stood. That night great shadows of primeval trees, thrown by a hundred campfires, flickered and interwove. If, as a patriot looked over the walls, his head was silhouetted against one of the encircling fires, muskets cracked.

At the present site of Rome, New York, but then far beyond the confines of ordinary settlement, Stanwix guarded a wilderness entry to the embattled colonies. Northward ran Wood Creek, the narrow watercourse through almost unbroken forest down which St. Leger had traveled from Canada; eastward the Mohawk stretched 110 miles to Albany and the populous Hudson Valley.

For a century and a half, settlement on the Mohawk had been impeded by the Iroquois nations that were now besieging Stanwix. The few villages huddled around stockades into which the inhabitants could flee with their cattle when war whoops sounded. Yet mansions stood by themselves surrounded with ornamental grounds, for the great families

---

*An earlier version of this essay appeared in *American Heritage*, 7, No. 2 (February 1956), 26–30, 101.

of the region had little to fear from the Indians. They had achieved their eminence through control of the Indians, whom they had now persuaded to join the Tory cause. St. Leger's Iroquois irregulars were commanded by members of the Johnson and Butler dynasties, one of them, Sir John Johnson, both a Mohawk chief and a British baronet.

These were cultured gentlemen, often educated in Europe. Associated with them in the Indian command was Hon Yost Schuyler, one of the coarsest and most disreputable inhabitants of the valley. Good patriot blood flowed in his veins—his father was a cousin of General Philip Schuyler; his mother, a sister of General Herkimer—but Hon Yost's parents, in the manner of frontier black sheep, had found their most congenial society among the Indians. As poor according to European standards as the tribesmen among whom they lived, these renegade Schuylers would have fallen into complete insignificance had they not the good fortune to produce in Hon Yost a son who was considered mad. Rising to strange exaltations, raving in unknown tongues, he appeared to the Indians to be in special contact with the supernatural powers, a prophet who spoke for the Great Spirit.

Hon Yost had adopted the manner and dress of his admirers. Adherents of the patriot cause despised him for this and for everything, but the Tory aristocrats employed the awe he inspired to increase their influence over the tribes; his lunacy was tempered by the ability to make his inner voices serve the interests of his friends. Prophesying to order, the madman was one of George III's more useful American supporters. He was to become, against his will, even more useful to the United States.

The invasion in which he was engaged was an added menace in a situation which had already cast gloom over the thirteen revolting colonies. The British seemed about to cut the nation in half at the Hudson River. St. Leger was scheduled to join up with a much larger British force that General Burgoyne had already led from Canada via Lake Champlain. The northern American army, commanded by General Philip Schuyler, was falling back before Burgoyne; it had not even attempted to defend Fort Ticonderoga, on which all defense plans had been based. Nor could Washington come to the rescue with the Continental Army, for he had to watch a third British force, under General Howe, that was based in New York City and might march up the Hudson to join the other two.

If St. Leger overwhelmed Stanwix, as seemed probable since his army so outnumbered the defenders, he could sweep on to Albany, cutting General Schuyler's supply lines and leaving him in the wilderness north of that city at the mercy of Burgoyne. Schuyler having been defeated, St. Leger and Burgoyne could march down the Hudson toward Howe, giving Washington the choice of abandoning the strategically invaluable river or being himself caught in a pincers.

Even before St. Leger had appeared from the forest, Washington had been in despair at Burgoyne's seemingly irresistible advance. The best he could suggest was that Schuyler's command be reinforced by one general, Benedict Arnold. The treason that was to change Arnold's fame to infamy lay in the unforeseeable future; he was the most brilliant combat officer either side boasted, and miracles could be expected of him, as he had done miracles before.

As they prepared desperately to stop Burgoyne's force, which was much more powerful than their own, Schuyler and Arnold relied on the militia of the Mohawk Valley to handle St. Leger; but on August 6 the militia, under General Herkimer, was defeated by the Iroquois at the bloody ambush of Oriskany. Arnold volunteered to set out with a few regulars—no more could be spared—to try to enlist from the shattered militia of the valley the thousand additional men that would enable him to drive St. Leger back into the Canadian forests. "You will hear of my being victorious or no more."

Cut off from the outside world, the garrison of Fort Stanwix did not hear that Arnold was endeavoring to save them, but St. Leger took care to notify them that Herkimer's force had been stopped. The three British officers appeared at the walls under a white flag, demanding a parley. They were blindfolded before they were led through the defenses, and only allowed to see again in a room where the blinds were drawn. Candles relieved the unnatural gloaming; a table was set with bottles of wine. For some minutes, the ritual of social call was adhered to, and then Major Ancrum delivered his sinister message. The Indians were "very numerous and exasperated"; if the fort surrendered at once, the British could control them, but should resistance continue it would be impossible "to prevent them from executing their threats to march down the country and destroy the settlement with its inhabitants. In this case, not only men but women and children will experience the sad effects of their vengeance."

"This garrison," the patriot commandant replied, "is committed to our charge. . . . After you get out of it, you may turn round and look at its outside, but never expect to come in again, unless you come as a prisoner."

The Tory officers who led the Indians thereupon signed a proclamation to the inhabitants of the valley: if the defenders of Stanwix adhered to their "mulish obstinacy," the Iroquois would "put every soul to death—not only the garrison, but the whole country—without any regard to age, sex, or friends; for which reason, it has become your indispensable duty to send a deputation of your principal people to oblige them immediately to what, in a very little time, they must be forced— the surrender of the garrison—in which case, we engage, on the faith of Christians, to protect you from the violence of the Indians."

The resulting terror was so great that Arnold, whose name usually worked like magic on militia levies, was able to add only some hundred frontiersmen to the few regulars he led. The fighter who would take any risk that promised a faint chance of success, who tried to capture the great fortress city of Quebec with a handful of men in a blinding blizzard, could not disagree when his officers voted to halt at German Flats (Herkimer, New York) and await reinforcements from some direction which hope said must exist, even if it was not visible.

The crucial reinforcement arrived unheralded and unrecognized, raving and in irons.

The Tory officers had become so bold that they held a recruiting rally behind the American lines. The principal speaker was Ensign Walter Butler; he was captured with the madman, Hon Yost Schuyler. Arnold appointed a court-martial which sentenced them both to death as spies. After the verdict, a wave of sympathy swept Arnold's local officers for Butler—they had been to school together—and Arnold was persuaded to send him to Albany for imprisonment.

But Hon Yost had no friends in Arnold's army to save him from the gallows. He was allowed to twitch and writhe unpitied, until bursts of female wailing advanced through the countryside, and a gypsy-like woman threw herself at Arnold's feet in an excess of grief and entreaty. Copious tears made pale valleys down her unwashed cheeks. Behind Hon Yost's mother stood a stolid young man who looked like an Indian: Hon Yost's brother, Nicholas.

As the madman seconded his mother's pleas, Arnold noticed that a vein of shrewdness seemed to direct his ravings. Arnold, his light eyes burning with menace from his dark face, asked Hon Yost if he could use his special powers to make St. Leger's Indians flee. Instantly the shouting ceased and the meeting got down to efficient business. Hon Yost expressed complete confidence in his ability to save Fort Stanwix; Nicholas agreed to remain as a hostage until the result was known. Having borrowed a musket, Hon Yost shot several holes through his clothes to give color to a story of a perilous escape from Arnold's camp. He threw down the musket and disappeared with the tireless lope of an Indian.

To help things along, Arnold wrote a letter addressed to Stanwix's commandant, but designed to fall into British hands. The militia, he lied, had flocked to him to make his force irresistible. "Howe with the shattered remnant of his army are on board ship . . . in the Gulf Stream becalmed. Burgoyne, I hear, this minute is retreating to Ty [Ticonderoga]. I have no doubt our army, which is near 15,000, will cut off his retreat."

At Stanwix, the situation had become desperate. Zigzagging forward, always at an angle that frustrated colonial marksmen, a British trench had advanced to within 150 yards of the northwest bastion. There the trench stopped, but continuing activity indicated that the enemy was digging a tunnel to place mines beneath the wall. When night fell, Ely Pixley and Ely Stiles dropped silently from the patriot ramparts, crawled past Indian sentries, and hurried eastward to report that help must come at once or it would be too late. Somewhere in the blind forest they passed Hon Yost, now accompanied by some Oneidas sympathetic to the patriot cause. Neither party saw the other.

When Pixley and Stiles beat on Arnold's door, his force was still hardly more than half of St. Leger's. However, he "determined to hazard a battle rather than suffer the garrison to fall a sacrifice." Before his little army lay thirty miles of wagon track and corduroy bridges so hemmed in with virgin forest, so thick with underbrush, so dark even at noonday, that the most painstaking care might not save these alert soldiers from ambush.

On the morning of August 22, St. Leger, surrounded with officers, chiefs, and interpreters, was happily surveying the approach to Stanwix for the best spot from which to ambush Arnold; it was an embarrassment of riches. He received scornfully Indian runners who came from his camp with rumors that kept increasing the size of Arnold's command. Only when a terrified Iroquois reported that "Burgoyne's army was cut in pieces and Arnold was advancing with 3,000 men" did St. Leger, as he remembered, begin "to suspect cowardice in some and treason in others." He hurried back to his encampment.

During St. Leger's absence, Hon Yost had burst into an Indian council, raving so loudly that it was clear he brought an all-important message from the Great Spirit. At first, no sense could be made of his babbling; then he pointed to the holes in his clothes and gave an account of his own escape. Only when anticipation was at fever heat did he begin to report on Arnold's army. Its might augmented as prophecy fell increasingly upon him, until he asked his hearers to count the leaves on the trees. Arnold's force was even more numerous; the tribes were doomed if this army once descended on them.

At a prearranged cue—Hon Yost had staged his production with care—an Oneida appeared matter-of-factly with a belt of wampum, which he said was from Arnold. He announced that the great Christian war chief had no quarrel with the Indians; if they would desert the British, they would not be harmed. Then the woods seemed to open. One after another, Oneidas rushed in, each with a more grievous tale. The last told of a talking bird which had croaked from a dead tree that the Indians had better flee before it was too late.

St. Leger had Hon Yost brought before him, but could not terrify the madman out of his ravings. A hastily called council of chiefs broke up at the news that 200 Indians had already deserted. Then an Iroquois deputation demanded immediate retreat; Arnold's army, as numerous as the stars, was within two miles. (Arnold was still at German Flats, preparing to march.)

Now certain that treason was afoot, the British commander refused to withdraw. At this, the Indians rioted, rifled the officers' baggage, seized the royal supply of rum, and became, so St. Leger remembered, "more dreadful than the enemy." There was no time to dismount cannon, pitch tents, or even awaken a sleeping bombardier. The invaders lurched for the forest.

Whooping horribly, the Iroquois encircled their fleeing allies; they killed and scalped stragglers. Nor were regulars who kept a semblance of formation saved from aboriginal tricks. An Indian would rush up to a platoon and shout that Arnold was just behind the nearest clump of trees. Taking off like sprinters, the soldiers jettisoned their packs, which the Indians plundered at their leisure. The British officers became frantic with humiliation and rage. They bandied recriminations, and would have skewered each other on their swords had they not been separated by the efforts of the Indian chiefs.

Hon Yost savored the excitement and encouraged the confusion—he was not above a little plundering himself—but he did not forget that his brother was a hostage. Eventually he abandoned the rout and vanished into the wilderness.

The madman had already vanquished the British when Arnold's troops set out grimly on the march they believed would throw them against terrible odds. After they had gone ten miles, a messenger appeared from Stanwix. He told how the defenders had become conscious of a strange hush in the British camp. When a cannonading induced no reply, a detail cautiously explored the deserted tents where dishes were still in place, the silent battlements where ammunition lay ready. They happened at last on the sleeping bombardier, but he was as puzzled as they. Evening had fallen before Hon Yost danced across the clearing to say that Arnold was on the march.

Even then the defenders of Fort Stanwix, who had been nerving themselves for a last-ditch fight, did not realize the incredible truth that victory had come—through the ravings of a madman.

British strategy was completely disrupted. Due to incompetence in the London War Office, Howe did not receive orders to advance up the Hudson from New York City until he had already committed himself to an attack on Philadelphia. The relief of Fort Stanwix completed the catastrophe by leaving Burgoyne in the wilderness above Albany unsupported. Furthermore, the flight of St. Leger's army did much to destroy the legend that the British regulars were invincible. Militiamen who had been hesitating by their firesides picked up hunting guns and swelled the northern army until Burgoyne and his British regulars were hopelessly outnumbered.

Hon Yost's prophecies were thus an important link in the chain that led to Burgoyne's surrender at Saratoga. Burgoyne's surrender finally persuaded the French that the Americans were worthy allies, and the French alliance made possible the victory at Yorktown which forced George III to acknowledge the independence of the United States.

Although he might have ranked, on performance, as a patriot hero, Hon Yost continued to hate the patriots. As soon as he had secured his brother's release, he rejoined the enemy; he took part in later raids on the Mohawk Valley. After the war, he lived with the Oneidas. That his reputation as a mediator with the supernatural powers remained unimpaired is revealed by his last appearance in recorded history: with the approval of the tribe, he tomahawked two Indian women to death as witches.

THE MOST UNFORGETTABLE LETTER
I HAVE EVER READ

The most humanly revealing letter I have found in my twenty years of research on American history is one written to Benedict Arnold by his sister Hannah seventeen days before the traitor met the British agent, John André, on the banks of the Hudson.

Daughter of a drunken, bankrupt father, Hannah Arnold developed as a young girl hero worship for her slightly older brother. She was handsome and charming, but failed to encourage most suitors—and the one whom she did encourage Benedict frightened away at pistol point. She came to live with her brother in New Haven where, when he was away on merchantile voyages, she handled his tempestuous business affairs. For a while, she was pushed aside—Benedict took a bride—but the marriage was unhappy and the wife died. Foster-mother to Benedict's three little ones, Hannah ran the general's house during the years in which he shone as a hero.

Crippled at Saratoga, embittered, and heading for disgrace, Arnold became commandant at Philadelphia. By the time Hannah joined him, he had set up an impossibly extravagent establishment and was moving in high Tory-minded society. He soon bundled two of Hannah's little charges away to school, and married a fashionable beauty, Peggy Shippen, who was young enough to be his daughter. Without Hannah's knowledge—she was a firm patriot—Benedict and Peggy offered their services to the British.

When Arnold secured the command at West Point with the intention of betraying it, Hannah and her sister-in-law were left behind in the Philadelphia house. Peggy continued to communicate through the British lines with André, received nervous letters from her husband, wondered every hour if the treason had been consummated, and was feverishly gay. Finally, she decided to join Benedict and be in at the kill. He sent his dandified aide, Major Franks, to get her.

As she set out for West Point and one of the greatest dramas in all American history, Peggy carried to her husband, without knowing its contents, a letter from his sister. It shows that Hannah, who had become an old maid in her brother's service, sensed, without guessing the truth, that something was terribly amiss:

Hannah Arnold to her brother, Benedict Arnold

Philadelphia Sept. 4th, 1780

Am once more set down my Dear Brother to ask you how you do? and to thank you for your three kind letters from Wt. point. Fashions I know nothing about: I have not a yuse of such knowldege—scandal I hate, and ever did—and ill nature I leave to you, as you have discovered yourself to be a perfect master of it witness yours of August 18th, 1780—as you have neither purling streams, nor sighing swains, at Wt. point 'tis no place for me—not do I think Mrs. Arnald, will be long pleas'd with it, though expect it may be rendered dear to her (for a few hours) by the presence of a certain chancellor [Robert R. Livingston]; who, by the by is a dangerous companion for a particular lady, in the absence of her husband; I could say more than prudence would permit—I could tell you of frequent private assignations, and of numberless billet doux, if I had an inclination to make mischief, but as I am of a very peaceable temper I'll not mention a silible of the matter.—your neighbor Mr. Md is or pretends to be very unwell he sees how matters are going, and will make sickness a pretence for discontinuing his visits, there's policy in war, you know—as for parties I have scarcely been in any, but at our house.—we have had one large and two, or three small ones, since your departure; the weather had been so violent, it has been as much as I could do to live, without seeing company.—

Marriages I know nothing about; deaths are very frequent but I know so little of Phila, that I know not whose,—we had letters from the little boys two weeks ago, poor fellows, they write in a most gloomy style, and appear to be exceedingly unhappy; their letter made me quite miserable for two, or three days, I am afrid to hear again for fear I should hear they had taken the same step as James Shippen did. they are not so old as he, and if they should 'tis not so much to be wondered at, they have always been us'd to the greatest kindness, and to have their necessary wants supplied, which I dare say from concurrent testimony, is not now the case—as for news of an(y) kind, must refer you to Mrs. Arnald and Major Franks, if they have none they can make you a little my word for it.—

Adieu—god bless you, give Edward [the baby] one hundred kisses for me and I shall miss the little dog terribly.

H. A.

The American World Was Not Made for Me

Alexander Hamilton's contribution to welding the thirteen semi-independent states which had won the Revolution into a unified political entity was greater than that of any other Founding Father, with the exception of Washington.* But this tells only half the story. The other half is that while Hamilton's genius built national unity, his psychic wounds caused disunion which was also absorbed into the permanent structure of the United States.

Hamilton's lack of balance was such that his greatest contributions were realized only when he was working side by side with another statesman, also brilliant but more stable. He had two major collaborators: James Madison and George Washington.

At the Annapolis Convention of 1786, Madison changed into what was almost a new document the over-aggressive and over-visionary summons Hamilton had drafted to call up the Constitutional Convention of 1787. And Madison was a collaborator on the *Federalist Papers* in which Hamilton supported and explicated, with such lasting effect, a Constitution that he had opposed as too mild and in which he was never really to believe. Hamilton's most impressive solo flight took place shortly thereafter when he dominated New York's ratifying convention, persuading that crucial but reluctant state to join the other states in the by then already established union.

Washington's role as what Hamilton called "an aegis essential to me" was divided into two extensive phases. Hamilton's most important contributions to winning the Revolutionary War were carried out as Washington's aide. And the achievements which have given Hamilton his greatest fame came, some years later, when he was Washington's Secretary of the Treasury. Then, he carried to fruition the fiscal reforms he

---

*An earlier version of this essay, entitled "The American World Was Not Made for Me: The Unknown Alexander Hamilton," appeared in *American Heritage*, 29, No. 1 (December 1977), 70–77.

had been advocating in vain for so long: payment of debts to the public creditors; the establishment of long-range federal funds which guaranteed that the government would stay indefinitely financially afloat; the chartering of a private national bank with federal support. He created all the institutions then needed to balance the lopsided agricultural economy, making possible a strong and permanent nation. In his *Report on Manufactures*, which was too far ahead of its time to receive Washington's sanction or pass Congress, Hamilton prophesied much of post-Civil War America. And, by a brilliant report to Washington that eventually won almost universal conviction, he established the doctrine of "implied powers," which unshackled the Constitution from its exact wording, enabling the government that rests upon that Constitution to change with the times, satisfying the needs of new generations as they come and go.

After Hamilton had resigned from Washington's Cabinet, he made his last major contribution, paradoxically in closer collaboration with his long-time chief than he had been since he had served as a youthful military aide. Putting on paper Washington's ideas, with which he had become so familiar through years of association, he drafted another of America's basic documents—Washington's Farewell Address.

Hamilton was born, almost certainly in 1757, on a British West Indian island, probably Nevis. His childhood experiences have been viewed by his biographers in a distorting light engendered by their affections and their desire to have their hero's career appear respectable throughout. Around the undeniable fact of his illegitimacy there has been constructed a saga of a warm homelife lived out in affluent surroundings. An impartial re-examination of the evidence turns the accepted story upside down. Not affluence is revealed but scrounging and relative squalor; not warmth within the home but fighting, the expulsion of the father, the betrayal of her illegitimate sons by the sexually wayward mother. Hamilton's position in the world was thus defined in local court documents— "obscene child." Having no true home to go to, standing up to obloquy, to silent sneers and surely open taunts from other children in the street, Hamilton learned to fight and to despise his fellow humans, and nurtured an ambition to prove himself immeasurably superior to them all.

As a shift in the grounding alters a projectile's flight, so the truth about Hamilton's childhood propels the biographer into previously unscanned skies. It becomes manifest that Hamilton appeared from the Leeward Islands to serve the emerging United States as by far the most psychologically troubled of the Founding Fathers.

Hamilton, who had been as a child, through no fault of his own, considered an outcast, brought with him to America an attitude, fundamental to his thinking, that was not shared by any other of the Founding Fathers: the conviction that the human race was not only unworthy, but to him a personal enemy that must be fought and conquered. This gave rise to his basic pugnacity, the adversary turn of mind that played such a major part in his successes, so major a part in his failures.

Hamilton had no experience of America before he arrived in New York in 1773 at the age of sixteen. Immigrants can fall in love with their new homes, becoming more vociferous patriots than many birthright inhabitants, but this was impossible for a youth already firmly conditioned to scorn and distrust his fellow man. Hamilton hugged to his breast the sensational opportunities offered by the environment where chance had thrown him, but he never appreciated or bothered to understand that environment. Thus, if he wished to be for once discreet and conciliatory, he did not know how to go about it. Much is explained by a statement he made when, as Secretary of the Treasury, he was at the height of his career and influence: "Though our republic has only been in existence some ten years there are already two distinct tendencies— the one democratic, the other aristocratic." The people of the United States, Hamilton continued, "are essentially business men. With us agriculture is of small account. Commerce is everything." How wrong he was in his assessment of the primarily republican and agrarian nation was soon revealed when he and his party were submerged by the Jeffersonian tide.

Had Hamilton cared, he would undoubtedly have learned how to analyze popular opinion. But he did not care. His weapon was the sword. In his romantic dreams it was a physical sword. But neither his body nor his true gifts were martial. The sword he was born to wield was forged in the brain.

Almost all people allow their primitive drives to be suppressed by prudence. Statesmen in particular think thrice before they act. Hamilton inspired wonder and also vicarious satisfaction by the freedom with which he slashed around him. But such a champion is truly valued only on his own side of the battle line. On the far side, sharpshooters squint through their sights to bring him down.

In realizing, during the Revolution, that the difficulties of the emerging United States were increasingly financial and governmental and in seeking apposite solutions, Hamilton was far from alone. In fact, the inexperienced and extremely busy military aide appeared on the scene

later than others. But he attracted attention (particularly among historians) by adopting extreme positions and putting on paper what others
considered it impolitic to disseminate. Every reform has such outriders,
although rarely persons as brilliant as Hamilton. To assess their effect is
difficult. They implant presently unpopular ideas in many minds, but at
the same time impede the efforts of more practical reformers to proceed
step by acceptable step.

Hamilton's pessimism about human nature did not extend to himself
or .to those who demonstrated what he considered their ability and integrity by agreeing with what he himself considered revealed truth. He
could thus share in the enlightenment doctrine of progress. Where Jefferson believed in the perfectibility of mankind, Hamilton believed in
the perfectibility of the few who were the rightful leaders of mankind.
Considering himself the leader of leaders, he was reluctant to make his
visions impure by compromising with the imperfect ideas that were acceptable at the moment. Progress, he believed, would demonstrate that
he was altogether right. Then a new generation of the most brilliant,
able at long last to carry Hamilton's inspirations to fruition, would follow
the torch Hamilton had lighted and kept unsullied.

The man whose youthful ambition had been for "literary pursuits"
published in newspapers and often as pamphlets hundreds of political
and polemical essays, almost invariably urging his compatriots to action.
These sallies covered a wide range of prophetic possibilities. At their
most achievable—as in such fiscal and constitutional ideas as he was in
his lifetime able to put over—he was in the vanguard, as he had wished
Washington would let him be in battle, of columns already forming
which were in need of such leadership. In his practical but visionary
phrases—as in his *Report on Manufactures*—he was defining the future.
But others of his ideas—such as his recommendation at the Constitutional Convention that the President and the senators should be chosen
for life by an electorate limited to the prosperous—were too alien to
America to have a chance of realization.

Hamilton's prophecies, whether practical or extreme, sounded together through the same eighteenth-century air, the grievously unpopular and wild discrediting the immediately advantageous and sane. His
Report on Manufactures seemed to the agrarian majority to reveal Hamilton as another Lucifer revolting to create a money-changers' hell. And
Hamilton's speech at the Constitutional Convention encouraged his opponents to diagnose monarchical scheming, although his financial pana-

cea exemplified middle-class conceptions which were to prove the greatest enemies of kings.

Hamilton enjoyed inciting contention. When Jefferson showed him portraits of Francis Bacon, Isaac Newton, and John Locke, saying that these were the greatest men in history, Hamilton replied that in his opinion the greatest man that ever lived was Caesar. There was no integral reason for his financial recommendations to be coupled with expressions of disdain for the common man. Nor was it necessary for the West Indian from a most dubious background to set up himself and the self-made money-men who were his followers as an American elite in opposition to the traditional aristocracy, as represented by inheritors of land such as Madison and Jefferson. In fact, Hamilton could hardly have sponsored necessary reforms in a manner more divisive.

In order to get his first set of financial plans through Congress, Hamilton was ultimately forced to make a concession to the South by agreeing to the location of the national capital contiguous to Virginia, but from this he learned no lesson. His plan for the Bank of the United States, the measures he proposed for fostering manufactures, flew—without any concessions—straight in the face not only of the Southerners, but also of the farmers who formed the vast majority in the United States. He outraged Jefferson by saying to him that corruption was an essential aspect of effective rule. Jefferson's reiterated accusation that Hamilton was subverting the federal government through a bribed "corrupt squadron" was only a paraphrase of one of Hamilton's often-stated contentions: federal financial institutions would stabilize the nation by cementing to the central power rich men whose prosperity would depend on federal authority.

One of Washington's greatest gifts to the founding of the United States was his perpetual concern with quelling dissension, drawing to the national standard every individual who could thus be drawn. This had been essential to winning the Revolutionary War, since, in the long run, the British could triumph only by dividing the patriot cause. His Excellency so controlled his young military aide that Hamilton got into no controversies of any sort, committed no indiscretions, while serving officially at headquarters. But as soon as Hamilton stepped into a private role—whether it was through unguarded statements at a drinking party in Philadelphia, or in yearning for an angry revolt, or his sometimes hysterical leadership in Congress—his fierce aggressions appeared.

As the President, Washington became the head of a government completely untried, supported by only a small majority of the people, with two of the thirteen states still unconvinced and staying outside. An administration that would pull together, that would create ever-mounting national unity was the overwhelming need, and this Washington established so effectively that Jefferson wrote, on belatedly arriving to become Secretary of State, "The opposition to our new Constitution has almost totally disappeared. . . . If the President can be preserved a few more years, till habits of authority and obedience can be established generally, we have nothing to fear."

Before Congress authorized the cabinet, Madison, who was in the House of Representatives, was Washington's closest adviser. To the Cabinet, Washington appointed the best men he could find, including Jefferson and Hamilton, who had previously not known each other. Madison, who was close to both, brought them together, eager to encourage what he assumed would be, under Washington's broad wing, a warm and fruitful partnership. Jefferson and Madison rescued Hamilton's first set of financial schemes by arranging the deal concerning the national capital.

Then came Hamilton's utterly unconciliatory recommendation for the Bank of the United States, which seemed to Jefferson's and Madison's Virginia constituency a naked power play in favor of men they saw as foreclosers of mortgages. Jefferson and Madison, still thinking in terms of cooperation, went along until the bill had passed Congress and was on the President's desk for signature. Then Madison, suddenly taking alarm and seeing no other way to prevent the signing, turned about-face on the doctrine of "implied powers," which he had supported in *The Federalist*. He tried vainly to persuade Washington to veto the bank as unconstitutional, since the establishment of such institutions had not been specifically provided for.

Thus began the famous fight, between Jefferson and Madison on one side, Hamilton on the other. Hamilton already had a newspaper, supported by Treasury advertising, that was his personal organ. With Madison's conniving, Jefferson gave Philip Freneau a job in the State Department that left him time to edit an anti-Hamiltonian newspaper. Freneau, also a born fighter, went for Hamilton like an angry hornet. Hamilton retaliated. As the charges and countercharges went back and forth, Washington became not only upset but puzzled. Convinced that there was no real basis for controversy, he could hardly believe that his two ablest Cabinet ministers were at each other's throats.

Washington wrote both Hamilton and Jefferson in almost identical terms: "Without more charity of the opinions and acts of one another in governmental matters; or some more infallible criterion by which the truth of speculative opinions, before they have undergone the test of experience, are to be forejudged than has yet fallen to the lot of fallibility, I believe it will be difficult if not impracticable to manage the reins of government or keep the parts of it together. . . . My earnest wish and my fondest hope therefore is that, instead of wounding suspicions and irritable charges, there may be liberal allowances, mutual forebearances, and temporizing yieldings on *all sides*. Under the exercise of these, matters will go on smoothly and, if possible, more prosperously."

Then came the wars of the French Revolution. Jefferson, regarding the upheaval as a continuation of the American struggle for liberty, was determined to support France in her conflict with aristocratic England. Stressing not the reforms but the excesses of the French Revolutionaries, and, in any case, led by considerations of national finance to favor cooperation with the greater naval power, Hamilton preferred the British cause. The result was a major controversy within the United States which deeply disturbed Washington. He believed that the correct role of the United States was an even-handed neutrality, and appealed to both Jefferson and Hamilton to keep the nation free from foreign entanglements that might lead to war.

Was Washington right in his belief that, with good will on both sides, the controversies that wracked his administration were unnecessary? There are reasons to think so. Despite daily donnybrooks and opposite brinkmanships, Hamilton and Jefferson were forced by the realities of the situation to agree that keeping out of the Anglo-French wars was greatly to the American advantage. And Jefferson, as President, continued Hamilton's financial measures, including the Bank of the United States.

Why then fight; why did not Washingtonian unity prevail? It is difficult, when the facts concerning Hamilton are in, not to see a trail leading back to the Leeward Islands.

Although Jefferson could be adept, and sometimes devious, in defending himself and what he considered the interests of the people who were his constituents, he was not a dedicated fighter. He had been a failure as wartime governor of Virginia. When he became President, he ran the country not by controversy but by manipulation. And Madison, despite a tendency to vociferous outrage, would rather read a book and think a thought than take part in a row. It was Hamilton who relished hand-to-hand fighting.

A really first-class fight requires, of course, already existing differences that can be incited. The divide along which the Hamilton-Jefferson belligerence developed had long worried Washington, whose election as commander in chief had in part grown out of it. (Since the Revolution was then being fought in New England by an exclusively New England army, Continental rivalry required a Southern, preferably Virginian, commander.) The South and the Northeast were naturally suspicious of each other, in part because of opposing economic interests. Endeavoring to reconcile all differences, Washington had hoped to hand on to his successor a profoundly united nation. He failed, and surely the major blame for this failure can be attributed to Hamilton, who exacerbated conflicts and suspicions that were, as generation followed generation, to eventuate in the Civil War.

All myths to the contrary, President Washington was not led by his Secretary of the Treasury. Nor was he—at least until, when an old man, at the very end of his battered second term—a partisan of the Federalists. Yet his value to Hamilton was immense.

Having suffered through the Revolutionary command (neither Jefferson nor Madison had been with the army), Washington realized how greatly the emerging nation needed, in order to be self-sufficient, a sound, central financial structure. His attitudes toward Hamilton's innovations were thus admiring and supportive. This persuaded Hamilton's opponents that they would have to reduce Washington's prestige in order to overthrow Hamilton. The tactic boomeranged. Hamilton and his supporters were enabled to reassure the American people by claiming identity with the long-time leader who was resolutely loved.

The seven years between Hamilton's appointment as Secretary of the Treasury and Washington's retirement from the Presidency were, indeed enchantingly fulfilling, the most fulfilling of Hamilton's career. Washington was to him no longer the all-controlling father he had been as commander in chief. Hamilton was now more truly self-confident; the scene was now much larger; Hamilton now possessed his own special field of knowledge.

As when he had been commander in chief, President Washington felt no desire to lead Congress. Although that body was now an integral part of the process over which he presided, he was so devoted to the separation of powers that he believed the President should not interfere with the functions of the legislators. His clear constitutional duty was to point out areas that required action and to decide, at the end of the legislative process, whether he would sign into law the bills that had been passed. Beyond that he was unwilling to go. This left a power vacuum into which Hamilton leaped, setting up, before Jefferson realized the possibility, his own block in Congress. For a while, Hamilton led Congress, and throughout Washington's Presidency, he remained puissant among the legislators.

It made Hamilton's role easier that the President admired his fiscal plans and operations, while his opponents lacked the financial know-how to interfere in more than a bumbling and usually ineffectual manner. Another opening for Hamilton in his pursuit of power was provided by the fact that Washington thought of his Cabinet as a unified body. Each secretary was given for administrative purposes his own specialty, but major decisions were made, under the President's final authority, by the Cabinet as a whole. This allowed Hamilton, who was endlessly energetic, intelligent, hardworking, and full of determination to move across the board, interfering in particular with foreign policy. When he could not operate openly, he went underground, communicating behind Washington's and Jefferson's backs with the British minister.

Hamilton, however, preferred to move with the maximum of visibility. Part of his satisfaction came from having all eyes upon him while, as an individual champion, he achieved, or seemed to achieve, heroic deeds. Jefferson was at first so far behind in these lists that it was Hamilton himself who made the Virginian a public figure by selecting him as the most conspicuous target of his resounding attacks.

Those were the years when Hamilton's youthful fantasies came almost altogether into being. Powerful men were his sycophants; women adored him; and if he made a flood of enemies, that was, as long as he could overcome, an integral part of his triumphant dream. Then the music stopped.

After Washington's retirement from the Presidency, Hamilton's life proceeded in directions which he could not traverse with pride or even with personal satisfaction. He had reached an eminence which demanded that he become, if there were not to be a letdown, the next President of the United States. But his warrior approach had made him so unpopular that even his greatest admirers realized he could not hope to achieve a top post in an elective government. To compound his plight, he had, in his determination to shine alone, failed to attract to himself followers of possible presidential stature. Where Jefferson, succeeded by his intimates Madison and Monroe, was to exert power in the Presidency for twenty-four years, Hamilton had no surrogate. When Washington announced his retirement, the Federalists nominated, to run against Jefferson, the archetypical New Englander John Adams, who owed nothing to Hamilton and was repelled by the West Indian's sword-waving flamboyance. After Adams had succeeded to the Presidency, Hamilton was reduced to the mean expedient of plotting behind the President's back with members of the Cabinet.

Then there arose the fascinating possibility that Hamilton might find escape from a "groveling" situation through the phenomenon he had longed for in his first known letter—a war. And from his point of view the right war—against France. The pendulum of foreign policy having swung toward England, the French were threatening to attack the United States. Congress voted to enlist a federal army. By intriguing mightily, Hamilton secured the post of second-in-command, which was in fact more than that, since Washington, the titular commander in chief, was far beyond his prime. Hamilton, who never achieved any deep satisfaction from his lucrative practice of the law, abandoned everything to lie with and preside over the embryo army. He inscribed such masses of "routine and even petty and trivial" orders that the indefatigable editors of the normally exhaustive Hamilton papers decided that to print more than a few samples would be a waste of time, ink, and paper.

Hamilton had visions of leading the army against the Spanish Southwest and perhaps even annexing part of South America to the United States. But Adams had never really wanted the army—he thought a navy a better defense—and had been outraged at being maneuvered into appointing Hamilton, whom he deeply mistrusted. The more orders the major general sent out in a mounting frenzy, the fewer soldiers there were to be efficiently organized. And then Adams, without consulting his Cabinet, which he now realized had been infiltrated by Hamilton, made peaceful overtures to France, abolishing the threat of war and exploding forever Hamilton's visions of military glory.

In 1799 the Federalists renominated Adams. In pain and outrage, Hamilton wrote a voluminous attack on Adams—more than fifty printed pages. Yet he preferred his Federalist rival to his ancient enemy Jefferson; he ended by urging his readers to vote for Adams anyway. He was, indeed, so upset by the indications of a Jeffersonian victory that he suggested to John Jay, the governor of New York, a method for stealing that state's electoral votes. Jay indignantly refused.

After Jefferson had won the election, the failure of the Constitution to distinguish between votes in the Electoral College for President and Vice President opened up a possibility for frustrating the will of the people by seating in the Presidency not Jefferson but the vice presidential candidate, Aaron Burr. Of the two, Hamilton despised Burr more; he opposed a Federalist drift toward using this loophole.

After Jefferson was seated, the Northeastern Federalists considered his Presidency so overwhelming a menace to all that was good and decent that they discussed taking their states out of the Union. Now Hamilton fought for the Union, helping to suppress the move toward succession. As part of this campaign, he intervened successfully to prevent Burr from becoming governor of New York.

Hamilton was still powerful in his own party in his own region; he still had his law practice to fill his mind to the extent that things which did not basically interest him could—but how small was the stage compared not only to what he had dreamed of, but to what he had once achieved!

The interaction of Hamilton's temperament with his formative experiences had not prepared him to create or enjoy a satisfactory private life. Although he yearned to escape from his storm-tossed ambitions to a warm and peaceful home, no walls that he could build were long impermeable to outside tempests; nor, even at home, could he keep from engendering troubles. Throughout his life, he continued to write his wife, Betsey, in the high style of romance and perfect love which had characterized his letters during their courtship. Again and again and again he stated that his one wish was to desert the great world to be forever at her side. Although Betsey insisted that she adored her husband, the evidence hardly points to a contented marriage.

Betsey became an extreme neurasthenic, grasping desperately, like a shipwrecked sailor, at supports that she feared were not steadfast enough to keep her head above the waves. She was often sick from nerves, and she was further separated from her husband's active life by a long succession of pregnancies. Apart from miscarriages, with which she was regularly threatened, she bore eight children.

After her husband's death, Betsey's health seems to have improved; she lived to be ninety-seven, a most redoubtable old lady. During her fifty years of widowhood, her husband was all her own: he could escape her no longer. Summoning various men to be his biographers, she repelled them all by her possessive effort to dictate what they should write. She even engaged in a lawsuit with one of her dead husband's most intimate colleagues to gain possession of papers which she believed would enhance her husband's reputation. Not until Hamilton had been dead for thirty-six years and Betsey was very old was a biography of Hamilton written—by their son, John C. Hamilton. It was reverent in approach and exaggerated in claims.

That the living Hamilton had been a dedicated and accomplished pursuer of women was implied by the documents of his young manhood and became standard gossip during his years of fame. How much Betsey heard or suspected, the records do not tell, but we know that two situations were forced on her attention. A close friendship went on, for all their relations and friends to see, between her husband and her dashing sister Angelica, who wrote Betsey in 1794, "I love him very much and, if you were as generous as the old Romans, you would lend him to me for a little while." Did Betsey believe Angelica's further statement that the wife need not "be jealous" since all the sister wanted was to "promote his glory" and enjoy "a little chit-chat"? In any case, the wife remained emotionally dependent on the sister.

Hamilton himself made as public as anything could possibly be what he asserted had been his affair with Maria Reynolds. He had engaged in financial dealings with this lady's disreputable husband which came to the knowledge of his political enemies. They concluded that James Reynolds had been serving as the Secretary of the Treasury's agent in buying up, at a low price, certificates which Treasury policy would make valuable, the owners to be swindled having been identified from Treasury records. To demonstrate that he had not been engaged in peculation but had, in fact, been paying blackmail, Hamilton published a pamphlet displaying a liaison with Reynolds's wife. The accepted judgment on his behavior is that expressed by Allan Nevins in the *Dictionary of American Biography*: the revelation "had the merit of a proud bravery, for it showed him willing to endure any personal humiliation rather than a slur on his public integrity."

Assuming only sex and blackmail were involved, Nevins's explanation would be the basic one. But overtones inevitably sound in the ears of someone who has from the start followed Hamilton's dilemmas. All that the situation had required of Hamilton was that he demonstrate enough factual information about the liaison and the resulting blackmail to convince the public. But Hamilton included in his pamphlet, which ran to ninety-five pages, the entirely unnecessary statement that he entertained Maria in his own home, and quoted entire love letters in which his paramour expressed the extremities of passion for him, and an almost suicidal despair when he neglected her. As one reads on and on, a feeling grows that there was a personal need behind all this quoting. Was Hamilton, probably unconsciously, identifying Maria with his mother? Was he trying to overcome unslaked humiliations by putting himself, as publicly in the great world as had been his disgrace in his childhood environment, triumphantly in the role of his mother's lovers who had incited his impotent jealousy and rage when he had been a child?

Not everyone was convinced, then or now, that Hamilton was in fact guilty of infidelity rather than some activity he was hiding. His contemporary tormentor, James Thompson Callender, wrote, "Those letters from Mrs. Reynolds are badly spelt and pointed [punctuated]. Capitals also occur in the midst of words, But waiving such excrescences, the style is pathetic and even elegant. It does not bear the marks of an illiterate writer."

When I myself was making preliminary survey of the Hamilton material, before I realized that any questions had been raised about the Reynolds affair, I was struck by the resemblance between the perfervid style attributed to Maria and that authentically used by Hamilton in his love letters to his fiancée and then wife. The modern historian Julian Boyd has pointed out that, despite urgings and expressed doubts, Hamilton kept hidden from all reliable eyes the originals of the letters he was willing to publish so widely. If Hamilton did write these love letters to himself, the implication of childhood fantasy is overwhelming.

There is no reason to believe that whatever love affairs Hamilton did have brought him anything but temporary surcease. And his legitimate family life mounted to a double tragedy. He had brought up his eldest son, Philip, according to his own ideas. And at the age of eighteen, Philip, having himself picked the fight, challenged to a duel a political enemy of his father's. Probably close to the spot on the Jersey Highlands where the father was to be mortally wounded, Philip received a fatal wound. We are assured by Hamilton's grandson, Allan McLane Hamilton, who was in his own lifetime famous as a doctor for the insane, that the shock of Philip's death drove Hamilton's second child—she was named Angelica after her aunt—over the edge into an insanity from which she never recovered, although she lived to be seventy-three.

Hamilton had, of course, his circle of male admirers—politicians and businessmen of ability, wealth, and influence—who accorded him all the esteem that, as a scorned and then disinherited youth, he had so passionately desired. But he could not translate this admiration into what he even more desired: power. Power not for its own sake, not for the license it gave to destroy, but for the opportunity to create order and system, to build. He had a vision of the perfect state, a vision orderly when he could hold onto his passions, and for a time it had seemed that he could turn that vision into reality. He could not foresee that his conceptions, which he believed had been defeated, would rise again, achieving in later generations dimensions in many ways above his most ambitious dreams. Before his living eyes the nation was dissolving into what he considered chaos—and he had lost the power effectively to intervene.

The French statesman Talleyrand became intimate with Hamilton during two years of exile in America and then returned to France to dominate, as Napoleon's foreign minister, European international affairs. He wrote, "I consider Napoleon, [the British statesman, Charles James] Fox, and Hamilton the three greatest men of our epoch, and if I were forced to decide between the three, I would give without hesitation the first place to Hamilton. He divined Europe."

Should Hamilton have settled in the Europe he had divined? Had it been an evil wind that had blown him from the Leeward Islands to a continent where the people, those vicious clods who had been his enemies since childhood, could prevent a man of vision from grasping the power he needed to achieve personal glory and also bring into being what he knew was best for everyone?

In 1802, Hamilton wrote his friend Gouverneur Morris, "Mine is an odd destiny. Perhaps no man in the United States has sacrificed or done more for the present constitution than myself; and contrary to all my anticipations of its fate . . . from the very beginning, I am still laboring to prop the frail and worthless fabric, yet I have the murmurs of its friends no less than the curses of its foes for my reward. What can I do better than withdraw from the scene? Every day proves to me more and more that the American world was not made for me."

A long-envisioned way out was left to him. He had written John Laurens, a friend now dead these twenty-two years, "I have no other wish than as soon as possible to make a brilliant exit." Aaron Burr had sent him a duelist's challenge. Although Hamilton admitted that dueling was the worst way of determining the justice of a quarrel, such encounters were part of the military, the ceremonial, the chivalric world. He would expose his body to Burr's bullet, but himself fire in the air.

On July 11, 1804, a bullet entered Alexander Hamilton's liver. The next day he died in great pain.

AMERICAN HISTORICAL MYTHS: JEFFERSON, HAMILTON, AND WASHINGTON

The extent to which special pleading has altered American historical reality cannot be better exemplified than by what has happened to the popular images of Jefferson, Hamilton, and Washington.

Jefferson is today considered to have been radical; Hamilton, conservative. This reverses historical roles. Social evolution was during their lifetimes moving away from the old aristocratic power structure based on the ownership of land to such a business society as Hamilton prophesied and that we have today. Jefferson wished that the money men then in Congress could be prevented, while agrarians and slaveholders voted freely for their own interests, from having any vote on fiscal matters.

Regarding cities as dens of iniquity, Jefferson tried to sink the beautiful plan for the national capital, designed by Pierre Charles L'Enfant with the backing of Washington, because it envisioned a metropolis rather than an enlarged rural village, like Virginia's capital, Williamsburg. However, legend assumed that Jefferson, as an acknowledged architect, was responsible for the extensive beauties of Washington, D.C.

Jefferson is considered the godfather of the New Deal and the other governmental social programs that followed. Actually, Jefferson would have been horrified by such accretion of federal power. He believed that the better the government, the less it interfered with how people conducted their lives, and that federal authority should rigidly respect states' rights. It was Hamilton who argued that the activites of the people needed to be controlled for their own good, and who advocated such a domineering federal government as modern "liberalism" has built.

Jefferson's eloquent expositions of the rights of man (as a slaveowner he did not include slaves) and his advocacy for the agrarian majority made him a popular hero in his lifetime. Hamilton's deification came after he was dead when businessmen took over the lead in American society. He was their obvious historical symbol, but his actual achievements, great as they had been, were not considered sufficient. Being themselves looked down on by older social groups, the possessors of new wealth wished their symbol to have been from birth a fine gentleman. But Hamilton had been illegitimate and a pauper. Myth was fabricated to change the squalor of his upbringing into high society and, erasing his illegitimacy, presented his wayward mother, who was for a while jailed for promiscuity, as a maltreated paragon of virtue.

Furthermore, the tycoons wished to justify their new and resented national power by having their symbolic father almost single-handed create the United States. This required shameless faking of history! As aide-de-camp at headquarters and Secretary of the Treasury, the mythological Hamilton steered in the right directions the dim-witted Washington. Their hero, they contended, invented the federal union and personally put it over. Anyone who has had the temerity to set out on a quest for a true understanding of George Washington undertakes a perilous adventure that requires climbing over hallucinary mountains and penetrating ghost-ridden forests. When in old age under attack by enemies who wished to discredit his policies, Washington wrote hopefully, "By the records of my administration and not the voice of faction I hope to be condemned or acquitted hereafter." The records voluminously remain, but his hopes have been only partially realized.

Basic to the phantasmagoria are two major roles that he has been assigned in the American psyche: first as "The Father of Our Country"; and the second as the human equivalent of the American flag.

Sigmund Freud has described how "infantile fantasies" concerning people's own fathers can shape their conceptions of historical figures: "They obliterate the individual features of their subject's struggles with internal and external resistances; and they tolerate in him no vestiges of human weakness or imperfection. Thus, they present us with what is in fact a cold, strange, ideal figure instead of a human being to whom we might feel ourselves distantly related." This exactly describes the marble image of Washington which has been made even more grotesque by the fallacious insertion into his mouth of wooden false teeth.

The confusion of the human Washington with the American flag has altered his image in differing ways down the years. When the people are happy with their nation, as they were during most of the nineteenth century, Washington was deified. When, as in more contemporary times, people are disillusioned, they enjoy suspecting Washington's integrity, even to the extent of welcoming with enthusiasm the false charge that as commander in chief he anticipated modern crooked business practice by cheating on his expense account. During this down phase, many have sought in Washington's presumed misdeeds justification for their own bad behavior. Mount Vernon has been plagued by visitors demanding to be shown the fields where Washington grew his marijuana crop. Washington, we are told, was known as "the stallion of the Potomac"; no pure woman could without danger be left alone in his presence. The famous English historian Arnold Joseph Toynbee vented his spleen concerning American disobedience during the Revolution by stating that Washington died because of a chill received while he was visiting a tasty black adolescent in his slave quarters. There is no evidence that Washington ever had sexual intercourse with a slave.

Innumerable are the legends that were fabricated and widely disseminated during the nineteenth century when his prestige was so high that zealots of all political and moral persuasions forged Washington's endorsement for whatever cause they wished to dignify. The reigning genius in this endeavor had been was Parson Weems whose *Life and Death, Virtues and Exploits of General George Washington*, an expanded Sunday School tract, went through more than eighty editions. Feeling a need to spice up the fifth edition, Weems invented a morality play about a cherry tree and little George, with a hatchet and an inability to lie. For generations, this goody-goody tale has darkened Washington's public image.

Alas, the most prolific forgers of statements for Washington have been ministers of the gospel. It sometimes seems that Parson Weems's biography has had almost as many successors as there have been poor parsons with flocks of children to feed. Propagandists for every variety of Christian belief have written for Washington prayers tailored to fit their particular sects. During the period after President Kennedy's assassination, when the air waves were devoted to nothing else, researchers desperate for material exhumed for broadcasting one spurious "Washington prayer" after another.

Great circulation has been given to an account attributed to a Quaker (who, it has been demonstrated, happened not to have been there) that at Valley Forge he had seen Washington lying on the ground, tears flowing from his eyes, as he called on God. This has resulted in a church's being built on the designated spot. The truth is that Washington, like Franklin and Jefferson, was a Deist. He avoided the word God, preferring "Providence," which he called sometimes he, sometimes she, and sometimes it. This did not mean that he was not, according to his own lights, a highly religious man.

Evidence presents a very strong presumption that Washington was, although not impotent, sterile: Martha had had four children in quick succession by a previous husband, but none by Washington. This has not prevented pretentious persons who have been troubled by a hole in their genealogy from insisting that the missing ancestor was George Washington, whose name had been omitted by later ancestors as a patriotic act.

Idolators of Hamilton, who have insisted (wrongly) that Washington had treated their hero as if he were an adopted son, have slipped over into postulating that Hamilton was in fact Washington's son. The future President had, as a young man, in truth gone to the West Indies where Hamilton was born, but at an altogether wrong date.

A major booby trap for a Washington biographer is the proud belief that "George Washington slept here." When a neophyte, I would benevolently inform hostesses that Washington had never been within a hundred miles of the place, and then (metaphorically) I would have to flee for my life. Now I smile and say nothing. Members of old Southern families outdo Northern claims by confiding that their ancestresses had refused Washington's proposal of marriage.

But perhaps the ultimate myth has been confided to me by two Southern blue bloods, independently of each other: Martha had revealed to one of their forebears that George Washington was, although he dressed like a man, actually a woman. A probable source for this can be ascertained. During the Revolution the Tory press teased the Rebels by printing that Washington had been seen unawares wearing petticoats.

The prevalence of misinterpretations concerning our major historical figures need not make us uneasy concerning the attitudes of our people toward our society. However fallacious, our historical symbols have never been codified into such a consistent myth as totalitarian governments use to lead the people astray. Contradicting each other, they blunt their impact, becoming no more than expressions of the diversity essential to a free society.

How strongly the true historical principles of the United States are still operative was recently revealed by an event that came to Americans so naturally that they did not realize that they were enacting a prodigy in history. Our head of state, the President of the United States, still in full legal possession of his powers was, because he violated traditional American values, forced out of office without the firing of a shot.

WASHINGTON AND SLAVERY

The record in relation to George Washington is a conspicuous demon-stration of how black history has been neglected.* One example: the two-volume index to the thirty-nine–volume set of Washington's *Writings* specifies almost everything except the names of slaves.

Ignoring this aspect of Washington's career has not only allowed "revi-sionist" historians, who have substituted their preconceptions for investiga-tion, to call Washington a racist, but it has also warped our understanding of major events not obviously connected with Negroes. History, for in-stance, has not realized that Washington's support of Alexander Hamilton's financial schemes against the protests of Jefferson was partly motivated by his desire to encourage an alternate economic system to slavery.

The first Virginian President met his greatest opposition in his home state. When an old man, he told a visitor: "I clearly foresee that nothing but the rooting out of slavery can perpetuate the existence of our union, by consolidating it on a common bond of principle." He foresaw the Civil War. Although exile from his ancestral acres would have torn his heart, he confided to an intimate that, if the issue became inescapable, "he had made up his mind to move and be of the Northern."

Washington had grown up in a Virginia which regarded slavery as preordained. (Not invented for blacks, the institution was as old as his-tory and had not, when Washington was a child, been officially chal-lenged anywhere.)

As a young planter, he felt no guilt. But before the Revolution broke, he had become so unhappy about trafficking in human beings that he could no longer bear to sell a slave, although natural increase was giving him a larger work force to support than he could profitably employ. In 1774 he wrote, drawing no racial distinctions, that, if the white Ameri-cans submitted to British tyranny, "custom and use shall make us as tame and abject slaves as the blacks we rule over with such arbitrary sway."

Washington's stint as commander in chief kept him in the North most

---

*An earlier version of this essay appeared in *The New York Times* on Thursday, February 22, 1973.

of eight years. Recognizing in a business economy a viable alternative to the slave-based agrarianism of his own background, he seriously considered disentangling himself from what he could not justify by selling his slaves and using the proceeds as investment capital. But such sales would have bothered his conscience, and he had been buoyed through so many hardships by the dream of reclaiming the peace he had known as a planter at Mount Vernon.

The Revolution won, Washington hoped that the American experiment—new, radical, unique—would serve as a model for the freeing of all mankind from kings and tyrants. Europeans asserted that, since people were incapable of ruling themselves, the natural harvest of republican government was anarchy. Refuting this contention required national unity—and no issue could be more divisive than slavery. Putting first what he considered the more comprehensive battle for freedom, Washington limited himself to stating that, if an authentic movement toward emancipation could be started in Virginia, he would spring to its support. No such movement could be started.

The thinking of Virginia's favorite leader, Jefferson, had moved oppositely from Washington's. In his younger days Jefferson had urged practical steps toward manumission, but, as he grew older, he receded into purely verbal libertarianism. He bred slaves for sale, and never freed more than a select few. His opposition to the financial measures Washington backed was to a considerable extent because he saw them as a menace to the Virginian way of life.

As the elderly President Washington was approaching the retirement which he had so eagerly anticipated, he made an effort to shatter his own ancestral way of life. He offered most of his Mount Vernon acres for rent. That his basic purpose was to be able to free every slave he controlled must, he confided, be kept secret for "reasons of a political and indeed imperious nature." He was already in enough trouble with the Virginia-led opposition.

A hitherto unnoticed letter (of which he kept no copy) reveals that, on his release from the Presidency, Washington secretly slipped some of his house slaves into freedom. The Mount Vernon acres did not rent, and Washington was unwilling to destroy his means of livelihood after so many years of public service. Furthermore, the very act of freeing all his slaves involved considerable obligations he would have to meet: the young blacks needed to be supported until they were old enough to work, the old and infirm for the rest of their lives.

Washington went no further with manumission during his lifetime. But in his will he freed all his slaves, with generous provisions for support.

WHY AMERICA WON THE REVOLUTION

The American Revolution was, like many conflicts that inflame the world today, multifaceted. An expeditionary force sent across the ocean by England implied a foreign war, the more because of the Hessian mercenaries. The Revolution was also a civil war, on not one but various levels. The patriots were revolting against their "rightful sovereign." In America, there was conflict between the loyalists and the rebels. The various states, which had as colonies always been kept by British policy politically independent of each other, did not find cooperation easy. And over all hung the perpetual danger of bloody confrontations inside the patriot cause between the haves and the have-nots, the conservatives and the radicals.

Toward victory in this multitude of conflicts, the determining battle-fields were not those we read about in history books: Brooklyn Heights, Germantown, Saratoga, or even Yorktown. The determining conflicts were tens of thousands of invisible engagements fought within the tiny compass of human skulls.

As could be foretold from the confusion of issues, the allegiance of the American people was far from settled when the war began, and it fluctuated as events unrolled. There were at the two extremes loyalists or revolutionaries so absolutely committed that they could not be budged, but the vast majority were pulled this way and that like small boats caught in a succession of whirlpools.

George Washington dreamed, of course, of a military stroke that would drive the invaders out of the continent, but he came to realize that, in the militarily indecisive conflict, the winning or losing of bat-tles—unless one was decisive—was primarily important for building up or losing public confidence. And, in the long run, the predominance of American popular opinion would determine the outcome of the war.

The British recognized only to a minor degree the importance of hold-ing or securing popular allegiance to the Crown. The ruling class suffered from abysmal ignorance of America, its geography, and its people. Throughout the several centuries of settlement, there had been no enticements in colonial life to lure across the ocean for any long period of time any Englishman of adequate status to have his voice audible in British governmental halls. Nor did the government take rising American unrest seriously enough to send over a commission or even one able statesmen to discover what was going on.

British aristocrats, of course, made money from America, but this had not induced them to visit there. Fine gentlemen did not sully their hands with business details. These they entrusted to social inferiors who also rarely crossed the ocean. They dispatched sea captains and super cargoes up southern rivers, and dealt in the north through loyal American merchants, usually native born, who in their prosperity regarded themselves as the American aristocrats.

In England the upper-class was so hemmed in by taboo that there were only three directions lesser birthright members of the aristocracy could follow if they were reduced to the straits of making their own livings: governmental service, the Church of England, or the armed services. None of these served to create truly informative contacts with America.

There were, of course, many governmental posts in the colonies to be filled. These were very useful in helping out with one of the clumsinesses of the British aristocratic system. Primogeniture, while preserving great families, concentrated wealth in a few hands. However, the actual inheritors had obligations to see that their younger brothers and other close relatives were taken care of somehow. An obvious solution for the support of poor relations, particularly those who drank and gambled too much, was to remove them from temptation by shipping them off to socially primitive America. It was understood that in their role as royal officials they would skim off enough revenue to make them no longer a burden on their families in England.

These upper-class office holders were interlarded in the colonies with bureaucrats of lesser rank and sometimes more ability. But they too had come to America to make money, and they were not inclined to damage their futures by showing any disrespect to the convictions of cabinet ministers who had never seen America.

In the Anglican Church, appointments were known (and still are) as "livings." They were fertile and much-desired sources of revenue. Once the persecutions, which had driven major divines from England to New England, faded, only ministers who could not get good jobs at home came to the colonies. The drinking of the Virginia clergy was a source of astonishment even to the bibulous planters.

Among the permissible upper-class pursuits there remained the armed forces and particularly, as far as America was concerned, the army. What garrison posts existed were, during peacetime, considered exile. But during the French and Indian War there was an influx of well-born and influential soldiers. They had acted on frontiers, and associated mainly with each other. In any case, the military mind is not tuned to the complaints of civilians, especially "inferiors." As the Revolution brewed, the principal adviser to the British government was Sir Jeffrey Amherst, who had been credited with winning the French and Indian War. He had despised the colonials, and was the epitome of an intolerant, narrow-minded martinet.

The advice of Benjamin Franklin, then resident in London, was scorned as he was considered one of the plotters. Much listened to in high places were those native-born Americans who held royal offices or were leading merchants trading with England. It was to their interest to be passionate loyalists. Wealthy, in a colonial sociey closely allied to the ruling country, they considered themselves the American aristocracy. Assuming popular support for their rank and all they stood for, they assured the Crown officials that the vast majority of Americans felt deep loyalty to the Crown. They were being terrorized by small but virulent groups of radical agitators.

The solution obviously was to· extirpate the agitators. Wishing to achieve this end as thoroughly and impressively as possible, the British dispatched to America the largest expeditionary force mounted by any power during the eighteenth century.

This military might drove Washington's inexperienced army before it as if they were overweening boys: out of New York City, all the way across and out of New Jersey, eventually out of the rebel capital, Philadelphia. But alas! Every British military triumph stirred up among civilians more enemies to the crown. Making little distinction between loyalist and rebel families, the English soldiers and particularly the hated Hessian mercenaries, who had been rented from German rulers, looted and raped. American prisoners of war were jammed into disease-ridden prison ships. Too prudent to go below, the jailors would daily call down the hatchways, "Bring up your dead!"

The British capture of New York City seemed a godsend to loyalists all over America who were having problems with the patriots. The Tory leaders sought refuge in New York, only to find themselves subjected to

a military government more oppressive than anything the patriot propagandists had succeeded in imagining.

While the British involuntarily helped, the patriot cause was burgeon-
ing from within, as much from instinct as from conscious thought. The
rebels themselves were coming only gradually to understand the basic
motivation for the acts that were to sweep them to eventual victory and
independence.

Vermont was as far from Georgia as England was from the tip of Italy.
Ever since they had been severally founded, the thirteen colonies had,
as they lay side by side on the long seacoast, lacked inner communication
except some between neighbors. Each colony had its own relationship
to the Crown, and lines of trade like those of politics had pointed across
the ocean to England. Yet the Americans from however far apart resembled each other more than they resembled Englishmen. They had been
made into a new breed by similar conditioning.

The settlement of the United States had been a continual process
of natural selection since almost every new arrival had committed the
revolutionary act of breaking with the long-established patterns of his
environment to toss himself into the unknown. And wherever on the
new continent he landed, a settler was faced with problems and possibilities that could not be dealt with by traditional recipes, that required
ingenuity, invention. The societies which the settlers created or which
they joined were not presided over by aristocracies or burdened with
almost impervious class lines. All freemen were presented with opportunities to rise. Shortages of land and food had given way to a superfluity,
narrow fields to seemingly boundless horizons. It was a land that called
for self-reliance, optimism, the freedom for which the revolution was
eventually to be fought.

The basic unity between Americans became more visible as the war
with England developed. George Washington caught on well enough to
recognize the forces that could be invincible. He sought to batter down
all impediments. He considered the still remaining rivalry between the
states more of a menace to winning the war than any belligerence Great
Britain had to offer. In his role as commander in chief (and in effect
chief executive since the Continental Congress was a legislative body),
Washington labored to bridge the gap not only between the various
colonies but also between the political left and right, making it clear to
all that their basic interests were in common. Individuals suspected of

being pro-British should not, so he argued, be persecuted; they should be drawn to the patriot cause by tolerance and kindness.

George Washington wrote and believed, "The misfortunes of war . . . to individuals are more to be lamented than avoided, but it is the duty of everyone to alleviate these as much as possible." Under his leadership, the Continental Army was inspired to respect the rights and property of non-combattants He annoyed Congressmen by his unwillingness to reduce the pressure on them to supply the army by requisitioning provisions from farmers at pistol point. He induced his soldiers to build from raw wood their winter encampment at Valley Forge because he was unwilling to add to the hardships of refugees from British-captured Philadelphia by billeting the soldiers in already crowded surrounding towns.

As the war advanced, the populace became more and more pro-patriot. This was of primary military importance. The only truly feasible method by which the British could pacify the extensive colonies was bit by bit: was to drive the "radical agitators" from one area after another, leaving behind garrisons which would help the "loyal subjects" protect themselves. Instead, disloyal subjects cooperated in extirpating the scattered garrisons. Washington's military intelligence proved to be ten times better than the British, since the neighborhoods through which the enemy marched kept him informed. And, if a British force got into trouble, as did Burgoyne's army near Saratoga, the population of the countryside rose against it like deadly-stinging swarms of bees.

In the Continental Army, there existed the most persuasive and the most emotional (all faced death together) intermingling of men from all over America. The soldiers were the first to recognize fully the emergence of a new American man. Washington realized that this recognition was a military resource far more important than the strategy taught in European books, than all the elaborate training and equipment the British invaders had brought with them across the ocean. The English soldiers, and even more the Hessians, had no interest in victory beyond personal advancement, spoils, and saving their own skins. There was a sharp limit to what they could be expected to do. But Washington's soldiers believed that they were fighting for a cause that was deeply their own, for the human freedom that had been inculcated in them by American land, for the self-determination of peoples as a noble principle applicable everywhere. They would accept any hardship of which the human body was capable. The success of the surprise attack on the Hessians at Trenton was made possible by the mercenaries' conviction that no army could be made to operate in such a storm.

History books, emphasizing battles, usually equate the winning of the Revolution with Cornwallis's surrender at Yorktown. However, that defeat would have been for the British a minor setback if the war had been going well. They had lost only a quarter of the troops they had in America. The most important circumstance that led to the debacle had been a freak: for a short time the French navy, although basically inferior to the British, had established dominance in American waters. This was unlikely to happen again: Admiral de Grasse had sailed away (as it turned out, never to return). Washington's army was still numerically several times smaller than the forces still available on the continent to his Majesty, George III.

The war dangled on for another year, but the British had in effect given up. They had come to realize that they could not subdue a people who were increasingly determined that they would not be subdued.

PICTURES FOR HISTORICAL PUBLICATIONS

Writers on history often regard the inclusion of illustrations as no more than a condescension to readers who should not be thus diverted from their own prose. A scholar who would shudder away from doctoring a quotation does not hesitate to reproduce any picture that comes easily to hand of an individual or an historical event. The illustrations they favor were often originally drawn for children's primers.

To simplify the process there have grown up commercial archives which defend writers from having to do their own pictorial research. I investigated one of the most successful. The proprietor, who recognized my name, was eager to display his wares. He was proud to have six renditions of Fulton's *Claremont*. Damn him, so I thought, I warned him that they were all spurious. Far from being grateful, he escorted me to the street and slammed the door behind me.

I joined with some of my colleagues in a campaign to induce historical writers to place illustrations on the same level as verbal quotations. We were getting going when libraries, museums, and historical societies decided that they had opened up a new source of revenue. Although they allowed quotation from documents free of charge, they added to the actual cost of the photograph a "reproduction fee." Although this does not faze popular magazines and advertisements, it is very destructive to conscientious scholars.

DRAMATIC PRESENTATIONS OF HISTORY

The scholarly community is naturally ambivalant about the fictionizaton or dramatization of history. Dedicated to citing facts for every statement, scholars have a natural suspicion of an art form invading what they like to make, as far as possible, a scientific study. Yet no scholar who is a humanist (as every scholar should be) should forget that much of literature—from the Greek dramatists through Shakespeare and Tolstoy to the present—has been created by the fictionalization or dramatization of history.

Those concerned with popular education must realize that most people are not susceptible to any dry scholarship. However, a history book that is well written can reach and persuade a large audience.

There is probably no scholar so withdrawn from the world that he would exclude all historical subject matter from dramatic presentation. The bind comes on the question of how far an historian should recognize and countenance the givens of dramatic form. There is no lack of scholars who believe that actors, accurately costumed for their period, should speak in paragraphs that could have been extracted from a learned journal. But such "dialogue," of course, could not be true to life or art.

Dramatic presentation must be in true dramatic form. It is obscurantism not to recognize that the means of the theatre are very different from those of the scholar's study or the printed page. Individual human beings move before the viewer, and thus action has to be presented in terms of personalities. These personalities cannot be abstractions. Any generalization has to be translated into the specific before it can be put on the stage. The appeal cannot be only to the intellect; it must also address the emotions. Nothing may appear before the viewer which the playwright cannot make convincing as an instantanous sensuous experience. And, furthermore, the theatre has its own tools that do not fit at all into the historian's hands: light as a physical entity; silence as a force in its own right; the impact of the actual physical presence of people and things; the use of "business" as a substitute for words. A scholar can only frustrate if he stands between a dramatist, director, or actor and dramatic art.

But this does not mean that the historian has to hide his face. Although he may not interfere with how the dramatic impact is achieved, he can and should demand that what this impact communicates is historically sound. Words must, of course, be put into the mouths of historical personages. Imaginary characters may be given secondary roles (which is much better than warping the roles of actual historical characters). Unimportant details and unsignificant timing may be altered for dramatic sequence. Anachronism should be avoided, not only in the obvious sense of not having George Washington send a telegram, but in the deeper sense of not attributing modern behavior and attitudes to the past. A particularly virulent form of anachronism is propaganda, which warps history to carry a contemporary message to glorify or debase.

THE HUDSON RIVER: ITS HISTORY, USAGES, AND RESULTING PECULIARITIES

The Hudson is unique, not matched in the variety and peculiarity of its manifestations by any other river on the globe.*

The Hudson rises precipitously among the northern mountains but during most of its extent it belongs to both the ocean and the land. It runs into a deep trench far under the Atlantic. However, in its now visible manifestation, its southern tidal boundary is where Sandy Hook marks off, like a parenthesis, the open ocean from the wide mouth of the Lower New York Bay. The tides advance inland through Gravesend Bay (north of Coney island), contract into the Narrows (now spanned by the Verrazano bridge), widen out again in the Upper Bay between Staten Island and the western shore of Long Island, pass Bedloe's Island (where the Statue of Liberty stands) and, having traveled some fifteen miles from the Atlantic, reach the lower tip of Manhattan Island. But the confrontation with one of the world's greatest cities does not stop the tides for a moment. They charge northward, up the Hudson River, passing between Manhattan and New Jersey, carrying the ocean's briny water some eighty miles inland. The pulse of the sea is felt all the way to the Hudson's upper city, Albany, some one hundred and eighty miles from the ocean and one hundred and fifty from lower Manhattan.

This deep tidal invasion of the sea is made possible by two phenomena. The Hudson drains only a restricted hinterland and amazingly is joined, during the entire trip to the ocean, by only one tributary of any dimension, the Mohawk River. On its broad trip to the sea, the Hudson fights the tides with surprisingly little water of its own, and the river bed is almost completely lacking in the declivity that would give the river a

---

*An earlier version of this essay appeared in Robert Glenn Ketchum, *The Hudson River and the Highlands: The Photography of Robert Glenn Ketchum* (New York: Aperture, 1985).

powerful downward flow. The head of a moderately tall man standing at sea level rises as high as Albany.

Some good soul with a taste for such measurement has made the following analysis which I am glad I did not have to attempt myself. Each of the ebb tides that flow out every twenty-four hours carries driftwood a dozen miles down the Hudson, but each of the intervening flood tides propels the driftwood back two-thirds of that distance. A drop of water takes three weeks to journey from Albany to New York City.

This languor presents us with a major paradox. So gentle and oscillating a flow could cut in the softest land no more than a shallow indentation, but the Hudson Valley is such a fissure as could be carved out of a rocky terrain only by a terrific current. Clearly, the valley must once have dropped much more steeply. But where did the imperious water come from? Historical geologists who spend happy careers moving mountains and continents around like chessmen, closing and opening oceans, have theory after theory. Perhaps the water that now fills the Great Lakes once drained into the Hudson.

A geologic formation which you can climb around on, if you please, behaves strangely in relation to the Hudson. The Appalachians have been an all-powerful dictator in American history. Extending from the St. Lawrence Valley to central Alabama, the line of mountains divides the Atlantic coast from the Mississippi Valley. Even if rivers in the eastern states start out as "tide-waters," in the manner of the Hudson, they soon come to a "fall line" beyond which water rushes down the Appalachian foothills and navigation becomes difficult. But the Hudson, flowing not from the west but almost directly southward, parallels rather than challenges the mountains. To this maneuver the haughty Appalachians are amazingly tolerant. Their offshoot, the Catskills, stop so docilely at the Hudson shore that the river is not deflected. But in one area about twenty-five miles long, known as the Hudson Highlands, the greedy mountains try to interfere by extending into the river's path.

There was an easy way out commonly accepted by even gargantuan rivers. Making a loop eastward, the Hudson could have flowed around the obstruction. But the river was determined to continue in the almost unbroken straight line that is another one of its unusual attributes. It broke its way through the Highlands with what is its narrowest and deepest channel.

How this was achieved is among the mysteries of the Hudson. A cheerful writer, William S. Gerke, had his own theory:

It is my belief that the Hudson was destined for the Sea as the sea was for the Hudson. . . . The Sea drove straight to the north as the River was driving straight to the south. Both struck at the heart of the mountains in their path as if impatient for the moment of the meeting of their waters.

Which was the strongest, the River or the Sea? The River, or so I prefer to think. In the winters, the River hurled its waters filled with grinding ice-floes against the wall. . . . There came a time when the wall was breached, when the River met the outstretched arm of the Sea and they were united at last. Now the tides of the Sea and the flow of the River combined in ceaseless rhythmic movement, in a meeting and mating of their waters. Well, no doubt, geologists will think this the merest romantic drivel. No matter; that is the way I think of it, that is the way it has always seemed to me.

The world traveler, Sir Robert Temple, described the Hudson Highlands as:

one of the fairest spectacles to be seen on the earth's surface. Not any other river or strait—not on the Ganges or the Indus, or the Dardanelles, or the Bosphorus, or the Danube or the Rhine, not the Neva or the Nile—have I observed so fairy-like a scene as this on the Hudson. The only water view to rival it is that of the Sea of Marmora, opposite Constantinople.

Washington Irving remembered:

What a time of intense delight was that first sail through the Highlands. I sat on the deck as we slowly tided along at the foot of those stern mountains and gazed with wonder and admiration at the cliffs impending far above me, crowned with forests, with eagles sailing and screaming around them; or beheld rock and tree and sky reflected in the glassy stream. And how solemn and thrilling the scene was as we anchored at night at the foot of these mountains, and everything grew dark and mysterious, and I heard the plaintive note of the whippoorwill, or was startled now and then by the sudden leap and heavy splash of the sturgeon.

At the northern gate of the Highlands stands its most imposing mountain, Storm King, 1,355 feet high. More than fifty years ago, when I was in my early teens, my mother, in her passsion for scenery, bought a summer house imbedded in the opposite declivity, Breakneck Mountain. Our little plateau, several hundred feet above the river, was some hundred yards long and wide, but cosy enough with its crotchety gabled house which Washington Irving would have admired, a large tree, and a miniature barn. A very steep driveway led down to a narrow dirt road (now a numbered highway) along the river. Overhead, the cliff was almost perpendicular, with some saplings hanging on with roots that had probed the rock-like spider's legs.

Breakneck did not feel kindly toward trippers who ignored its name. I was home alone one Saturday morning when there appeared at the door two terribly shaken young men from the city. As they were climbing around above, the footing had given way under a companion, who was lying far below motionless. I sprang on my bicycle and pedaled madly for the local doctor. I have never seen a man less pleased to see me: he was just setting out with his family for a picnic. But the Hippocratic oath is the Hippocratic oath. Having unloaded his family, he set out resentfully in his car. But he was not held for long. The man was dead.

There is often a macabre side to great beauty.

Although the Highlands are acknowledged to be "the gem," there is hardly a reach of the Hudson where the navigated shores and their reflection in the placidly moving waters do not (except where defaced by modern building) excite or charm the eye. Stretching on the west bank, beginning opposite Manhattan and extending north for twenty-five miles, there is an impressive geological oddity. It is as if whatever spirit rules the Appalachians, wishing to restrain his territorial greed, had build himself a high fence that stopped at the very edge of the river's flow. Geologists, who have no belief in ruling spirits, postulate that once upon a time molten lava had poured into a deep crack in the earth where it hardened and remained after the surrounding sandstone had washed away. The cliff, three hundred to five hundred feet high, made up of vertical strata, looks like a gigantic picket fence of rock, thus earning its title, the Palisades.

Near the Palisades's northern end, the river opens up into a miniature ocean called by the Dutch the Tappan Zee, encircled with hills and valleys but now ruined by road builders who found it cheaper to direct the New York Thruway over the shallow water on a hideous viaduct. North of the Tappan Zee in the highlands is the only sharp curve in the whole length of the river, the site of the West Point Military Academy.

Closer to Albany, the variously peaked Catskill Mountains rise from the west bank.

Its eccentricity in lacking, during all the miles between Albany and the sea, any downward current worthy of consideration made the Hudson the most amenable of rivers. Before the application of steam or gasoline power, it was impractical for boats of any capacity to advance against currents, and there was no practical way to transport bulky goods except by boat. One might assume that, during the generations when the northern end of the Hudson butted wilderness, there had been little need for trade or travel. Yet the most lucrative trade in British America sailed the Hudson's waters.

Furs which could not be produced on the European side of the Atlantic sold for large prices there. Operating out of Albany, the Dutch inhabitants of New Amsterdam had established a trade alliance with the puissant Indian confederation the Iroquois. Unlike agriculture, which sits comfortably within the boundaries of its fields, the harvesting of furs requires large expanses of forest. Armed by the white man, for generation after generation the Iroquois subjected distant tribes and inflamed the wilderness with mercantile wars against other natives like the Hurons whose partners were the French traders in Canada. Into Albany came a harvest almost worth its weight in gold.

Why, the reader may ask, could not that compact harvest have been carried to the sea in canoes? Of course it could. The problem was that the Indians had to be paid. This did not mean pouring gold out of portable money bags. The Indians had no understanding of or use for money. All the more because the fur traders discouraged all Indian activity except hunting and fighting, the tribes had to be completely supported: they were given not only trinkets and guns and ammunition and firewater, but the clothes they wore and almost all their food except the meat brought in by hunters. "Indian truck," the currency of the forests, was bulky, and so were the requirements of the fur traders themselves. Furthermore, as time passed, farmers with their products began (over the opposition of the fur traders) settling in the Mohawk Valley.

In 1807, the Hudson River fostered a new prime mover that was utterly to change the history of the world. As every schoolboy should know, Robert Fulton gave the first really practical demonstration of steam navigation by sending the *Claremont* puffing all the way from New York City to Albany. The Hudson's contributions to this feat were its rigidly controlled waterway—no rolling waves to get machinery off balance—and, since Fulton had not worked out how to build a really powerful engine that would not swamp his boat, no opposing current. As Fulton improved his invention in further vessels and competition appeared, the Hudson, because of its physical peculiarities, remained for years the world capital of steamboat navigation. No boat successfully steamed up the Mississippi until 1817, and the Atlantic was not crossed altogether by steam power until 1838.

Competing for passengers, the owners of the Hudson steamboats overloaded their saloons (public rooms) with such complications of Victorian decoration as were achievable privately only by the very rich. However, the owners had no interest in the local passenger trade, stopping rarely and charging heavily for short runs. Furthermore, their boats were still too crowded with machinery to carry much merchandise. Sailboats remained the normal Hudson River craft.

Although the river argued only with foreseeable tides against the pull of sails, skippers were bedeviled by irrational winds. On open water or in an estuary surrounded with fields, an experienced navigator can trim his sails with assurance, but the Hudson does not go in for tranquil edges. The sailor finds himself in a long, roofless tunnel lined on both shores with irregularly shaped mountains, confused hills, and burrowing valleys from any one of which, when strong winds are blowing, a burst can ricochet at any conceivable angle. If a skipper is not paying the strictest attention, or even if he is, his boat may be endangered in a trice.

Since the human mind prefers the supernatural to the random, the sailboat men attributed the aerial vagaries to Indian curses against the encroaching white man or, more commonly, to mischievous spirits left behind by the Dutch after the British capture of New Amsterdam. Of the resulting folk tales, Washington Irving is the immortal chronicler:

> The captains of the river craft talk of a little bulbous-bottomed Dutch goblin, in trunk hose and sugar-loafed hat, with a speaking trumpet in his hand, which they say keeps the Dunderberg [a mountain below the Highlands]. They declare that they have heard him, in stormy weather, in the midst of turmoil, giving orders in low Dutch, for the piping up of a fresh gust of wind, or the rattling off of another thunder-clap. That sometimes he has been seen surrounded by a crew of little imps, in broad breeches and short doublets, tumbling head over heels in the rack and mist, and playing a thousand gambols in the air, or buzzing like a swarm of flies about Antony's nose [a headland]; and that, at such times, the hurry-scurry of the storm was always greatest. One time a sloop, in passing by the Dunderberg, was overtaken by a thunder-gust, that came scouring round the mountain, and seemed to burst just over the vessel.

Though tight and well ballasted, she labored dreadfully, and the water came over the gunwale. All the crew were amazed, when it was discovered that there was a little white sugar-loaf hat on the mast-head, known at once to be the hat of the Heer of the Dunderberg. Nobody, however, dared to climb to the mast-head, and get rid of this terrible hat. The sloop continued laboring and rocking, as if she would have rolled her mast overboard, and seemed in continual danger of either upsetting or of running on shore. In this way she drove quite through the Highlands, until she had passe Pollepol's Island, where, it is said, the jurisdiction of the Dunderberg potentate ceases. No sooner had she passed this bourne than the little hat spun up into the air, like a top, whirled up all the clouds into a vortex, and hurried them back to the summit of the Dunderberg, while the sloop righted herself and sailed on as quietly as if in a mill-pond. Nothing saved her from utter wreck but the fortunate circumstance of having a horseshoe nailed against the mast, a wise precaution against evil spirits, since adopted by all the Dutch captains that navigate this haunted river.

There is another story told of this foul-weather urchin, by Skipper Daniel Ouslesticker, of Fishkill, who was never known to tell a lie. He declared that, in a severe squall, he saw him seated astride of his bowsprit, riding the sloop ashore, full butt against Antony's nose, and that he was exorcised by Dominie Van Gieson, of Esopus, who happened to be on board, and who sang the hymn of St. Nicholas, whereupon the goblin threw himself up in the air like a ball, and went off in a whirlwind, carrying away with him the nightcap of the Dominie's wife, which was discovered the next Sunday morning hanging on the weathercock of Esopus church steeple, at least forty miles off. Several events of this kind having taken place, the regular skippers of the river, for a long time, did not venture to pass the Dunderberg without lowering their peaks, out of homage to the Heer of the mountain, and it was observed that all such as paid this tribute of respect were suffered to pass unmolested.

Geography made the Hudson Valley the most strategic area during the American Revolution. From before the Declaration of Independence until after independence had been officially granted, Manhattan Island served as the main base of the British army, the harbor as the main base of the British fleet. Furthermore, the broad, currentless river, extending all the way from the ocean to the northern wilderness and potentially navigable by the British fleet, presented invaders with the opportunity to divide the rebellion into two separately subduable parts.

Realizing that the only way to win the war with a bang was to drive the enemy from their bases on the lower Hudson, General Washington concocted expedient after expedient, trying to lure his French allies to join with battle plans they always considered crackbrained. And indeed the geographic strength of the fortress defied attack.

Yet solid British control hardly extended beyond the Harlem River, which closed in the top of Manhattan Island. For the next twenty miles or so, the territory east of the Hudson was a no-man's-land, subject to incursions over land and water from either belligerents, and perpetually wracked by the guerrilla warfare that did not exclude robber bands, which is so effectively described by James Fenimore Cooper in his novel *The Spy*. But, except to the tortured inhabitants, this was all small potatoes compared with the strategic issues.

Transportation of supplies across the Hudson was essential to the patriot cause, but the ragged or mountainous hinterland and shoreline made such ferrying feasible only at widely separated crossings. Most convenient was King's Ferry, about twenty-seven miles above Manhattan at Stony Point. This was fortified by the patriots, captured, recaptured, captured again, and finally evacuated by the British when their forces became too engaged elsewhere to hold the intervening territory.

The overwhelming issue was control of the entire navigable river. It first arose in virulent form when Burgoyne marched down from Canada for Albany, presumably to be joined by a powerful army advancing up from Manhattan. The offensive went awry because of confused orders and impractical strategy. The main army in New York City sailed off for Philadelphia, and Burgoyne, unable to keep his supply lines open to Canada through the wild upper Hudson and beyond, surrendered at Saratoga. However, a minor foray from Manhattan revealed that the forts Washington had built to hold the Hudson closed could not resist assault. This resulted in the erection at West Point of the stronger fortifications, expertly designed by the Polish engineer Thaddeus Kosciusko, that were the major engineering feat of the Continental Army.

During more than three years of hard labor, the soldiers shaped the towering ramparts. Inflated dollars, anguishedly raised, were spent by the millions. The fortification seemed to slant backward as it precipitously mounted the Hudson's west shore. Close to the water, the main redoubt clung to a sheer crag like a monstrous crab. Above, there was a maze-like interweaving of ramparts pierced for cannons. Far overhead, three peaks were topped with semi-independent forts. If you looked downstream, the river seemed to disappear into the hills. This only sharp turn in the entire Hudson River would force any British warship to come almost to a stop under fire from the fortress's cannons. To complete the impediment, a tremendous iron chain was here extended under the river's surface from bank to bank.

As the war was going less and less well for the British, their expeditionary force sinking under its own weight without achieving anything decisive, the commander-in-chief, Sir Henry Clinton, became obsessed with the conception of bisecting the rebellion at the Hudson River. But his spies reported that West Point was too strong for capture, Then Clinton's favorite, Major John André, whom he had raised beyond ordinary process to the rank of adjutant general, reported that a disgruntled and partially crippled American general was offering to sell his services to the British. André advised Benedict Arnold to make use of his disability to secure the stationary post of commandant at West Point, which was a piece of merchandise for which His Majesty would pay well. Arnold secured the post. In a sequence of events played out on the Hudson that is unsurpassed for melodrama in all American history, Arnold met with André on the banks of the Hudson. The warship to which André hoped to return was forced by cannon fire to fall downriver. As he attempted to ride back to Manhattan, André was stopped by some of the marauders who haunted no-man's-land. They were probably after his gold watch, but they found incriminating papers in his stockings and turned him over to a patriot post.

The officers there suspected that Arnold was implicated, but felt obliged to follow routine by informing their general of André's capture. However, they sent the incriminating documents to Washington, who was on his way to Arnold's headquarters. It was a race to see which messenger would arrive first. Arnold's did so, enabling the traitor to make his escape downriver to the enemy, although Wasington, informed only shortly thereafter, sent his aide Alexander Hamilton galloping to try to have him intercepted. But André was well caught. To the regret of Washington and all the other American officers the charming young man encountered, he had to be ruled a spy. André was hanged at Tappan, in the Hudson Valley, two miles inland from the great river.

Much more significant than Arnold's treason was the crisis—it affected the future of human institutions everywhere—that developed during 1783 in the American encampment at Newburgh, close to the northern gate to the Highlands. As the war was clearly coming to an end, the thirteen states that had joined together to drive out the British turned their attention to establishing their individual independence. Skimping their representation at the Continental Congress, they refused to give that central body funds with which to pay its debts. The two major groups who were being defrauded were the financiers, supporters of the cause who held extensive obligations, and the army, fighters who were owed quantities of back pay. There developed a strong movement, led by Robert Morris and Alexander Hamilton, to have the army impose continental rule on the elected governments of the states.

Here was the beginning of a process that has been repeated again and again in history—it has produced Napoleon, Lenin, Mao Tse-tung, Khomeni, Castro. After a revolution, old institutions have been destroyed and all is chaos. The solution has been to raise a strong man and have him establish order by force. In America, the only possibility for dictator was George Washington. He was offered, in the name of his suffering soldiers, universal power. There are indications that the army was ready and indeed eager to rise. But Washington was immune to the lust for power. At a mass meeting, with great difficulty he persuaded his soldiers to rely on democratic means. Thus was the United States enabled to become, for all the world to see, a beacon light of human freedom.

In its preemptive northward march across the United States, cutting the eastern seaboard off from the central valley, the Appalachian range relaxes only once, in the area of Albany. This break was to have the profoundest effects on the Hudson River and the city at its mouth.

The barrier was of little importance until, after the Revolution, settlers, many of them released veterans, began homesteading beyond the mountains. They found fertile land in abundance, but the great Ohio-Mississippi river system was dominated by a strong downward flow. Produce could be rafted down, but it was a long journey and at the end there was only isolated New Orleans and the Gulf of Mexico. Nothing to speak of could be moved the other way, up the river.

The vast financial and political need of tying the new West with the eastern seaboard by navigable water rather than mountain trails became clearer every year, as did the fact that whichever community was established as the eastern terminus would be immensely profited. George Washington's major activity between the victory over Britain and the Constitutional Convention was an effort to create at his doorstep in Virginia a Potomac Canal that would climb the Alleghenies in some navigable manner and meet a navigable watercourse on the other side. But geography was too strong even for Washington.

The Hudson River held the cards. Its only major tributary, the Mohawk River, flowed in from the west, and there were a series of minor watercourses that haltingly connected it with Lake Ontario. That the entire system was close to being level with no insurmountable physical impediments opened the way for the Erie Canal. In the third volume of my *History of American Painting*, I thus described the ceremony that marked the joining of the waters of the West with the eastern seaboard and the Atlantic Ocean:

> Governor De Witt Clinton, balancing on the gunwale of a canal-boat, poured water into the Atlantic Ocean from a green and gold keg labeled "from Lake Erie." New York Harbor reflected a surrounding circle of frigates, barges bright with banners, and, most exciting to the American imagination, all the fiery spirits that frequented the Hudson River and the Bay. Where else in that November of 1825 could so many steamboats have gathered together as here, where eighteen years before practical mechanical navigation had been born?
>
> "The elements," so poetized the official report, "seemed to repose as if to gaze on each other and participate in the beauty and grandeur" of what appeared "more a fair scene than any in which mortals were engaged." Yet the elements were principals in a surrender as basic to America's future as Cornwallis's at Yorktown. At this opening of the Erie Canal, Distance was handing its sword to Public Works. The East was now linked to the West, and New York City crowned King of the United States.

New York City's long-established ruling class had their eyes directed across the ocean since their prosperity was largely based on trade with Europe. They had founded the New York Academy of Fine Arts dedicated to elevating American art and taste by the importation of correct esthetic conceptions. These included the neo-classical belief that the proper study of man was man and that therefore landscape painting, at best an inferior art, became the more unworthy the less the scene had been fashioned by human hands. It followed that the wild banks of the Hudson were not worth painting at all.

Opening to New York City an endlessly prosperous trade with the broad American continent, the Erie Canal created a new class of merchants, usually farmboys who had graduated from behind the counters of country stores, whose eyes turned not to Europe but inland. Uninterested in or ignorant of imported theories, they loved the American landscape in which they had been raised. They were joined in New York City by painters, also self-graduated farmboys, whose views of Hudson River scenery they greatly admired and generously bought. Although the old-fashioned connoisseurs objected, the resulting artistic movement pleased the broad American public which was both nationalistic and romantic; it saw, in depictions of unspoiled nature, a hand much greater than the hands of man—the hand of God. The Hudson River School became the only group of painters in the entire history of America who were admired by a majority of the citizens of the United States. Their works, copiously bought, widely distributed in engravings, and inspiring illustrators of every variety including Currier and Ives, established the Hudson Valley as the capital of American natural beauty.

More modern times have erased the practical importance of many of the Hudson's attributes. The fur trade as early New York knew it is dead. A currentless river or canal can no longer make determining contributions to inland trade. The dictatorial Appalachian mountains have been dethroned as railroads and trucks speed eaily through or over them, and airplanes need not notice them at all. Yet what the Hudson basically wrought remains.

West Point, chosen for its geographic location as the best place for closing the Hudson to the British, now houses the United States Military Academy. The government General Washington protected from secession at Newburgh still protects and fosters us all. Modern railways, highways, and airports continue to pay obeisance to the centers of population and trade erected before their invention. New York City still reigns as America's major center of commerce and culture. Hudson River School paintings, although for several generations eclipsed by new esthetic importations from Europe and our own development of Abstract Expressionism, have returned to their stature as the most beloved (and among the most valuable) exemplars of American art. And the Hudson valley still inspires, although in new mediums such as photography, important artistic creators.

THE CITY IN THE AMERICAN LAND

During the first two hundred and fifty years of settlement on this continent, community building was a basic physical activity of the American people.* Every area wished to grow in population and importance. Of this activity the city was the ultimate expression.

However impressive, and wherever situated, all American cities were in recent history tinier than can be factually illustrated. The early inhabitants cherished their growing community not because of how it then appeared but in anticipation of what they hoped it would soon be. But, in any case, the basic requirement for the creation of an engraved image—the existence of a market for a considerable number of impressions—was hostile to beginnings. Thus our earliest pictures of nascent cities show them at least a generation after the first ground was broken and the first house built.

American history as it is written and taught tends to obscure the unity of the process according to which our communities grew. We get the impression that the frontier emerged as a new phenomenon when settlement crossed the Alleghenies after the Revolutionary War. Actually, the "Wild West" opened on the Atlantic coast when the very first settlers lighted their first fires on American soil. Thence, the frontier began its march to the Pacific, moving most rapidly along the banks of rivers, temporarily halted where mountains rose. Different areas and climates demanded different solutions to immediate problems—some settlers had to battle to conduct sunlight to the ground through primeval forests, others to find shade and wood in a parched land—yet in every region the progression from small community to large was in essence the same.

Although much celebrated in song and story, the front wave of settlement was likely to be ephemeral: the true pioneer was more an adventurer than a builder of institutions. But we should not visualize him as an adventurer in the romantic sense. Men who came to the frontier to

---

*An earlier version of this essay appeared as the Introduction to *American Views: Prospects and Vistas*, ed. Gloria-Gilda Deak (New York: The Viking Press, 1976), pp. 11–15.

test themselves, feel strange new sensations, were usually visitors from more stable areas who would return east to rehearse their stories to shining eyes in warm drawing rooms. The true frontiersman was a poor man of limited outlook who had often failed in more civilized pursuits. He achieved satisfaction from the rigors around him in exact proportion to his temperamental aversion to the institutions of organized society. When settlement began to collect around him, the archetypical frontiersman moved on to a farther frontier where social amenities were not required or even observed.

Left behind were those of the original inhabitants who had least enjoyed and been least fitted for original pioneering. They became part of the second wave of settlement into which their children completely merged. It was this wave that built roads, established banks and law courts and libraries, that put on the ground prepared by the pioneers the true seeds of community growth.

Once a community was rooted, the issue was how large it would grow and what functions it would serve. Villages separated themselves off from farmland, and some of the villages expanded, upon occasion slowly, upon occasion with explosive violence, to become cities. On a small scale the location of the center could be altogether determined by the settlers, as when the location of a church established a village, but the larger the eventual growth, the more it was influenced by geographic absolutes. The most ubiquitous of these was the behavior of water. If water concentrated itself into a considerable stream and then dashed down a declivity, there was a site for mill wheels—industry small or large was beckoned. Even more influential was water broad enough to be navigable and quiet enough to be navigable in two directions.

Before the invention of the railroad there was no practical way to move large cargoes except in boats. (Whiskey became a very important commodity beyond the Alleghenies at the end of the eighteenth century because only when distilled did grain become compact enough to be carried across the mountains in pack trains.) But navigable water was not by itself enough to make a site for a city. The river had to go from a source of marketable goods to a place that had access to the market. And since a boat that sailed by a community without stopping contributed nothing, there had to be some geographic reason for the shipping to come to a halt. Prosperity would be best served if cargoes had to be unloaded: changed from one size of boat to another, or between water and land transport. Then the local inhabitants could, if they had what was known as "git-up-and-git," build warehouses. They could reship goods to other parts of the world, or they could buy wholesale and sell retail to country merchants. Competition sometimes arose between sites that had the same (or almost the same) advantages, but without cooperative geography, no true urban growth was possible.

Cities thus grew up where rivers entered the ocean through harbors in which merchant ships could easily unload and remain safely anchored during storms; or at the fall lines of rivers, where navigation by ships had to cease. Boston, New York, San Francisco, New Orleans were great ocean harbors. Hartford and Philadelphia were examples of cities that grew up at the farthest point that ocean vessels could penetrate upward on rivers. The various cities on the Mississippi and the Ohio had to wait for true expansion until steamboats were invented that could navigate up the river system as well as down.

Although railroads, after they had taken over in the mid-nineteenth century, fostered some cities of their own and killed off others, in areas where urban patterns were already well established (as on the eastern seaboard) the rails served concentrations of population that already existed. In fact, the greatest metropolis of all was handed on to the railroads by a previous invention.

At the beginning of the nineteenth century New York was a secondary center, far behind Philadelphia and Boston in riches, in population, in political and cultural influence. It had been occupied by the British during most of the Revolution and was suffering from an aristocratic land-owning system that had descended from grants made by Holland when New York was New Amsterdam. The lordly Hudson, so flat that Atlantic tides pulsed all the way up to Albany, ran nowhere but to newly opened areas on tributary rivers or to the northern wilderness. However, an undeveloped opportunity existed: if a boat turned left onto the Mohawk River, and then was carried across a narrow piece of land, and then proceeded through the tortuous but still flat waters of Wood Creek, it came out on the Great Lakes. And access could be achieved from the Great Lakes to river systems that dominated the central valley of North America.

From the time that numbers of people began moving across the Allegheny Mountains, it was realized that any eastern center could achieve unbounded prosperity if it could open water transportation between the central valley, the mature settlements on the eastern seaboard, and a comfortable outlet to the Atlantic Ocean. George Washington tried boldly to create a canal along the Potomac River which would bring world trade to Mount Vernon's doorstep, but the Potomac flowed too steeply down mountainous declivities. Nature had put in her silent and irrevocable vote for the almost level route from the Great Lakes to the Hudson. The opening in 1825 of the Erie Canal finally carried western water to the city of New York. New York was elevated overnight into the great American metropolis, achieving such hegemony that, although canals have become obsolete and inland water travel has almost died, it is still the economic and cultural center of the United States.

Since people get bored without division, envy, and distrust, there has long been a tendency in American life to postulate a fundamental conflict between urban and rural society. It is difficult, however, to say where one ends and the other begins. How large does a center have to be before it becomes an enemy of the hills and fields? Actually, although there are differences of function and interest, there is no more basic a conflict between city and country than there is between a man's arms and legs.

The development of centers—village, town, local city, regional city, national city—has been as much an integral part of the growth of America as the spread of rural areas. And always the function of centers has been the same. They have never been economically or culturally self-sufficient. They have received impulses from the world around them and pulsed them out again in a synthesized form. The difference between the large centers and the small is that the former carry out this process on a larger scale.

American cities have always drawn to them people from their hinterland: the larger the hinterland, the greater the area from which the urban population comes. New York draws from all over the nation and also from all over the world because it opens so many opportunities to those who wish to rise in so wide a choice of endeavors.

The outlanders who come to a city, whether it be large or small, are, of course, changed by their new environment. The most important changes are caused by a mingling together, from day to day, often from moment to moment, of people and ideas from many sources. In presenting these, the city functions as a container being perpetually refilled. How much do traditions that have risen within the city itself impinge? The answer seems to be, at least in the United States, that the less extensive the hinterland a city serves, the more it presents and imposes a specific flavor.

The contrast between Boston and New York presents an apt example, since the very geographic happening that made New York the national city isolated Boston. The route of the Erie Canal, as it proceeded down the Mohawk River, pointed directly at the New England city, but water could not flow that way. The Berkshires stood in the path. And so the route turned, almost at a right angle, south into the Hudson River. That turn separated Boston from the whole western expanse of the continent. Losing all claims to being a national center, Boston became (except for the nearby universities that have established their own hinterland) an epitome of one admirable aspect of American culture.

What happened to New York when it was thrown high as the national city can be extrapolated from the history of American painting. It was to be expected that the city would produce a school of artists who were, like itself, national in their influence, but it might have been also expected that the school would reflect in its outlook and subject matter the rise, the glories, and the squalor of urban life. In fact, the New York school, which emerged almost simultaneously with the opening of the Erie Canal, was less concerned with urban taste than was the art that had reigned in the smaller and more local earlier New York. The megalopolis nurtured America's first school of landscape painting, the now famous Hudson River School.

What seems a paradox is not a paradox at all. The trade of New York had previously been a swapping back and forth with Europe, and the leading dwellers had been much more familiar with London than with any of the communities to the west of them. But now New York had become the capital (except in politics) of a vast, rural continent. The change brought flooding in a new population. Since the city had become in effect a huge rural store, men trained in rural storekeeping became the rising merchant class and were soon rivaling and even pushing to one side the former leading families. And also into New York came painters who had communed with Nature humbly, reverently, and at first hand—the contact of country-born artists with country-born patrons in a city that was, like a burning glass, concentrating the rays coming in from a still-rural America.

The artists spent their summers hiking through wild nature, filling their sketchbooks with material to be painted. But their actual canvases were created in the city. Working side by side in a few studio buildings, they solved practical and philosophical problems in unison, creating that communal achievement which is a school of painting. But this was only one aspect of the advantages presented to the painters by urban life. Artists in other fields—writers and sculptors and musicians and architects—dropped in of an evening. Through proximity the painters were enabled to educate (and be educated by) a group of patrons. They were brought into contact with informed leaders of many aspects of American and international life, including artists from other climes. And they had access to media of communication which made their reputations and their works better known even in the counties whence they had come than would have been the case had they not moved to the national city. Although none of the Hudson River School was born in New York and none painted the city, the school could not have existed without the city.

It is tremendously important for our understanding of American life to take into serious consideration the phenomenon this exemplifies. Cities are not inhabited by a special race; they do not spout ideas alien to their rural neighbors. Cities are part of the countryside, centers where the feelings and conceptions are gathered in and concentrated. It is this concentration that establishes culture. Should American cities be allowed to fall apart, they would carry down with them American culture.

THE PRESIDENCY:
WHERE MORE IS LESS

The executive staff of the first President of the U.S. rarely consisted of more than two men.★ When George Washington did not have the heart to keep his secretaries from going on vacation, he penned all the presidential correspondence himself. President Ford's executive staff totals 535.

Washington had no need of organizational charts or doorkeepers to prevent his staff from interfering with each other and becoming an irritation to him. Ford, wishing to replace Nixon's sealed chamber with an "open presidency," announced that nine designated advisers would have direct access to him at all times. but this attempt at simplification did not work out in practice; there were still too many people clamoring to see him, too many interruptions, too many demands on his time. The President still needs a kind of traffic cop, and Chief of Staff Donald Rumsfeld is entrusted with deciding who should see him and when.

Although the men who drafted the Constitution were familiar with the tyranny of kings, they gave the President great power, largely because they tailored the office to fit the man who they knew would be the first incumbent. Trusting George Washington, they made him—and all his successors—commander in chief of the Armed Forces, ruled that he could be removed from office only for treason or criminal behavior, and gave him veto power over the Legislative Branch. Since then, other Presidents have increased this inherently powerful office in size, panoply, and functions, but not in effectiveness, public confidence, or contact with the people.

In setting up his own staff when he became President, Jefferson described with admiration how Washington had handled official correspondence. Each Cabinet minister received all letters relevant to his department. Should he decide that a letter required no reply, he would

★An earlier version of this essay appeared in *Time*, August 4, 1975, pp. 49–51.

nonetheless communicate it to Washington "for his information." Other letters were sent to the President with the proposed reply attached. In most cases, Washintgon returned them without comment. "If any doubt arose, he brought it up at a conference." Jefferson commented, "By this means he was always in accurate possession of all facts and proceedings in every part of the Union . . . and met himself the due responsibility for whatever was done."

Letters now come into the Executive by the millions. There are eleven Cabinet posts to Washington's four. Ford, like Nixon, has avoided Cabinet Secretaries who possess any political clout on their own that would give them substantial independence (the exception is Kissinger). Washington's chief Cabinet members were the nation's two outstanding leaders after Washington himself: Jefferson and Hamilton. As long as they stayed in office, Wasington kept them under control. Under Washington, the personnel of the total Federal Government was 350. In March 1975 the number of employees in the Executive Branch alone totaled 2,815,670.

During Washington's presidency, the national capital was first in New York and then in Philadelphia. In Philadelphia, he occupied a cramped three-story house built as a private residence. There was no place for public offices except on the third floor, and callers climbing the stairs passed through the Washingtons' living quarters. Since the kitchen was in the visitors' plain view, when he had moved his headquarters from New York City he had left his cook and her daughter behind; their "dirty fingers" would not be a "pleasant sight." Most of the official furniture was brought from New York where it had been inherited by the Federal Government from the congressional president. Much of it wore out so completely that Washington had to use his own money for replacements.

There are 132 rooms in the modern White House. The President's personal domain occupies much of the second story: 13 rooms, $6^{1}/_{2}$ baths, two sitting halls. Each incoming President can draw on furnishings left over by his predecessors and kept in bulging storehouses.

Washington had no budget to supplement his annual salary of $25,000. The current White House has an operating budget of $1,695,000—but that is just the beginning for today's President. He has an annual salary of $200,000, plus a personal expense allowance of $50,000 a year. Other departmental budgets also help cover presidential expenses. For example, if Ford gives a dinner for Britain's Prime Minister Harold Wilson, the State Department foots the bill for the state dinner. In addition, such expenses as the operation of Air Force One, which Ford uses now exclusively for his travels, are paid for by the Air Force. Thus the President gets all of his travel free.

When his Government was moving to Philadelphia, Washington sought a small farm to work on near the new capital because his doctors believed he was endangering his life by lack of exercise. He had no available cash, but offered in exchange 3,000 of his western acres. The exchange was not considered adequate. At Washington's command, his need was never made known to anyone in authority. Nor was it ever satisfied. Nixon, according to the General Accounting Office, spruced up his homes in Key Biscayne and San Clemente with $1.3 million in tax money.

When Washington decided to make a three-month trip through the Deep South, how many Secret Service men and other guards, how many publicity men and speechwriters, how many advisers, aides, and secretaries, how large a press corps did he take with him? None. In addition to the men who handled his horses, his entourage consisted of his valet. The army of advancemen who set up the situation for Ford wherever he goes, where were they? Tavern keepers were amazed when a carriage turned unheralded into their dooryard and out stepped a tall man who proved to be the President of the U.S. The coachman would then investigate the stables; the President, the rooms. If both proved too dirty for beast and man, the President would set out again, once in the middle of a torrential rainstorm although he did not know where on the deserted road he would find another tavern. He was puzzled that he received no dispatches from the capital. It turned out that due to a confusion of mails and roads, his Government did not know exactly where he was for almost two months.

Ford's jet, Air Force One, is tended day and night by a ground crew of about 25. Well before a scheduled trip, an Air Force advance agent goes to the destination and checks out all landing details. Moments before the presidential plane takes off or lands, Secret Service agents drive down the runway to make sure it is clear of debris and to check for bombs.

Although the staff that accompanies Ford varies with the purpose of the trip, there is always a crowd; top personal advisers, one or more military aides, speechwriters if there are to be speeches, members of Mrs. Ford's staff if she goes along, political aides if politicking is intended, foreign policy aides if the direction is overseas. Secret Service men abound.

As he rushes through the air, Ford can pick up a radio telephone to speak to anyone in the world, his voice bouncing off a satellite. Since these conversations can be overhead by those who tune in on the right frequency, Ford also has available a teletype system whose secure method of communicating with the ground is classified top secret. In an atomic age, the President cannot afford to be out of touch for as much as a split second.

Every schoolchild who has studied American history knows that Washington was accused of showing royalist leanings by cavalier treatment of his fellow citizens. Actually, modern Presidents are far less accessible—even Gerald Ford, despite his genuine efforts to create a more open presidency.

Each week the Washingtons had two entertainments open to anyone who appeared in respectable clothes: the President's "levees," for men only, every Tuesday from 3 to 4; and Martha's tea parties, for men and women, on Friday evenings. Washington thus described his levees: "Gentlemen, often in great numbers, come and go, chat with each other and act as they please. A porter shows them into the room, and they retire from it when they please and without ceremony." At their entrance, Washington saluted each, "and as many as I can talk to I do." At the tea parties, he spoke to every lady, and spent as much time as he could with the pretty ones.

Jefferson tells us that at one of Washington's early levees, his secretary, David Humphreys, shouted as Washington entered the room where his guests waited, "The President of the United States!" Washington was disconcerted. When the occasion was over, he told Humphreys angrily, "Well, you have taken me in once, but by God, you shall never take me in a second time!" From then on, Washington was found waiting when the first guest arrived.

When Ford makes an entrance at the least conceivable ceremony the cry is, "The President of the United States!" Although the Fords like to appear before groups, for an ordinary citizen to see either of them on his own initiative for purely social reasons is virtually impossible. Most presidential entertaining is official to the highest degree, lists of guests being initiated and determined long in advance. Should someone ask to see the President, he must have both important business and important connections if he is to have the slightest chance.

Ford has at his beck every facility of modern communication. To distribute his State of the Union message, squadrons of every kind of functionary that a public relations society can imagine were mobilized, and batteries of every machine for disseminating words that a technological society has been able to develop were brought into play. Translators scratched away in 36 languages. No politican of any influence, no corner of the world, was not instantly supplied with Ford's sentences, sometimes even before they had been delivered.

Poor George Washington! When he had completed his Farewell Address there was only a single copy, written out in his own hand, and not one publicity man to bless (or curse) himself with. He entrusted the manuscript to David Claypoole, the owner of a four-page Philadelphia newspaper. After Claypoole had set up the address, he expressed a reluctance to return the manuscript. Washington gave it to him, leaving the Executive without a copy. The text appeared exclusively in this one newspaper, under a small head, on the second and third pages (the front page was as usual devoted to advertising). There was no editorial comment or indication that this was one of the greatest scoops in history. Washington was unavailable for comment. He was in his coach on the way to Mount Vernon.

As soon as the newspaper hit the street, other Philadelphia editors grabbed copies and ran to their racks of type. By foot, by horse, by wagon, by boat, the text spread. Wherever there was a printer, it was set up anew. It took months to reach the American back country, a season or two to reach and percolate through Europe. How poky! Yet what statement of a modern President ranks in influence and prestige with Washington's Farewell Address?

The growth in the size and ceremoniousness of the presidential office is by no means a direct result of the growth of the nation. Between Washington's and Lincoln's times, the population enlarged eight times and the area of the nation $3^{1}/_{2}$ times, but Lincoln managed the Civil War with a staff hardly larger than Washington's. By 1914 the whole continent was inhabited and the population was 24 times that of 1790; yet President Wilson's staff was still about the same size. The modern presidency was a creation of Franklin Delano Roosevelt. Faced first by a horrendous depression and then a horrendous world war, Roosevelt developed a new political philosophy and a new foreign policy, both of which are still dominant.

Although Hamilton disagreed, Washington, Jefferson, and a majority of the Founding Fathers insisted that the better the Government the less it had to do. People should and would want to take care of themselves. This conception remained powerful in the American pysche until the 1929 depression made clear that ordinary men could not, without help from Government, stand up against the vast complexes of force that had grown up within the nation and the modern world. Self-reliance was thus frightened away, and with it individualism. Coincidentally, the "knowledge explosion" encouraged the replacement of wide-ranging minds with specialists who emerged periodically from their burrows to sit around tables with troglodytes from other specialties.

Washington, Jefferson, and their contemporaries believed that the U.S. should avoid "foreign entanglements." That conception lingered as the U.S., impregnable behind its ocean ramparts, moved across its own continent to ever-increasing prosperity. Under Wilson, this dominant policy was broken by World War I, but the concept regained force until it was finally shattered by World War II.

We now feel that it is the duty of the Government, led by the President, not only to sustain the American people but to act as guide and protector for as much of the world as our influence can be made to reach. This requires huge conglomerations of federal employees.

There can be no doubt that the popular trust of presidential incumbents has decreased with the multiplicity of the demands made upon them. When George Washington was in office, he was very conscious of the danger of a collapse of confidence if he allowed too much to be expected of him. Unlike modern Presidents, he never tried to whip Congressmen into line. He accepted their separate function as one of the facts with which he had to cope—and in the process allowed them to take off his shoulders responsibility for many aspects of the Government. (Washington left it to Congress to set up a federal court system, for example, and did not interfere when the legislators enacted a customs bill that he disliked.) Thus did Washington manage to keep his objectives to the minimum—and to achieve almost all.

Modern Presidents are inundated with not only possible but impossible tasks; they are asked to cure, for every individual and the human race in general, all the ills that flesh is heir to. Being considered universal problem-solvers, they have become universal scapegoats. Their voices may sound across the nation and the world, but what they put forward will not impress a listener who feels that the speaker has failed to straighten out, as he should have done, the listener's own particular problems.

No rational individual would want to go back to the presidency as it was before F.D.R. The world has become so complex that there are many important areas where Government must help men to determine their own destinies, and the oceans behind which American isolation once flourished have shrunk until they would be mere passing specks beneath intercontinental missiles. But it is possible, particularly after more than 40 years have passed, for even the most valuable of reforms to defeat its own objectives by going too far.

Perhaps the major reason the Bicentennial has created visible uneasiness across the land is that it inevitably calls down from the heights of our history an old ideal that frightens many contemporary Americans: self-reliance. It is a measure of our situation that a call for individual or even community action so often results, in fact, in no action at all. Whatever the problem, it is left for the Government to solve. Americans hesitate to acknowledge that perpetually passing the buck to Government may not indicate an enlightened concern with the plight of our fellow citizens so much as an easy way for an individual or a community to cop out.

Every new demand on the presidency, and on the Federal Government as a whole, increases its size and unmanageability—and also our taxes. No other living organism, not even crabgrass, has the lust for life and growth of a bureaucracy. George Washington wrote, "Whenever one person is found adequate to the discharge of a duty by close application, it is worse executed by two persons, and scarcely done at all if more are employed therein." But nowadays, if four prove indadequate, eight are assigned and then sixteen and so on and on.

It seems counterproductive, for example, for the President to have so large a staff that he has to have a watchdog to protect him from his own aides. The fear of assassination has necessarily hampered presidential freedom of movement; yet there is a strong indication that in other and unnecessary ways the lifestyles of modern Presidents are unduly determined by those who cluster around them.

Given the awsome (and vastly expensive) scaffolding that we have built around our Chief Executive, do we have cause to fear that we have created an "imperial presidency" capable of trampling democracy down? The fact is that the American people have just, for the first time in history, forced a President to resign. Nixon made every use he could of the prestige and power of his office; yet his fall was achieved, simply and bloodlessly, by the will of the people. That would have been impossible had he been a true emperor.

If the Government has become larger, more remote, more complicated and expensive than necessity warrants, it is partly our own fault.
We have the ballot as one remedy. Congress, moreover, is showing signs
of becoming more assertive and is taking some steps toward re-establish-
ing itself as a separate center of power. Individuals, community groups,
and private organizations must speak out and be prepared to assume
responsibilities if the unceasing growth of the presidency and its functions is to be limited. Though some Government officials may look on
themselves as members of an anointed group, all of them are (to revive
a phrase that has fallen out of common usage) "public servants." And
that includes the President. Should we desire a simpler presidency,
should we wish to take more responsibility on ourselves whenever possible, we have to ask for it—rather, to insist—and it will have to be
granted.

PERSONAL

MY FATHER, SIMON FLEXNER

In 1976, Rockefeller University staged a symposium on its predecessor the Rockefeller Institute for Medical Research. Starting with my father, as the creating director of the Institute, they invited me to open the session with a familial account. Rereading for this volume, I feel embarrassed by how much I have talked about myself and wondered whether I ought to suppress. But then I remembered that Rockefeller University has for more than twenty years distinguished my speech with a listing in Books in Print.

I was born in 1908, when The Rockefeller Institute for Medical Research was seven years old.* I hesitate to claim that I was conscious of the Institute in my cradle, but as far back as anything registered in my memory, the Institute was there. It was indeed the most pervasive phenomenon, outside of my own personal life, with which I grew up.

I must confess that my childhood attitude toward the Institute was simplistic. I knew that the institution had not existed before my father became the director. I knew that its beginnings had been small, and that under his guidance it had grown great. I knew that he had contributed to that greatness with his own scientific discoveries. He was still at the helm. It was natural for me not to take into adequate consideration the contributions of others.

The biblical statement that "A prophet is not without honor, save in his own country and in his own house" was not exemplified by my father. I was brought up to revere him as a great man and, as a member of my particular generation, I could do so naturally, without the resentment a child might feel today. All the adults with whom I associated respected my father. The admiration of our German governess for the "Herr Direktor" was indeed so comically extreme that family memory cherished the occasion upon which Fräulein laughed at the great man. While greasing the automobile, my elder brother, suitably named William Welch Flexner, handled his implement—it was known as a grease

---

*An earlier version of this essay appeared in *Institute to University: A Seventy-Fifth Anniversary Colloquium* (New York: The Rockefeller University, 1976), pp. 3–12.

gun—so carelessly that father was inundated. Responding with fury as grease dripped down his forehead and from his nose, he shouted that William should not be entrusted with dangerous weapons. The proceedings continued in a spirited vein until they were interrupted by the amazing sound coming from Fräulein's lips. In an instant everyone, including my father, was laughing, too.

The sense of father's greatness was the romance of my childhood. We were not poor, but there were many things I should have liked to have that I was told we could not afford. I remember particularly—those were the days before plastics made toys crude and cheap—that I yearned for a little metal automobile with interior peddles in which a child could go whizzing along. My regret at my deprivation was tinctured with pride when I was told that I could have a dozen such expensive toys if my father were willing to abandon his scientific career to become a consultant whose presence would be considered a necessity whenever a rich person was very ill. The slightest step in that direction would have horrified me.

As I grew older, I became increasingly conscious of my father's gratitude to the Rockefellers for the opportunities they had given and were continuing to give to him. He felt toward the founders, father and son, a very strong sense of loyalty. My parents and the Rockefeller Jrs. were friends, although only my mother's relationship with Mrs. Rockefeller included any intimacy.

The presence of the Institute in my childhood, and particularly the benignity of the presence, had much to do with my mother. She was a true collaborator, discussing with my father his problems, being gravely and helpfully concerned. But she was by no means overwhelmed. Living with a powerful husband, two sons, and a male sexist pig of an Irish terrier, she kept the feminine element afloat with no difficulty whatsoever, partly because my father always treated her not only with love but with respect. Her personal interests were literary. Standing here as a lifelong writer, I need not say how deeply she influenced me.

However, one of the many things about me that concerned my parents was that I was slow in learning to read. It was a family recollection that, when I was goaded, I would state emphatically, "I will not learn to read until I am twenty-one and then I will read the newspaper." Nevertheless, I was worried, too, and it may well have been the greatest triumph of my life when I actually read to myself a volume dealing with Peter Rabbit. This was an achievement which I felt should not be overlooked, and where could I make a greater splash than in the family center of concern, the Rockefeller Institute?

Father was to make a speech, and as I went to the auditorium—I think it was a room in the Hospital building where movable chairs could be placed—I carried conspicuously my copy of *Peter Rabbit*. I was asked why I had brought the book. Embarrassed to confess that my true objective was a boast, I said that I feared that the speech might be dull and so I had brought along a book to read. This statement achieved, of course, great currency at the Institute as a joke on my father. I hope none of you has brought along a copy of *Peter Rabbit*.

By the time I was old enough to have firm memories and some understanding, the Institute had grown. Although my father was continuing his scientific work—I was awestruck at how many times he washed his hands when he emerged from his laboratory to take me to lunch—much of his time was spent in consultations with the scientists, whom he called his prima donnas. Some, but not many, were intimates of our house. Closest to my father was Peyton Rous, who, with his ebullient wife, Marion, seemed members of the family. Dr. Noguchi was always in and out, almost a boy like my brother and me. I remember that after he had given us opera glasses for Christmas, he stood at the far side of the room with his mouth open to see if we could focus on his tonsils. Dr. Carrel, who still exhibited the military crispness of his service in the French army, never stooped to such shenanigans, but had a warm and flattering interest in my father's two sons. Alfred Cohn, who was my father's personal physician, brought into the house what an outsider might have considered a suitably pompous note. Dr. Levene talked about literature and art to everyone's pleasure. Dr. Landsteiner I did not know, but my father pointed him out to me one day on the Institute grounds, and told me to remember the moment, as I was looking at a very great man.

When I reached adulthood and my father was dead, various of the major scientists who had worked with him began to confide in me. I was amazed to have these distinguished men tell me that they had been afraid of my father, unable to sleep during the nights before they were to have an interview. This made me speculate about myself: had I also been afraid? Certainly, I had formulated no such idea during my childhood, but equally certainly I had, as soon as I was old enough, come to the conclusion that he was not to be crossed lightly—indeed, not to be crossed at all. If I wished to go in some direction of which he might not approve, I was careful to see that he was not concerned or informed.

Once, on an idle afternoon, my brother and I, dropping water out of our Madison Avenue window, splashed a lady's fancy hat. She rang the doorbell and left a message with the maid. I remember my intense terror until mother agreed to receive the message and not tell father.

But I knew that we could count on my father's loyalty, as I am sure his associates at the Rockefeller Institute could. This fact cannot be better exemplified than by what could be considered a truly outrageous incident. My uncle, Dr. Abraham Flexner of the Flexner Report fame, was often in our house, where, to my brother's and my outrage, he continually played practical jokes on us and, if we tried to respond in kind, insisted on his untouchability as a distinguished adult. One afternoon he appeared, dressed to the nines, in order to glean admiration before he delivered an important lecture. My brother and I had been working on our skill as pickpockets: we handed people their watches, which they had thought were in their pockets. It was child's play for us to extract Uncle Abe's handkerchief and put in its place a long, greasy rag. He went off blithely to his lecture. In mid-flight, he felt a need to wipe his brow. The result was not what he had foreseen. Shortly after the lecture was over, he came pounding into the Simon Flexner household, demanding condign punishment. Father said to him, "Abe, if you will play practical jokes on my sons, they can play practical jokes on you." There the matter rested.

A favorite family reminiscence, which my father loved to repeat, concerned a stately German scientist who had come to pay a formal call. Father was escorting him to the door of our house when a derby hat came sailing down the stairwell and landed, to the sound of childish laughter, at a crazy angle on father's head. When he removed the hat with unruffled good humor, the German was doubly taken aback. "America," he exclaimed, "ist das Paradies für children!" Father undoubtedly took pleasure in this anecdote, because his own childhood had been so far from a paradise.

The stories he often told about his early years were always humorous in tone, yet they almost always depicted him as a victim. He told us, for instance, that, after he had hung around yearning to play with some older boys, they had called him in and offered to give him a starring role in one of their games. An egg was to be so expertly hidden that the other boys could not find it. It was sequestered under Simon's hat. But no sooner was it there than one of the boys smashed his hand down on father's head, breaking the egg so that it dripped over his face and clothes.

Sometimes Simon struck back. He had saved pennies that were very hard to come by to procure a particularly lurid dime novel. He was reading happily when his older brother Jacob, who was the tyrant of the family, disapproving of the book, snatched it and threw it into the furnace. Some weeks later, father came on Jacob asleep in his chair. A noiseless trip to the kitchen, a noiseless return with a bottle of ammonia, which he placed under Jacob's nose. As the tyrant sprang up in asphyxiation and then in wrath, father fled and locked himself in the bathroom. We children wondered how he got out safely, but he would carry the story no further.

Although never lacrimose, these reminiscences indicated an unhappy childhood. That a miracle was taking place in the small house in a poor neighborhood of Louisville, Kentucky, was invisible to all the inhabitants, and particularly to my father. His father had emigrated from the neighborhood of Prague and set up as a peddler, carrying hats on his back as he wandered the Kentucky roads. Eventually, he earned enough money to buy a horse, and then he established a wholesale hat store. In the Jewish community of Louisville, he wooed a young woman who had been born in Alsace and had worked for a while as a seamstress in Paris. The couple, as they produced many children, prospered modestly until the business of my father's father was wiped out during the panic of 1873. The father became a clerk in the hatshop of a former rival, and the sons were sent out to work as soon as they were old enough to earn anything.

Simon was the slow child and eventually the despair of the large family. He could not even finish elementary school without repeating a grade. His formal explanation was that "I was slow in growing up." To me he confided that, as he entered adolescence, he was too disturbed by the presence of the girls to keep his mind on his studies. After he had, at long last, escaped from elementary school at the age of thirteen, an effort was made to find him a job that he could keep. While clerking in a drygoods store, he pulled the chair out from under a particularly pompous and obnoxious customer. He was fired. Surely he could be entrusted with keeping an eye on the enlargements which a photographer was allowing to develop, each for its right number of minutes, in the sunlight! But Simon, who had acquired a jigsaw, forgot time as he drew designs he would cut out of the cigar-box tops and bottoms he could easily procure. So much for that job. He became the chore boy in a drugstore, but now he was writing an epic: *A Dying Arab to His Steed*. Not only did he, as he inscribed his flowing verses, use up quantities of wrapping paper that cost money, but he was too busy with his Muse to sweep the floor. His father felt it necessary to take him for an admonitory visit to the county jail.

The break came when, at the age of sixteen, Simon Flexner almost died of typhoid fever. He rose from the brink of the grave with the ambition, possessed of the energy, direction, and abilities that were to carry him from his inauspicious beginnings to so unforeseeable a destiny. He was not to travel alone. Everyone in this room knows that his brother, Abraham Flexner, made as great, although different, a mark on the development of American medicine. And there were other distinguished brothers.

In his new manifestation, Simon Flexner found himself again in a drugstore, but not now as a boy of all work. He was an apprentice. This involved his being sent to a college of pharmacy at night. He brought home a symbol of his changed destiny: the college's gold medal. The medal became a favorite possession of his mother's. She gave it, when my father married, to his bride as the ultimate sign of welcome and renunciation.

Now a graduate pharmacist, my father went to work with his older brother Jacob, who owned a flourishing drugstore. Jacob possessed a microscope, which he used to examine urinary sediments, and the instrument became Simon's obsession. He began by examining random small objects—insect wings and eyes, etc.—but soon he was reading books, teaching himself normal and pathological microscopic anatomy. The local medical profession brought him for examination tissues removed at operations and autopsies.

"The system of the time," my father remembered, was that a drug clerk had "one evening and every other Saturday afternoon free. It was on these evenings at home that I studied or worked most uninterruptedly with the microscope. The domestic picture is still vivid in my mind. The table in the dining room was cleared. My mother sat under the gaslight with a basket of articles to be mended—sewn or darned; the younger children at the table with books and lessons, and I with microscope and its paraphernalia, working away."

Eventually, Flexner went at night to the medical school associated with the University of Louisville. This was the kind of school that his brother Abraham was to put out of business. It was run by the doctors whose prescriptions my father filled during the day. He used to say that he graduated in obstetrics without ever seeing a baby born. "I did not," he later wrote, "learn to practice medicine. Indeed, I cannot say that I was particularly helped by the school. What it did for me was to give me an M.D. degree."

Already he was conscious of the scientific revolution, in the later stages of which he was to make important contributions. At that time, professors, even in major medical schools, were often unwilling to admit that germs could cause disease, but the Kentucky drug clerk had, before he even went to Louisville's humble medical school, read Tyndall's *Essays on the Floating-Matter of the Air, in Relation to Putrefaction and Infection*. This book steered him to a life of Pasteur. One of the practitioner-professors at the local medical school gave two lectures on pathology. Discovering to his surprise—he did not yet know much about professors—that the lectures had been cribbed in their entirety from Dr. Prudden's *The Story of Bacteria*, he turned passionately to the book. How gratified he would have been to know that Dr. Prudden would eventually be a close friend and colleague.

(My own memory of Dr. Prudden was that he lived during the summers on the top of so steep a hill that our Dodge touring car could not get up without boiling over. As the family chauffeurs, my brother and I learned to anticipate the various places beside Dr. Prudden's road where we could find water with which to appease the steaming engine.)

When my father was still working in his brother's drugstore and experimenting with the microscope at home in the evenings, there occurred an event so amazing that, as a seasoned biographer, I should doubt that it had actually taken place were I not confident of my father's truthfulness. A traveler for one of the drug houses appeared sometimes in Louisville and was a trustee of the New York College of Pharmacy. He talked with Flexner and then offered the obscure drug clerk the professorship of pathology at the New York College. But this is not the most amazing aspect of the episode. The obscure drug clerk turned the offer down. Father's explanation was that he realized he did not know enough to accept. But it may be that the youth felt, now that he was moving so fast, drawn toward a different and greater destiny.

Not that he had an exact idea of where he was going. He felt no call toward the practice of medicine. He wished to stick to his books and his microscope, to pathology, to science—but how in that environment, when his weekly salary was still needed at home, was he to achieve so strange an objective? He knew of no place—there was, indeed, in all the United States hardly any place—where a person could make his living by such endeavor. Prophetically, the youth who was to do so much to create the laboratories of The Rockefeller Institute for Medical Research considered founding a one-man laboratory in Louisville. He would back up with scientific studies the local medical practitioners. Perhaps the local medical school would pay him for giving a few lectures annually. Perhaps—he began teaching himself German.

The Flexner family was disentangling itself from its financial difficulties. Simon's younger brother Abraham had suffered from no such youthful confusion as had retarded Simon. He was a true-blue infant prodigy. There is a story, probably only slightly exaggerated, that he had corresponded with President Eliot of Harvard on the most erudite matters at the age of twelve. He had discovered that a university on the most advanced principles was being founded in Baltimore. Money to go there was forthcoming: the family could only back so shining a light. Abraham graduated in the classics from Johns Hopkins and, soon after his return to Louisville, established a school, also on advanced principles, which prospered, adding more money to the family possibilities.

Word came back to Louisville that the Hopkins was opening, as the first step toward establishing a medical school, a hospital that would admit some graduate students and teach the new scientific medicine— mostly imported from Germany—that was not yet rooted on these shores. Abraham lent Simon enough money to go to the Hopkins for one-half-year's term.

The young man, he was now twenty-seven, who appeared at the hospital shortly after it opened its doors, seemed in many ways an allegory of the New World seeking in its own way the wisdom of the Old. Although he appeared with the M.D. degree necessary to procure him entrance, he had no formal education to speak of. Almost everything he knew he had taught himself, and in the process he had developed a tremendous hunger for knowledge and an almost Herculean ability to absorb it. With what energy he listened to and took part in the scientific demonstrations; how exhilarated he was by the library full of books that had been unavailable in Louisville; how eager he was to learn everything—codes of behavior and general culture, as well as science—from the more knowing associates with whom he was now thrown! He was observed with wonder and some amusement, and then he made his own small discovery, based on sections of an eye tumor he had brought with him from Louisville to examine when he knew better how to do it. A comet seemed to be starting on its course—but it stopped dead still.

Flexner went to his principal teacher, Dr. William Henry Welch, to announce that he had to go home. Welch said that was ridiculous. Flexner explained that he had run out of money. "I'll lend you the money," said Welch. Flexner expressed gratitude but he could not accept the loan; his one term at the Hopkins had already put him too deeply in debt. Welch said, "We have only one fellowship, but it is free for next year. Will you accept it?"

Those words laid a cornerstone on which this great institution was built.

IN DEFENSE OF THE MALIGNED
CITY DOG

My own city dog, Pye, is a cream-colored standard poodle.* Her resemblance to a lamb is not lost on the six- to twelve-year-old set. Herself fond of children and also of being petted, she is likely to be surrounded, when we appear together on the street, with little people. Even smaller people as they are rolled by in their strollers, reach out fat arms and make a brave atttempt to say "doggie." If a glance at the mother reveals that she is smiling, I will call the poodle over to nuzzle the baby. The resulting screams of delight assist me in carrying through sometimes discouraging days. However, there is a darker side to the picture. When I am caught on the street without the dog, I am severely criticized and even threatened. It is fortunate for me that eight-year-olds do not come in larger sizes.

It is in the nature of children to love dogs. However, cities contain a surprising number of older people who hate dogs, often hysterically. Efforts are made to bar dogs from parks and apartment houses and housing developments. Perpetual pressure is put on the police to harass dog owners, and hardliners make no secret of their hope to achieve complete banishment of all dogs from cities.

To my view, these attitudes demonstrate how large cities alienate some inhabitants from their ancient human roots. Men and animals have lived together since the human race emerged at the beck of the Darwinian wand. During my own New York City childhood—and I am still spry—there were as many horses on the streets as automobiles. Policemen's horses were the pets of the neighborhood children. Horse droppings sustained a multitude of English sparrows, who enlivened the air with chirpings and the beating of little wings.

The domestic cats that are now housebound would then slink out at dusk to raid garbage cans, while in the small hours toms would serenade

---

*An earlier version of this essay appeared in *The New York Times*, July 3, 1983, Op-ed page.

the moon in close harmony from back fences. But now, except for fat, lethargic pidgeons, dogs alone represent in city public places man's ancient kinship with the rest of animal creation. But even their sole presence stirs up outrage. That nonhuman animals should gambol publicly around the city in company with human beings who are their friends and protectors seems to dog-haters unsuitable, immoral, and emotionally disturbing.

The psychological disquiet, plus the fact that they are easy targets, has encouraged making dogs scapegoats for many less solvable urban problems. Dogs are particularly denounced for polluting the streets. It is alas true that some owners neglect their responsibility to pick up after their pets, but the real damage is minuscule within the overall pollution of the modern city environment.

Although having to scrape off your shoe can be very annoying, you are not menaced, as by smoking chimneys and belching automobiles, with lung cancer. Dogs are attacked for being destructive to parks, but they are no more destructive that sporting adults or children at play, infinitely less so than human vandals.

Since dogs take on the coloration of their masters, vicious people create vicious dogs, but trying to handle this problem by banning dogs is no more reasonable than stopping drugstore holdups by abolishing drugstores.

Abandoned dogs must fend for themselves. The trouble does not originate with the animal. Dog lovers do what they can. In my poodle's and my circle, the heroes are not the owners of pedigreed animals but persons who have rescued, on the streets, strays often grotesque in appearance.

The age-old cooperation between dog and man is signaled by the wide variety of breeds, each one developed to serve a particular specialty. In the city, distinctions between breeds are largely irrelevant. Although some owners favor large dogs to scare away muggers, the city dog has only one basic function: to love and be loved.

The city dog, if reasonably treated, is the perfect citizen. More than any human beings who are not saints, dogs are immune to prejudice. They love and sustain their masters irrespective of color, creed, social or economic position, age, sickness or health, appearance, eccentricities, infirmities.

Receiving the love of a dog is a comfort for any human being capable of loving back. Dogs, being a specific for the endemic urban malady of loneliness, warm the lives even of people without major troubles. Yet the dog's power to heal grows with need.

At both ends of the human progression dogs shine. Although mothers corrupted by metropolitan living deny and denounce, dogs, who alone among city pets can accompany children out of doors, are a boon to growing up. While providing companionship, they teach kindness and respect for the animal kingdom. For the old, from whom the human world is drifting, a dog is an ever-present companion whose dependence on his master can give a purpose to life. In the middle years, the wounds that need healing are as various as the landscapes through which the humans walk and the traumas that haunt individual brains. What canine traumas the dog suffers he cannot communicate, and he responds to simple pleasures, leaping with joy when, after even the briefest absence, his friend returns.

Such societies of dog walkers as my poodle and I frequent are the most various and democratic gathering in our big city neighborhoods: little children and septuagenarians, stockbrockers and janitors, dowagers and waitresses. All worldly divisions are obliterated by everyone's affection for everyone's pet. If two dogs get into a tussle, there are no recriminations: each owner apologizes to the other.

A NEW SCIENCE: HOW TO FALL

One person falls a quarter of a mile and survives; another sprawls on a bathroom floor and is killed.* In finding why, science is giving valuable tips to paratroopers.

A man and his wife were flying over the snow fields of Alaska at fifteen hundred feet. They were talking cheerfully, but suddenly a remark of the husband's received no reply. Turning from the controls, he saw the door of the plane swinging open; his wife was gone.

In a flood of horror, he realized that she had fallen, without parachute or protection of any sort, more than a quarter of a mile. That was certainly the end. Yet, with the stubbornness of the human mind that will hope against all logic, he circled back, landed on an ice field, and began a despairing search for the woman he loved.

During two hours he stumbled on through the heavy drifts, his eyes half blinded by the flaring whiteness, and then he happened on a deep hole in the even surface of the snow. Peering down, he saw at the bottom, fifteen feet below, the body of his wife.

Rapid digging brought her to the surface, and when at last he held the woman in his arms unbelievable joy flooded his veins: though unconscious, she was warm and breathing. He staggered to a nearby Eskimo village, where he borrowed a dog sled.

The wife was treated first by a native doctor and then by an orthopedic surgeon rushed up from Seattle; it was two months before she was strong enough to be carried to a hospital in Canada. But in the end she limped from the hospital doors, able to return to active living.

This woman had fallen more than a quarter of a mile and had survived; yet strong men are killed daily by slips on the sidewalk or a parlor rug that involve falls no greater than their own heights. The capriciousness of chance could seem to go no further.

We all know that luck seems to preside over every accident. A

---

*An earlier version of this essay appeared in *Science Year Book of 1944*, ed. John D. Ratcliff (New York: Doubleday, Doran, 1944), pp. 193–200.

crowded limousine rips into a telegraph pole; three of the occupants are killed, one spends six months in a hospital, and the fifth walks out of the wreckage unscathed. Yet all were subject to the same catastrophe. Under the pressure of war, science, which has never been willing to give luck much credit for anything, is seriously investigating the reasons for such variations of destiny.

Aviators, parachutists, motorcycle cavalry, tank troops, dashing young men in jeeps—all these are being continually subjected by accidents to violent, death-dealing impacts.

In order to find out why some people survive and some die in a fall or crack-up, it was necessary to determine exactly what happened to each individual during the split second of impact. How to do this seemed at first an insolvable problem. In an accident everything happens instantaneously; no one has time to telephone a research worker when Grandmother is tumbling down the cellar stairs. And even if a doctor were there, he would concentrate on effect and treatment, not cause.

A solution was finally offered by a study of suicides who leaped from high buildings. It is possible to tell with precision from what altitude they started; to chart the line of their fall. One despairing young man, who willed his body to science before he leaped, gave a much greater boon to science by rising unscathed from the ground ten stories below. He assisted Hugh de Haven in his valuable investigations on non-fatal leaps.

The young man had jumped from a ten-story window, hitting the ground ninety feet below with a velocity of about fifty-two miles an hour. If an object falling at this speed is stopped instantaneously by striking an unyielding surface, at the moment of impact the normal pull of gravity is increased three hundred times; in other words, the body of the young man would have weighed forty-five tons. Certainly no human frame could withstand such a force as this.

But, as De Haven discovered, it did not have to. The young man had landed stretched out flat in loose, sandy soil; when he rose he left in the ground an impress of his body five or six inches deep. Instead of being stopped in one-twentieth of an inch, let us say, his fall had been slowed down through a space of six inches. The tiny deceleration, lasting much less than a second, cut down the force of the impact so mightily that he did not weigh forty-five tons; he weighed only twelve. And the force had been spread out evenly over his entire surface, since he landed flat.

From this young man's miraculous escape, de Haven drew two conclusions: first, that the smallest cushioning at the moment of impact can make a tremendous difference; and, second, that the body can stand much greater stresses than science had formerly believed possible.

Hugh de Haven is a research associate in the Department of Physiology at Cornell University Medical College in New York City. He's a mild, quiet-spoken man, and he knows as much as anyone about what will happen when Aunt Filomena falls over the oil mop at the head of the cellar stairs. More than Aunt Filomena, at any rate.

He flew with the Royal Flying Corps, the R.A.F. of the last war. He and a bomb crew were coming in on a wing and a prayer when their ship crashed from 1,500 feet. De Haven was badly hurt. So were others. One or two escaped without injury. That interested this shy scientist. He went back to the plane. After studying the wreck, he came to the conclusion the reason he was injured was that there were ten lethal instruments jutting in front of his position in the plane.

De Haven decided to eliminate, or circumvent, as many of those as he could. He began to study falls and their effects on the human frame. He hasn't stopped yet.

He became interested in the safe landings of frustrated suicides. He reports that a forty-two-year-old woman, having finally summoned up the courage to jump from a window forty feet high, landed spread out, rose on her left elbow, and remarked bitterly to the janitor who rushed toward her, "Six stories and not hurt!" She had struck soft ground—this time a garden plot.

But yielding earth is not the only cushion that saved the lives of plummeting people. Two whom de Haven studied landed on the roofs of automobiles, caving in sheet steel just enough—a matter of a few inches—to escape death.

Others went through the roofs of low buildings, one girl landing headfirst, her skull shattering three-quarter-inch pine boards. She escaped with a lacerated scalp and a fractured vertebra. Sky lights, ventilators, and awnings—flimsy structures that tend to crumble—all saved a case or two.

Most remarkable, perhaps, was a thirty-six-year-old woman who jumped from the eighth floor and fell seventy-two feet, landing at the rate of forty-five miles an hour in a jackknife position over a wood and wire fence. Her chest and abdomen struck the narrow edge of one-inch boards, but as the boards crumpled easily, she was able to walk unassisted to a nearby clinic and ask for first aid. Examination revealed no material injury.

We may now understand how the wife who dropped more than a

quarter of a mile in Alaska managed to survive. Although she fell a phenomenal distance, her fall received a phenomenal cushioning when she sank fifteen feet down in the snow.

The basic principle herein involved has, of course, long been recognized: it is the principle of the net which the fireman spreads out for people who jump from flaming buildings. But de Haven has shown that death can be frustrated by a cushioning so tiny that it would seem to be completely insignificant. A dent in the steel roof of an automobile, a little mark left in the ground—these are the symbols of a lifesaving force.

Where you fall is not the only consideration: how you fall is also of importance. We know that a high percentage of accident deaths are due to a blow on the head which causes concussion of the brain. The researches of two scientists at Oxford University, Drs. D. Denny-Brown and W. Ritchie Russell, have given us new light on the causes of concussion.

Having anesthetized small animals in such a manner that they would feel no pain, the scientists struck their heads with pendulums under carefully controlled conditions. Soon they made an amazing finding. If the head is pressed against a solid object when it is struck, you would expect the result to be much more serious than if the head is swinging free, its motion taking up part of the impact. But not so.

Concussion is caused by damage to the soft tissue inside the skull. When the head is held rigid, the bone protects like armor plate, and even if it is fractured, serious damage does not necessarily result. But if the head is allowed to swing, the skull itself takes over the force of the blow. Receiving the impact first, it starts to move while the brain within it is still stationary; the soft tissue is driven against the near side of the bone. And should the moving head be stopped suddenly by striking against a hard object, the skull again stops first, the sudden deceleration smashing the brain tissue violently against the far side. Thus is caused the deadly concussion which is the worst single hazard of accidents. It now becomes clear why a slip in the bathroom or on the street may kill, while a fall from a high building does not necessarily do so. Should a man who drops fifty or a hundred feet land on an object which slows down the impact ever so slightly, he will not be subjected to forces so great as those met by a man who, after a fall of five or six feet, strikes an object completely unyielding. And if it is the head which strikes bathtub or sidewalk, the sudden stopping of its movement may easily jam the brain against the skull to cause concussion. This also gives us the scientific secret of the boxing glove. The inch or so of padding keeps a blow to the head from starting the skull into motion so rapidly that the brain tissues are injured.

The findings of de Haven and his English colleagues can be used by every one of us to save our own lives should we ever become involved in accidents in automobiles, buses, trains, airplanes, or any speeding vehicle. When a fast machine strikes a solid object, the split second of slowing down which cheats death is usually supplied by the crumpling of the machine itself.

The research of the scientists has confirmed the wisdom of a trick long pragmatically employed by daredevils who deliberately smash up automobiles moving at high speeds.

Just before the impact the stunt man jumps into the back seat and lies hard against the rear of the front seat, with his hand or arm between the side of his head and the solid structure. The crumpling of the seat slows down the speed with which his body is brought to a standstill, while his head is shaken up as little as possible.

Anyone who finds himself involved in a crack-up should imitate this procedure. He should press his torso against some solid object forward that will not receive the first shock of the crash, and be especially careful to squeeze his head tightly against the object so that a quick swing will not cause concussion.

Since fatalities in crashes are not directly due to the impact of the vehicle itself but rather to a second impact, that of the passenger against the structure of his machine, many injuries can be avoided by redesigning the insides of airplanes and automobiles to reduce the number of objects that can be struck, and to give the passenger something to flatten himself against. This is already being done in the design of airplanes. In new automobiles such safety provisions will undoubtedly be included.

From de Haven's findings on non-fatal suicide leaps, we may draw some hints on how to make tremendous falls. The first rule, of course, is to avoid them altogether if it is possible to do so, since even under the best conditions a drop from a sixth-story window is extremely dangerous. But if jump you must, remember that any object which will give, even only a few inches, is a potential life-saver. If there is an awning somewhere beneath you, you are very lucky, for awnings can be almost as effective as a net. It is better to land on an automobile than on paving or sidewalk; metal ventilators may crumple beneath you; the roof of an old shed may give way; and the soft earth of a spaded garden plot may save you. Furthermore, you should try to land as flat as possible. Do not put your arms and legs out in front of you to ward off the blow, since, at the great speed you will be traveling, the long bones will be likely to be driven into your body like swords.

The technique for meeting long falls differs from the best procedure, should you find it necessary to drop not from the sixth but the second story of a building.

The paratrooper who bails out a half-mile up in the sky is, from the point of view of his landing, dropping a distance of six or eight feet. Due to the action of his enlarged umbrella, he strikes the ground with a velocity no greater than if he had taken a free fall of a little more than his height. To bring him to the ground without the slightest injury is one of the primary concerns of the Paratroop Command. If you sprain your ankle when you trip over the baby's toy, it is not serious: you hobble around for a week or so until your ankle gets well. But if a soldier sprains his ankle when he drops behind the enemy's line, it means death or capture, since he cannot fight efficiently.

The question of how to land with the velocity of a short fall has thus received major attention from the armies of the world. And it has been answered so successfully by the American forces that less than two injuries are suffered per thousand parachute jumps. And the soldier must handle not only a downward shock, but also a forward, backward, or sideward velocity.

If you wish, like the hero of a Western story, to spring with impunity from the door of a rapidly moving train, you had better be an expert tumbler, as the paratroopers have to be. Men have instinctively tried to keep their feet when they feel themselves falling. Paratroopers have to eradicate this deeply ingrained habit. Should the force of their fall pull them off the vertical, they do not fight this tendency, but go jubilantly with it, landing in an acrobat's tumble. Their model is the circus performer who, when he dives head foremost through a flaming hoop, lands first on his hands, then goes into a somersault, and finally, after this long maneuver, regains his feet.

Fortunately for the average citizen, straight drops do not require this technique; you need merely imitate a much less complicated part of the paratrooper's regimen. Like the soldiers, you must learn to use your legs efficiently as shock absorbers. Try to make a two-point landing, both your feet hitting the ground at the same instant. If your toes or heels land first, either may be fractured. The correct points of contact are the balls of your feet.

The human tendency to get better protection from the ground by holding the legs rigid must be fought at all costs; land with your knees slightly flexed and plan to go down on your haunches with the force of the shock. If your knees are stiff, you may tear the ligatures of your legs or dislocate your hips; if your knees are bent too greatly, you lose the shock-absorbing effect and are in danger of spraining hip, knee, or ankle. Should you be forced to land hands first, bend your elbows slightly, just as for a foot-first landing you bend your knees. If you fail to get your hands or feet beneath you, if you are not expert enough to go into a paratrooper's tumble, you still have one protection left, provided you have the will to apply it. Relax! Imagine, if possible, that you are going to land on a feather bed, and let all your muscles go limp to receive its delightful softness.

According to an old proverb, Providence takes care of children and drunkards; certain it is they are much less likely to get hurt when they fall. The reason is that, in contrast to coldly sober adults, they relax naturally. Tense muscles tear, and the bones behind them are likely to fracture; loose muscles give in to the force of the blow. It may seem like advising the inhabitants of a fiery furnace to keep cool, but the fact remains that avoiding muscular tenseness is a most important secret in falls of every kind, be they of five or five hundred feet.

MY FRIENDSHIP WITH
EDWARD HOPPER

My friendship with Edward Hopper stemmed from my purchasing in 1948 from a drugstore rack for twenty-five cents *The Pocket Book of Old Masters.*★ It was an attractive paperback, illustrated with good plates, and undoubtedly available in innumerable ordinary places across the continent. In those days, when American art was still a subject of scorn to our academics, esthetes, and critics, I liked to contend that, if it were possible to get past the barricade set up by these Europeanized intellectuals, the American people at large would enjoy and appreciate the art of their own land. I suddenly visualized a chance for testing my assumption. Pocket Books had then the largest paperback distribution in the United States. Supposing they could be persuaded to float on their waters a history of American painting?

I mailed out the proposition as a forlorn hope, but almost immediately found myself lunching grandly, in an expensive restaurant, with the editors and executives of Pocket Books. They expressed enthusiasm. The result was *The Pocket History of American Painting*, published in 1950, with four adequate color plates and forty-eight good black-and-white illustrations. Cost: twenty-five cents. Copies were sold by the hundreds of thousands; the book was translated into more than twenty languages, and a copy came into the hands of Edward Hopper.

Since the taciturn semi-recluse was so pleased with what I had written that he sought out my acquaintance, it must have expressed to an unusual extent how he liked to think about himself and his work. The passage is short enough to be quoted in its entirety. It picks up from the last statement in the preceding paragraph: "We admire Sheeler's paintings but are not emotionally stirred."

Edward Hopper (1882–) strikes richer overtones. Trained not in the estheticism of Chase but the humanism of Henri, Hopper thinks technical

★An earlier version of this essay appeared in *Art Journal* (Summer 1981), 133–35.

experimentation an empty exercise unless it grows from an artist's urgent need to transcribe his "most intimate impressions of nature." However, he has not worked in a traditional manner. Unlike his fellow student Bellows, he could not make the methods they had both learned from Henri express his own emotions. While Bellows turned out a flood of art, Hopper engaged in a lonely search to find himself. As impervious to outside influence as was Winslow Homer, he adopted no ready-made recipes, either French or American. His technique and his vision matured together with the slow certainty of organic growth. Bellows was almost at the end of his career when Hopper emerged from retirement, the possessor of a major and original style.

Hopper had discarded Henri's romantic outlook and dramatic brushwork for a firm, laconic realism. He depicts American cities with love, and yet with unflinching exactitude: the garish stores, the jumble of architectural styles, the contrast of brightness and shadow on blank or overdecorated walls. When he shows people—diners at an all-night restaurant . . . a woman undressing under the glare of an unshaded bulb—we see them in a flash, as if we had gone quickly by a lighted window. The pictures are alive with the mystery and loneliness of a great city. In landscapes as in urban scenes, Hopper gains solidity from geometric compositions similar to those Sheeler borrowed from Cubism, but he denies any borrowing: "Angularity just comes naturally to me." Living in the same age, he had reached some of the same conclusions as the Parisian masters. Like theirs, his art is moving and forceful because it evolved from his own temperament and his own experience.

Authors breed paper as copiously as cockroaches breed cockroaches, and it would be useless to burrow in my piles of old file boxes to find the letters Hopper wrote to me. However, I am sure he did not summon me by telephone. (To my knowledge, he never used the telephone, although his wife, Jo, did.) I surely did not delay.

My generalized memory of my fifteen-year friendship with Hopper is of sitting with him in silence, either total or stretching between us under the perpetual chatter of his wife, Jo. He communicated, so it seemed to me, affection, intuitive understanding, and sympathy. My own naturally ebullient nature—no one had ever accused me of being taciturn—was led by the force of his personality to welcome, warmly and contentedly, this wordless communication. Having lived all my life in an environment of talk, where custom requires speech even if there is nothing to say, I have never with any other human being even approached such a relationship as I had with Hopper.

On one occasion, I saw the force of Hopper's silence cow a noisy cocktail party. The American Academy of Arts and Letters has two marble buildings with, between them, a broad marble terrace. The terrace is overlooked by little porches fronting doorways in each building. The party was proceeding on the terrace. Hopper stood motionless on one of the porches. When I went up to him, he asked me whether I had seen Jo. She had disappeared. When I said I had not seen her, he asked me to go down into the crowd and look for her. This I did, asking various people. Several other of his friends were also searching. It did not take long for everyone to realize that Hopper's wife was missing. All eyes turned to the tall, silent figure standing there motionless and forlorn. His wordless anxiety made people speak in whispers. All gaiety died. Finally, he put on his hat and walked off alone with gestureless melodrama. (Hopper had disagreed with Jo about something, and she had bustled off in a rage. When he reached home, he found her waiting for him there.)

Hopper liked to say that all his paintings were an expression of himself. Surely without conscious intention he had himself acted out in tableau one of his paintings, dominating a cocktail party with the laconic power that makes his canvases dominate the museum rooms in which they hang.

It was commonly regarded as Hopper's misfortune that he was married to Jo. She was particularly disliked by reporters and critics who had by hard effort achieved interviews with Hopper only to find him hidden behind a barrage of Jo's talk. I particularly remember the loud complaints of an interviewer—I think from *Time*. After an hour or so of frustration as Jo answered all questions directed at Hopper, he was delighted to see her get up to leave, presumably for the bathroom. The reporter's heart leapt: here was his chance! Although Jo told her husband to say nothing in her absence, the reporter did not doubt that Hopper would grasp his opportunity to burst into speech. He refused to say a word. Such stories fed the rumor that Hopper was hopelessly henpecked.

During the opening of the last show the Whitney gave Hopper during his lifetime (1964), he did not feel up to standing during the long hours. He was seated, when I came to him, with Jo prowling before him. Then Alfred Barr, the sacrosanct long-time director of the Museum of Modern Art, appeared. Being unable to get past Jo, he said to her that he was proud that he had discovered Hopper by giving him his first major exhibition. When Jo looked blank, I said, "Surely, Mrs. Hopper, you know Alfred Barr." She finally stretched out her hand: "Any friend of Jimmie

Flexner's is a friend of mine." As Barr retired discomforted, Hopper's usually inexpressive features glowed with satisfaction.

Far from trying to increase Hopper's isolation, Jo tried (at least in my experience) to edge him out of it. She would often call me on the phone, asking me to come down to their Washington Square flat in the morning. I had to begin each visit by admiring some of Jo's own paintings, which resembled Hopper's but were vastly inferior. Then we would have our three-cornered session. Hopper did join sparsely in the conversation, but it was evident that the words were not for him an effective medium of communication. I can remember very little of what he said. The one subject concerning which he spoke volubly was his angry and sad feeling that the younger generation of painters who were pursuing abstraction were debasing art and pushing his own achievement aside. I was one of many who tried to persuade him that because of the formal structure of his painting, he was one of the few representational artists whom the abstractionists admire, but he was inconsolable. Perhaps this was because of a deep psychological drive within him toward loneliness. Yet he was deeply hurt.

In Hopper's presence, and with him seemingly indicating approval, Jo told me one day that he wanted to paint another picture laid in a movie theater, but they did not know how to get into one when it was, as he wished, shut and empty. Would I arrange it? I said, "Of course," although I had no idea how I would arrange it. As it turned out, nothing was ever easier. I called my literary lawyer, she called a theatrical lawyer, and within forty-eight hours I was personally telephoned by the president of one of the largest theater chains in New York (I wish I could remember his name), who said that any one of his theaters would be available to Hopper at any time he pleased, day or night. The idea of another theater picture by Hopper had excited everyone. But when I got Hopper on the phone, he said laconically that he had no intention of painting another theater picture. (Among his very last paintings were two theater interiors, but neither seems detailed enough to have required his actual presence in a theater.)

One morning when we were having a most agreeable time, Jo suggested that they take me out for lunch. Hopper objected that that would be expensive, and they had an argument. Sure that the Hoppers could not be broke, I listened with amusement for a while before I departed. I suppose it was an indication of my sense of security in my relationship with Hopper that I did not feel the least put out or offended.

In 1961, when he was seventy-three, Hopper was worried that he

was losing his ability to paint. He was very pleased when he completed
a picture to his satisfaction. I received a letter expressing his pleasure and
asking me to go to the Whitney Museum to see a painting of his, and
let him know what I thought. I set out knowing that whatever I thought
I would have to be enthusiastic. My own pleasure was great when I
discovered that this would be no problem: *Second Story Sunlight* ranked
very close to his best pictures. I wrote him a letter of which my copy
has long since disappeared. But the original has turned up in the Whitney Museum archive. I have been urged to publish the significant passages because of the upshot, but I confess to some embarrassment in
doing so.

The letter, which was not intended for publication, must be judged
in its context: it was written to give the maximum encouragement to an
old and revered friend who, I knew, was becoming unsure of himself.
My praise of Hopper's art was altogether sincere—I consider him the
greatest American painter since Eakins and Homer—and my interpretation of the painting reflected accurately what I felt, even if in revision I
would have toned down the overblown phraseology. But I did it to
please Hopper, who viewed the Abstract Expressionists in a very unfair
light.

May 13, 1961

Dear Mr. Hopper:

Thank you very much for letting me know that your picture is on
exhibition at the Whitney. I have been down to see it, and agree that it
is one of your best works—which is saying a lot. It has the tremendous
strength which I so admire in your paintings. Had I been one of the other
artists whose work is being shown, I would be very annoyed, since in
comparison with your canvas most of the other pictures looked hopelessly
wishy-washy, and even the most effective seemed to be in a minor key.
It is the difference between major painting and pictures, like those of the
abstract-expressionists, that are primarily decorative. The contrast confirmed my growing suspicion that one reason those painters are being so
successful is that their art dresses up rather than dominates a room. Their
pictures will cooperate with interior decorators towards a consistent
"decor." Your picture would be acceptable only in the drawing room of
someone who loves art so much that he is willing to have his environment dominated by it.

What can be more foolhardy than to write a great painter one's own interpretation of his picture? However, I have always been one of those fools who rushes in where angels fear to tread. (one advantage is, you don't have to associate with angels!) So here goes: I felt both in the formal and emotional tensions of your painting a pull between restraint and the opulence of nature. Restraint represented by the peaked architecture and the old lady for whom all passion is spent; opulence, by the line of trees, the sky, and the marvelously buxom young lady sitting on the edge of the porch, not waiting for anything in particular, yet fertile and sure in the movement of the seasons to be fulfilled. I felt it was an allegory of winter and spring, life and death. Did you have any such idea as that?

The archives at the Whitney Museum reveal that Hopper made what was for him a surprising and perhaps unique use of the letter. He wrote the director of the Whitney Museum:

Dear Goodrich:

I am enclosing a photostat copy of a letter by Thomas Flexner that I received from him a few days ago. As it is mostly about the picture of mine which you recently acquired for the Museum I thought it would interest you.

Since I took the trouble of having the photostat made, it may indicate that I am not as modest as I am said to be.

Yours sincerely,
EDWARD HOPPER

But to me, Hopper was disagreeable about my letter. I had, he stated, completely misunderstood his painting. It showed a tuberculosis sanitarium.

Not knowing what I now know, I have often remembered my letter unhappily, sorry at the thought of having made a fool of myself before a revered friend, and even sorrier to be convicted of windy absurdity as a writer on art.

I can remember no other occasion in my long association with Hopper when he was disagreeable to me. Why did he express hostility rather than thanking me for a letter that gave him so much satisfaction and pleasure?

My guess is that the letter, too accurately aimed at its targets, carried out its reassuring mission too well. Moved to break his restraint by sending a copy to the director of the Whitney Museum—an act he may subsequently have regretted as a confession of weakness—he felt that the extreme pleasure I had given him was dangerous: he was being invaded

from outside. His emotions had to be always under his own control, and
the only person allowed in his control room was his alter ego, the other
half of his circle, his wife, Jo.

As they both told me, and many preliminary drawings reveal, the
model for his female figures was always Jo. It is fascinating to observe
how, as the sketches get increasingly close to the finished composition,
Jo is transmuted into the often radically different figure he eventually
painted. Thus she posed in the nude, when a dumpy lady in her late
seventies, for the tall, slim, firm-breasted, naked young woman in *A
Woman in the Sun* (1961). The current explanation of his behavior—that
Jo was a household tyrant too jealous to let her husband work with any
other female—trivializes a profound psychological phenomenon. There
is a fierce sensuality in Hopper's paintings of women, particularly when
they are naked. This sexual drive, if indulged, would have thrown him
on the mercy of the world. He needed to keep it within rigid inner
bounds. By making his female alter ego his starting point in creating his
image of any woman, he remained, however much he subsequently
altered the image, on his own terrain, with a path of retreat stretching
behind him to his personal fortress. He could safely let himself go. But
if he had painted directly from the body of any other woman, or, like
Pygmalion, pursued his own unanchored erotic visions, he would have
found a need to pull back lest he be launched on a wild, uncontrollable
ocean.

Hopper, as Gail Levin has pointed out, carried in his wallet a quotation from Goethe which states that art "reproduces the world around
me by means of the world within me." The application of this principle
to Hopper's works can seem difficult because he presents an image so
realistic that it can be misinterpreted as impersonal. Actually, far from
inviting the exterior world to inspire into artistic expression as Winslow
Homer did, Hopper worked his way tortuously and slowly from his
inner self out into the exterior world. The motivating force was the
exact opposite of what is ascribed to Hopper by those who misjudge his
work as cold and brutal. The basic psychic fact was hypersensitivity, an
extreme vulnerability that, only because of need and always with a sense
of danger, exposed itself outside his protective armor. This psychological
phenomenon goes a long distance toward explaining Hopper's paintings.
The environment he has entered, being dangerous, cannot be lax. These
forays from himself, achieved with much difficulty, carry with them
excitement, romance. Loneliness is in counterpoint with its opposite.
And the paintings are infused with an inner fire which is the more moving because it burns in a frightening, alien world.

WILL BARNET

Will Barnet and I have long been good friends. I greatly admire his pictures and he has kind opinions of my books. Feeling himself very much an American artist, he thought of me to write the introduction.*

I have always sought, in writing about artists, to find what I consider the inevitable interrelation of the work with its creator's personality and experiences. Will and I had had many previous talks, but always on a purely convivial level. So we agreed to get together for a more serious interview.

We met in his high-ceilinged studio in the National Arts Club on Gramercy Park in New York. Knowing that Will receives constant phone calls, I had made it a condition that he remove the receiver from the hook. (Several calls slipped in while I took off my hat and coat and got settled—it was too early for the drink he offered me—and then he did remove the receiver.) He did this a little regretfully, I judged, as if he were feeling rather shy. But once we got talking, he entered into the conversation with an enthusiasm that matched my own.

My first question concerned certain recurring subjects in his work: Why were so many of the female figures in his paintings topped with his wife Elena's face (easily recognizable because of her distinctively slanted, brilliant turquoise eyes)? He answered that he considered family relationships fundamental to human existence. Even in the semi-representational paintings of his earlier days, although the figures verged on the abstract, they had represented his first wife and their three sons. Subsequently, his growing daughter, Ona Willa, had been a favorite subject.

He often included cats, he explained, not only because he sees their curves as echoing those of a recumbent woman, but because cats had long inhabited his households. Why parrots? His father had bought parrots from sailors back from tropical seas. Domestic associations, he added, although not directly communicated to his viewers, brought, because of his feelings, a warmth to his images.

---

*An earlier version of this essay appeared as the Introduction to *Will Barnet* (New York: H. N. Abrams, 1984).

This raised an obvious question: Had his childhood been characterized by warmth? His parents, he told me, had migrated from Eastern
Europe. They had brought with them to America three children: two
daughters and a son. But the American-born Will was so much younger
than his three imported siblings that he was, in effect, an only child.

It has been common in the history of the United States for children
in poorer immigrant families to be offered during their upbringing little
sustenance from the European cultures from which their parents had
fled. Young Will had to find roots for himself in the New World.

Will's mother, although sickly, provided her son with an alcove, so to
speak, of warmth and understanding. It cannot be a coincidence that
Will's paintings again and again celebrate the relationship between
mother and child. From his domestic paintings, men are almost without
exception excluded. Yet the male presence is very much there: the
painter himself viewing the scene with deep emotion from outside the
picture space.

Cut off from most ancestral traditions, growing up among over-
worked poor from many lands, Will wandered abroad in Beverly, Massachusetts, where he was raised, and there discovered a handsome and
rich environment, deeply imbued with the traditions and history of the
nation into which he had been born. Beverly had a fleet of seafaring
ships, often moored at the wharves that Will frequented. Situated across
a narrow inlet from picturesque Salem, Beverly too had once been a
whaling community, and there the time-ripened mansions still stood,
built by merchants whose fortunes had been earned in what seemed to
the boy a world of dreams. Because the great houses abutted on the
shore, there was opened to the wanderer along the waterfront such an
intimate view as could never be glimpsed from the street. By climbing
over rocks and threading his way through reaches of sand, Will could
partake visually of the gracious life of the privileged inhabitants. He
remembers "beautiful ladies strolling through gardens adorned with stat-
uary."

Not long after he was old enough to get around by himself, Will came
on what seemed almost a fairy palace. Miraculously he found himself
not excluded but welcomed. He could climb the marble steps to a ro-
tunda that gave access to rooms built of marble. In the Beverly Public
Library there was a chamber especially devoted to children. Here he
became particularly fascinated, so he remembers, with boys' stories laid
in New England's past: tales of the Pilgrims, the Green Mountain Boys.

Reading Hawthorne's *The House of the Seven Gables*, he was even able to visit the house itself, it was that nearby.

Barnet told me that he had become an artist at the age of eight: he set up his studio in the family cellar. When the little boy confided to the librarians that he was an artist, they gave him full use of a room that contained portfolios of Old Masters reproductions. There were also "great books on each period of art history," Will remembers. This room, closed to the general public, served Barnet as "an inner sanctum where I spent my youth in company with the old masters."

Barnet likes to recall the many artists and cultures—European, Japanese, Oriental, primitive—whose influence shaped his work. It is a significant aspect of his career that he came to know these styles almost altogether on American soil. He did not cross the ocean to Europe until he was in his forties. In this he harked back, although not consciously, to the practice of artists of the Hudson River School, who, when they at last went to Europe, went as full-fledged professionals rather than, as was the practice after the Civil War, beginning their studies in European ateliers.

Barnet's base became the Art Students League in New York, America's most effective art school, which urged on its pupils no single consistent style. Although he won scholarships, he needed further income, and he fell into another American tradition by turning for his livelihood to a craft side of art. Almost all the members of the Hudson River School had begun artistic life as engravers: Winslow Homer had earned his first fame making drawings for woodcuts.

Barnet made his living as an expert printer of lithographs. He soon became the official printer for the Art Students League. And, naturally, he also made lithographs of his own, which he found he could sell for fifteen or twenty dollars. This was during the very depths of the Great Depression, when many American artists, particularly Barnet's contemporaries, lost their faith in American society and institutions. Barnet remembers that he voted for Franklin Delano Roosevelt in 1932 as he wanted a president who could get things done within the American system. Few of his lithographs—remarkably few, considering how moving was the result—dealt with the tragedies wreaked on individuals by the Depression. In *Conflict*, he depicted with horror the brutality of street fighting without making any value distinction between the antagonists.

Barnet responded to the spirit of the times by finding his subject matter in the unexalted lives of ordinary New Yorkers. He refers to these lithographs as "social statements," but neither barbed satire nor angry humor accord with Will's temperament. Will is most conscious of the influence of Daumier, but the prints seem to be in the benign tradition of the Ash Can School, although gaiety and lyricism have given way to a gentle melancholy suited to Depression times.

When Barnet married and began fathering children, his own life merged with the lives of the tenement dwellers around him. His most cramped scene of the tenement life, *Makeshift Kitchen*, shows a woman, her tiny room festooned with laundry, using as a kitchen table a board balanced across the bathtub. She wears a neat black dress protected with an apron. She is his wife. Barnet here communicates the domestic warmth of cheerfully resourceful Bohemian living rather than any sense of social outrage.

Remembering that the Hudson River School as engravers had relied on black-and-white values and later used those values as the underpinnings of their paintings, I asked Barnet what effect the technique of lithography had on his later work. He replied that it had been a hindrance, because of the concentration on detail that it demanded. But another aspect of printmaking, which he took up in the late 1930s, taught him very valuable lessons. This was the woodcut, a medium that did much for Winslow Homer. Working with the large masses of the woodcut enabled Barnet to translate these forms into large painting planes.

Barnet increasingly moved away from the depiction of realistic space, substituting "a compressed space based purely on the rectangle." When I asked him why he had discarded the illusionistic depth that has been used by realistic painters, he replied that in order to dominate the image completely, it was necessary to recognize that the canvas was flat and that the vertical and horizontal tensions create the basic structure of the painting. In searching out shapes and positions that formed their own relationship, Barnet eliminated recognizable images. The shapes were surrogates for emotions which he labored to communicate through the totality of the image.

As I compared the chronology of Barnet's life with that of his art, I became aware that the abandonment of images as they exist in nature coincided with the breakup of his first marriage, and his return to figurative subjects followed his marriage to Elena and the birth of their daughter. His new wife had re-created for him that most potent human force, the family.

Barnet now applied to figurative art "the language of painting," of

harmony, balance, and tension, which he had developed through working with geometric forms in his abstract works. The result is visual paradox, a convincing realism that yet is not real. Without any loss of
verisimilitude, human figures, cats, or birds are two-dimensional structures. A single stretch of color, imperceptibly modulated, covers from
edge to edge his forms, whether large or small. Planes are compressed,
one upon another, without any sense of violating space: a cat may, indeed, sit with comfortable assurance on a stoop that is two-dimensional.
Major images, widely separated, are not connected with one another by
any of the normal expedients of composition. Often there is nothing
between them but what appears to be blank space. And yet the total
picture locks into a harmony that is all the more exciting to the viewer
because the means are not communicated. Nothing in Barnet's pictures
is arbitrary—although the adjustments are not apparent. "The viewer,"
so the artist himself says, "does not have to understand; he feels."

To achieve a compositional scheme can take Barnet a decade. "Not
emotion," he states, "but feeling grows with working time." He makes
innumerable drawings, which to my eyes are handsome works of art,
but which he rarely lets out of his hands because he regards them as
only preparatory studies. The poses, the outlines implying masses, the
costumes worn by his characters have to be universal, of no particular
time or place, and adjusted again and again in order to achieve "intimacy
without description." "Just to paint a picture," Barnet summarizes, "is
not enough for me."

My favorites among his compositions are those that hark back to his
childhood spent on the edge of the sea in an old whaling town: pictures
of female figures staring out over the water from wharves, porches, or
the captains' walks on the roofs of houses. These canvases have been
variously interpreted, the obvious gloss being to conclude that the
women are watching for approaching sails bringing their men home
from long voyages. But most women in this situation would be convers-
ing with one another. In Barnet's pictures each stands, even when in a
throng, utterly isolated and alone. Barnet feels that direct communication between the protagonists in any of his pictures would trivialize his
work into anecdote. His female figures remain abstract symbols but possess a stronger symbolic significance because they clearly connote the
human condition.

Barnet thus explains his ocean pictures: "I was involved with the new
problem of trying to deal with the sky, ocean, and great distances. I felt
the need to come to grips with the radiant light found in the atmosphere

without being realistic or literary. I want to disassociate from normal activity the relationship between the figure and nature, and deal instead with the mysterious poetry of the two. I want to give the sense of great distances, yet keep the paintings two-dimensional."

The resulting compositions contrast the infinity of a symbolic ocean with human hopes, strivings, and mysterious destiny. In this, Barnet has an obvious affinity with an earlier painter from a Massachusetts whaling town. Albert Pinkham Ryder also brought his compositions to maturity with great deliberation, allowing them (as he put it) "to ripen under the sunlight of the years as they come and go." Like Barnet, he gradually made the minute adjustments on which the effect would rely.

Yet there are differences as significant as the similarities. Ryder was a full-blown romantic: his semi-abstract shapes of sail and cloud call up Wagnerian overtones. But in Barnet's compositions there is nothing explosive; nor is there anything vague or relaxed. With the austere beauty of mathematical formulation he makes us experience the interplay between the personal and the universal.

INVALUABLE PUBLIC LIBRARIES

At the very heart of that American dream which has created all that is most admirable in our society lies education.* It is, of course, necessary in a democracy that the voter is fed and clothed, not so that he can become fat and fancy, but so that he will have the opportunity to improve himself, enlarge his knowledge and judgment, and help lead the nation aright.

Does education mean only taking courses? There is today, when institutionalization is conquering American life, a discouraging tendency to regard self-education as obsolete. But surely self-education, once universally recognized as basic to the American spirit, remains basic to all learning. Who should give courses? We hope not a professor who is reading the notes he took from lectures by a previous professor who is reading the notes *he* once took, and so on back to what Eve said to Adam after she bit into the apple from the Tree of Knowledge.

Every time a person—student, professor, or whoever—reaches out for a personal conclusion or a new idea, he is engaged in self-education. Libraries are the capitals of self-education. The young today speak of "doing your own thing." In the arena of knowledge, the most universal and flexible tool for doing your own thing is the library.

Why does the government regard sending citizens to school and often on to college as so important that the opportunity should be furnished free by the state and yet allow libraries to languish? It is hard to believe that this generation has become so mean-spirited that it regards education merely as a means of gaining social status and securing a job. If education is more than that, if it is an expansion of the mind, elementary schools and high schools and community colleges and four-year colleges and graduate schools are tools of major importance; but at the core are libraries.

Public libraries accompany the citizen from childhood to the grave.

---

*This essay originally appeared as the Foreword in *For the People: Fighting for Public Libraries*, ed. Whitney North Seymour, Jr., and Elizabeth N. Layne (New York: Doubleday, 1979), pp. xiii–xv.

The preschool child can find on the shelves picture books to excite his curiosity and wonder. If he is lucky enough to have an adult to read to him, books for that purpose abound. And the more underprivileged the home of a boy or girl, the more restricted the budget of the school attended, the more importantly the public library offers otherwise unreachable riches.

The public library must be enabled to call as well as offer, to lure into its rooms those who would not normally find their way there; but for an eager child once arrived and acclimated, what a haven he has found! It is a haven not only because of the volumes on the shelves but because of the aura their very presence spreads, because of the quiet, because of the space, because this is an oasis from all the physical turmoil of the world. Children living in crowded homes, playing on crowded streets can here in dignity and peace seek what they are and believe, seek to find themselves.

Particularly now, when universal education is a national desire, the library has a usefulness that no formal educational institution can rival. "Open admission" has been inaugurated in colleges as a tool to bring learning to all, but it has proved a very unmanageable tool. It demands what is impossible: instruction that will simultaneously serve students whose experience and preparation vary widely. But for public libraries open admission is not a new experiment but the fundamental principle. It is the essence of a library that each individual studies what most suits his interests or needs at his own rate. Guidance is sometimes necessary to show the newcomer where he can best begin to drill his own well of knowledge, but from then on he can at his own pace dig as deep as his time, interest, and ability allow. The most rudimentary information is available and the only limit to the depth achievable in a great library is the ultimate limit of the abilities of mankind as a whole.

The hours adults spend at work are becoming progressively shorter. There was no need to worry about the use of leisure a few generations ago, when men worked from dawn to dusk; when housewives not only had a long progression of children but furthermore ran manufactories of domestic goods in their homes. Now people have more time than they know what to do with. The Connecticut town I inhabit in the summers contains a covered bridge which used to span the Housatonic in quiet dignity, giving off only an intermittent rumble as some vehicle passed through. Now the bridge is so thronged with sightseers that the town has had to supply, on weekends, two deputy constables, one at each end, to keep order and make passage through the barnlike interior possible.

Individuals wander around the bridge long after their interest has waned; they can think of nothing else to occupy their time. How helpful would be a library book, read under one of the trees on the Housatonic shore! Libraries are, of course, not only a source of knowledge, but enhancers of imagination, suppliers of diversion, of pleasure.

Science has greatly extended the span of human life, while our society has been encouraging or forcing individuals to retire at earlier ages. Even when desired, jobs can be scarce. The nation includes an ever-augmenting number of persons who have no essential occupation to fill even part of their days. Public libraries beckon.

Public library doors are open to all free of charge, with no requirement for admission, and irrespective of wealth or race or any worldly condition. When we see people, as various as the community is various, sitting side by side at library tables, each intent on his own dream and desire, we seem to hear the beating of the vast heart—tolerant, compassionate, appreciative, wildly exciting—of a nation dedicated to liberty and conceived on the principle that all men are created free and equal.

But great as this function is, libraries have what is perhaps an even greater function. Libraries are the memory of mankind, the storehouse that contains all which is known and has been thought. Were some holocaust to destroy all intellectual institutions except libraries, all could be re-created. But if the libraries were destroyed, all other institutions in the world could not re-create them.

MOTHER'S IMPORTANT COUSINS

My mother's important cousins were a problem.* They lived abroad, so that I never had a chance to get used to them, and, when we did meet, most of them did not approve of a boy who was taught in New York's most progressive school to question authority and express his disagreements.

My reactions to Cousin Bertrand Russell extended back to before I saw him. My mother loved to tell, as a demonstration of how she could outwit her sons, an anecdote from a previous visit of her old friend to New York. The philosopher was expected for dinner when our family nurse fell suddenly ill. Since no one had then heard of babysitters the crisis was severe. I was so small that I could be exiled to bed, but there was no way to prevent my elder brother from coming to the table. He was also modernly educated and Mother feared the worst.

Again and again she would describe to some smiling middle-aged audience how she had told Brother William that Cousin Bertie despised Americans. When Bill had worked himself up into a vociferous Lincoln School indignation, Mother inserted the remark that one of the most usual English charges was that American children talked too much. "How perfectly ridiculous!" William replied. With heroic patriotism, he was silent during dinner. To the grown-up laughter which always greeted this anecdote I decided I did not like Bertrand Russell.

When he reappeared in New York and I did now meet him, I saw no reason to change my opinion. His greatness was beyond my comprehension. I might, of course, have accepted it on faith, but I had been taught to take nothing on faith. I based my judgment on what I saw and heard.

I saw a thin man with no chin and a great deal of hair. His endearing resemblance to a cockatoo lasted only while his mind was in neutral during the boredom of having to shake hands with a medium-sized teenage boy. Then he launched into the brilliant talk for which he was

---

*An earlier version of this essay appeared in *Blackwood's Magazine*, 319, No. 1923 (January 1976), 25–31.

celebrated, but which I could only partially follow. As his mind turned over and over ever more rapidly, his eyes took on the ecstatic glaze of a driver enjoying the power of a mighty machine that carries his effortlessly past everything on the road. If I interjected a remark, I was hooted at as if I were a wandering chicken that makes a great car check in its course.

When my family took me to Europe after I had graduated from high school, when I had just turned seventeen, I met the remainder of Mother's important cousins. By this time, I had selected the vocation that I still pursue—I was determined to become a writer—and the magazine I had edited at the Lincoln School was given an award as the best high school literary magazine in America. Doubleday was publishing an anthology from its pages in which my own precocious poetry was liberally strewn. Thus my mother was particularly anxious to bring me together with one of her cousins who was an important literary figure in London, Logan Pearsall Smith.

Cousin Logan had been copiously informed by the female correspondents who kept family communications open that on the American branch a young writer was beginning to leaf out. If he had been actually inflicted with anything I had written, he never mentioned it to me. He could have been nothing but put off by my crude if energetic effusions. For my part, I read his most famous book, *Trivia*, with a feeling that I was being unfairly treated. It was nice to have a literary cousin whose name made my English teachers gasp—but why did he have to write epigrams and prose poems that seemed to me drops of elderly vitriol or artificial garlands of delicately withered flowers?

Mother's favorite fact about Cousin Logan was that he had so successfully lived down his origins as a Philadelphia Quaker that he had been appointed by the British Government to serve on a committee to keep the language free of transatlantic barbarisms through supervision of the speech of the announcers on the Government-controlled radio. To Mother, who tried to persuade me to pronounce "dog" so that it rhymed with "hog," this seemed a great feather in the family cap. I was not so sure.

However, there was no doubt that cousin Logan was a much-admired writer, and, for all my brashness, I knew I had much to learn. It was with a nervous hope that I could bridge the gap between myself and the author of *Trivia* that I accompanied my mother through springtime London to the family settlement on St. Leonard's Terrace. From King's Road with its roaring traffic, we advanced a block toward the Thames and, in a manner amazing to a New York bred boy, found ourselves, there in the center of a great city, surrounded with green. St. Leonard's Terrace faced the extensive grounds which front on that ancient foundation for retired soldiers, the Chelsea Hospital. The hospital itself had been designed in part by Sir Christopher Wren, and over the trees rose a dome.

The terrace was too much of a backwater to attract traffic; our cab advanced through rural silence and emptiness. The houses looking across the roadway to the gardens were low and narrow and clearly old; they seemed to breathe in the sunlight and exhale it in the most delicate of varicolored glows. During most of my seventeen years time had seemed to be at my elbow, bustling, and yet—for I was very young—an altogether delightful companion. Now time seemed suddenly to have been left behind, a few hundred yards back on the King's Road.

I had been surprised on my arrival in London to find that my imagination automatically people the busy streets with characters from Dickens's novels. I would seem to see Mr. Micawber slouching along the pavement, rubbing his hands. However, Dickens's dramatis personae would have been, on St. Leonard's Terrace, incongruously strident and grotesque.

Mother had paid the cabby and was now standing on the sidewalk, her face alight with happy memories. Finally, observing my anxious look, she smiled with a mingling of affection and amusement. "I'm sure you'll get on with Logan," she said. "After all, you're both writers."

Thus complimented, it was with a certain confidence that I awaited the opening of the door and then followed the maid down a narrow hall to a drawing-room where I saw a sight that delighted me: my first Englishman with an eyeglass! He proved, on introductions, not to be Cousin Logan but a disciple. Cousin Logan had not yet made his entrance.

We had been received by Cousin Alys, who had brought Bertrand Russell into the family by marrying him. They had been long divorced, and Alys lived with Logan, her brother. She was a large woman, still handsome, dowdy in the ineffable manner which contributes so much to the impressiveness of British matrons. She had twin passions: charitable work and the family. She and Mother were soon deep in discussions of some distant relatives about whom I had never heard. The man with the eyeglass, motionless as if stuffed, showed no desire to recognize my presence. I was too nervous to notice much about the living-room except that it was small and filled with objects which, had they not been so tastefully fragile, might have been summarized as a clutter.

Eventually, there was a shuffling sound and in came an elderly man who, I realized, must be Cousin Logan. He was taller than I had expected from the delicacy of his writings. However, he was stooped; he peered near-sightedly through glasses, and all his movements were blunted, as if he were contained in an invisible bell jar that prevented him from taking a long step or gesturing far from his body. He gave me a limp hand and said in the impeccable British accent which had made him a monitor of the B.B.C., "I understand that you wish to be a writer."

"That's right," I replied, beaming.

"I hope you will not produce bestsellers."

"Why not?"

"No good writer has ever produced a bestseller."

This was too much for my modern education. "What about Byron?" I asked. "And, of course, Dickens?"

"Byron and Dickens were not good writers."

At this, the man with the eyeglass suddenly came to life. He laughed heartily, as at something devilishly clever. Logan simpered. I observed them with amazement, for once completely tongue-tied.

On our many subsequent meetings Cousin Logan and I never achieved a closer *rapport*. As I look back on it now, I believe that he would have been pleased to have added to his disciples the red-headed literary sprout on the American branch. But he had no idea how to proceed. I remember that he lent me, as the best book recently published by a young Englishman, an autobiographical account by a delicate youth who had found peace in the countryside associating politely with sunsets, quaint peasants, and twittering birds: a sort of Etonian *Walden*. I could think of nothing to say to Cousin Logan about it, which made us both nervous. There was nothing old in me, and in him nothing young. We touched nowhere.

All the more because my mother was disappointed, I was not happy about my failure with Logan Pearsall Smith. However, he was not the family literary connection in whom I was most interested.

Cousin Ray, Logan's and Alys's niece, was married to the brother of the biographer Lytton Strachey. Although I was still too young to appreciate Cousin Logan's irony, Strachey's prose style—clear, simple, yet capable of all emotion—came to me as a perfection I would like some day to reach. Ray explained that Strachey was very shy, that he would never knowingly allow himself to meet a teenaged admirer, but she added that, as he was staying at her house, she would slip me in unannounced to breakfast.

I arrived in the early morning to be seated with my cousins at a table with one chair vacant. Eggs and toast were tasteless as I waited. At last, an amazingly perpendicular figure—tall, narrow, emaciated, drooping a red beard—appeared in the doorway, clad only in trousers and an undershirt. Startled eyes fixed on me. "I see you have company!" And Lytton Strachey vanished, never again to be seen by me.

Experience somewhat tempered my enthusiasm over my mother's announcement that while in Italy we would stay at I Tatti, the villa of the famous art historian Bernard Berenson, who was married to Logan's and Aly's sister, Mary. When we arrived, it was manifest that I would at least enjoy the surroundings: a hillside outside that most beautiful of cities, Florence; a garden designed in the Renaissance manner, that was more lovely than any garden I had ever seen; a sumptious mansion on the walls of which I glimpsed, as the butler showed us to our rooms, a succession of great paintings. It was with a high heart that I began to unpack.

Then there arose a sound of rushing water. A knock on the door and a maid appeared to announce, intelligibly although in Italian, that my bath was ready. I was still young enough to resent having anyone tell me to take a bath, but I was grimy from the train and agreed.

No sooner was I dry and back in my bedroom than rushing water again sounded. Another knock on the door; a different maid but the same announcement. I tried to tell her in my halting Italian that there had been a mix-up. My bath had already been run. I had taken it. She listened uncomprehendingly, repeated her announcement, and, with a look that implied "you dirty pig," departed.

What to do? I had no intention of taking another bath, but the water was in the tub, unctuously, accusingly waiting. I felt like a complete fool as I tiptoed out into the elegant hall, shut the bathroom door behind me, and surreptitiously pulled out the plug. Back again in my room, I could not help straining my ears apprehensively for another gurgle of flowing of water. But what I heard was the luncheon gong.

I was still somewhat flustered when in a huge crowded drawing-room I met Cousin Bernard. To my boyish eyes, he appeared to be the worst of them all. He was a small, delicately featured man with a soft, white beard. Obviously proud of tiny, manicured hands, he moved them when he talked with precise, self-conscious gestures. Surrounded with an admiring group of very stylish middle-aged ladies, he accorded me no more than a handshake.

Finally, bored with sitting silent and unnoticed, I rose to look at the pictures on the walls. They were so beautiful that, as I stared, I forgot the company. Once, as I turned to move from one masterpiece to the next, I thought I saw Berenson's eye upon me, but, if so, it returned instantly to the ambassador's wife who was grinning at him.

Lunch in a large, ornate room was more populous than my mother's grandest dinner parties. I was seated near enough to Cousin Bernard to eavesdrop on his ritualistic flirtation with a striking brunette, whose middle-aged face was so expertly made up to appear young that it presented a disturbing double image. She seemed to have a facial tic, but I could not be altogether sure, since every time her mouth began to pull out of shape she would absorb the movement in a dazzling smile.

No one paid the least attention to me. Eventually, the human spectacle palled, and I become conscious that I had been sitting clodlike in the middle of chatter. Mother's favorite story of how she had silenced my brother in the presence of Bertrand Russell arose in my mind, trailing irritation. I resolved that I would speak up, although it seemed certain that I would be immediately squelched. When reading Reinach's book on Italian painting, I had been skeptical about a statement I had found there. I would ask Cousin Bernard.

Into a momentary pause, I launched my voice: "Is it true that there are only three existing paintings by Cimabue?"

Berenson's mouth had been opening to speak to the lady by his side, and his little hand had been preparing a gesture, but with the quickness of a cat he dropped his hand and turned his head to face me. "You got that statement from Reinach, didn't you?"

"Yes."

"Reinach got it from me, but I've changed my mind." He was suddenly chuckling. "It's the most ridiculous statement I ever heard."

As the party filed back toward the sitting-room, Cousin Bernard appeared at my side. "These people will be going home soon. Nickie"—he nodded in the direction of his handsome companion-secretary—"is expert at shooing them out. Don't you go anywhere. I've told Nickie. I have a plan."

When we were alone with the sweet-smiling Nickie, Berenson explained that it was time for his rest, but then he would take his afternoon walk. Would I come along? He would show me some fine views of Florence. He seemed genuinely pleased when I assented.

"While I rest"—and he was already leading the way—"you might like to read here in the library. I noticed you looking hard at my Piero—at least *I* call it a Piero. It does present problems." He was pulling books from a shelf. "You might like to see what I say about it. And also what the fools"—the word was altogether gay—"write who disagree with me. You've got a fresh, unspoiled eye; at least, I had when I was your age. Tell me later what you think."

When I looked up from the volumes he handed me, he had vanished, it seemed miraculously, since no means of exit was visible. I was in an unbroken circle of books, tier on tier rising to where high windows intervened. When he came to get me an hour later, a section of the bookcase swung back. It was so delicately cantilevered, as I subsequently discovered, that it moved at a touch.

How well I remember that library where day after day I read as he rested! How well I remember our daily walks! Berenson could be a prickly companion for pompous adults. I can still see him standing on his toes, looking like an angry bantam rooster, beside the huge column of flesh that was an English general. The general had said that a good beating never hurt any man. Screaming with rage, Berenson might well have physically assaulted his gigantic adversary had not Nickie intervened. But with me he was all joy and gentleness.

As I look back on it now, I see that, chameleon-like, he took on himself my youth. Although his shiny car with its immaculately respectful Italian chauffeur usually let us out where the walk was downhill and met us again before the road turned sharply upward, how jauntily he strutted down the slope, how gaily he leapt on rocks to secure a better outlook, how boyishly he swung his cane! He was not really old then—only sixty—but to me he seemed frail. He would have been deeply hurt had he known that the contrast between his capers and those of my usual adolescent companions gave me, perhaps because I came to love him, my first deep sense of the tragic physical weakening that comes with passing years. But there was nothing weak about his talk—that was pure excitement.

I remember that he tickled me up by saying that my Italian was so execrable that I should instantly get an Italian mistress; it was the only way to learn a language, and himself had had—this statement was accompanied by a little histrionic gesture—several mistresses by the time he was seventeen. As a politely bred American boy, I would have been confused and embarrassed by an Italian mistress, but I was complimented by BB's suggestion.

Of art we talked by the hour. He took me sometimes to the galleries in Florence, and never expressed an opinion until he heard mine. If we disagreed, we would argue. He never talked on a level on which I could not follow him, or spoke with any note of authority. If I was usually convinced in the end, that was because he had won in a fair debate. For his part, he seemed interested by my untutored reactions, eager to absorb what little I could teach him. He had me write out for him my favorite sonnet by Edna St. Vincent Millay, and he seemed edified by my demonstration that certain angels, in I have forgotten what picture, were doing a dance step that I had learned in New York. But sometimes our debates became heated, and then visitors to the Uffizi or the Pitti would be horrified to hear a boy shout at the great Bernard Berenson, "You're crazy!" and to have the great BB shout the insult right back.

Thus Mother's important cousins played in the end a vital role in my education. Had it not been for my boyhood encounter with Berenson and my friendship with him which extended down the years, would I have written books on painting (albeit schools of American painting with which BB was completely unconcerned)? Perhaps not, and, since I have enjoyed writing those books, I am grateful. But my boyish friendship with Cousin Bernard did further encourage in my modernly educated young mind tendencies which have made me, within the graver purlieus of art history, somewhat of a maverick. I have never been able to feel that art is apart from life, something to be analyzed with the impersonality of a scientist or tiptoed toward with religious reverence. Always it has seemed to me that a great painting is, as Berenson had been, my friend, to be argued with as well as admired, and to be laughed with when spirits are high. You can have no idea how much trouble this attitude has given me where gravity bows to suitable correct scholarship and taste.

ACKNOWLEDGMENT

The author and publisher herewith render thanks to the publishers of previously published materials for permission to use such materials in this book. Every effort has been made to contact the publishers of these materials and to make full acknowledgment.